D0892000

A BRITISH ACHILLES

To our great and gracious God and for the Jellicoe family

A BRITISH ACHILLES

The Story of George, 2nd Earl Jellicoe
KBE, DSO, MC, FRS
Soldier, Diplomat, Politician

by
Lorna Almonds Windmill

Pen & Sword
MILITARY

First published in Great Britain in 2005 by
Pen & Sword Military
an imprint of
Pen & Sword Books Ltd
47 Church Street
Barnsley
South Yorkshire
S70 2AS

Copyright © Lorna Almonds Windmill, 2005

ISBN 1-84415-354-1

Typeset in 11/13pt Sabon by
Concept, Huddersfield, West Yorkshire

Printed and bound in England by
CPI UK

For a complete list of Pen & Sword titles please contact
PEN & SWORD BOOKS LIMITED
47 Church Street, Barnsley, South Yorkshire, S70 2AS, England
E-mail: enquiries@pen-and-sword.co.uk
Website: www.pen-and-sword.co.uk

Contents

Part One: Soldier
(September 1939 – December 1944)
[The Admiral's son; the Coldstream Guards; action in the Western Desert; the SAS; the SBS; SAS Raids on Crete, Sardinia, SOE mission to Rhodes, Sea raids and action in the Greek Islands; 'Bucketforce'; the Peloponnese; the Liberation of Patras and Athens; 'Pompeforce'.]

Part Two: A Different War
(January 1945 – December 2004)
[Washington; Brussels; the Soviet Desk; the Baghdad Pact; Lord-in-Waiting; Minister of Housing; Home Office Minister; First Lord of the Admiralty; Opposition; Member of Cabinet; Resignation; The British Overseas Trade Board; Medical Research Council and Aids; Prevention of Terrorism; The House of Lords 'Committee on Committees'.]

I burn my candle at both ends;
it will not last the night.
But O my foes and ah my friends
it gives a splendid light!

Emily Dickens

Foreword

For children born early in the Great War, as I was, the name of Admiral Sir John Jellicoe and the Battle of Jutland rang in our ears like the echo of a conflict of giants. Children a few years older could remember – or said they could – the thunder of the guns of our Grand Fleet and the enemy's High Seas Fleet rolling inland from the mists of the Dogger Bank. By the time we could take all this in, Jutland had risen through history into myth; the name was murmured in the same breath as Trafalgar and the Armada. We learnt how the great battle had kept the enemy locked in port and out of action for the remaining years of the war and how, when they surrendered at the end of it, the High Seas Fleet of our enemy scuttled itself in the depths of Scapa Flow.

Admiral Jellicoe's son is the subject of this book. The second Earl Jellicoe – 'George' among friends – first loomed in my case during my first infiltration into occupied Crete at a few minutes past midnight on 23 June 1942. Loomed is the right word, for it was pitch dark and he was no more than a shadow in a rubber dinghy heading for the rope-ladder up the side of HMS *Porcupine*, the ten-ton motor-boat which had briefly dropped anchor with its engine ticking over, now almost inaudibly, under a steep southern inlet of Crete. I was heading for the shore in another dinghy, and for a moment we were almost within touching distance. There was just time to exchange names and greetings. Then he boarded and was gone; the only one to make it back from a five-man SAS raid on Heraklion aerodrome, leaving behind them a chaos of burnt-out aircraft and exploded petrol and ammunition dumps scattered over the enemy's airfields.

By the time my signaller and I stepped ashore, the vessel had vanished and I didn't actually see this new acquaintance till fifteen months later; the dark upheaval inland swallowed us up for the next fourteen of them. We were the latest addition to a handful of SOE who comprised a military mission to help the Cretan resistance. Some of them were waiting on the beach all armed and we headed up a canyon. It was the start of a strange peripatetic cave-life.

The war was at a critical phase. Rommel and his Afrika Korps were advancing fast across Libya, so fast that, two days earlier, *Porcupine*, instead of setting off from Bardia, had shifted in haste to Mersa Matruh, 100 miles further east. Except for an occasional submarine, we were now cut off by sea; but somehow tales of the activities of George Jellicoe and his fellow-raiders made their way to our wintry grottos. The deeds of the Long Range Desert Group, the Special Air Service and then the Special Boat Service cheered us up, under the stalactites, and the names of David Stirling, Paddy Blair Mayne, Andy Lassen, David Sutherland and George Jellicoe became household words to us.

Thanks to our meeting in the dark, George's interested us most. When we met the following year in Cairo and became friends, I caught up with his adventures, and those of his fellow-irregulars, and filled in the gaps – or thought I did, until recently I began reading the typescript of Lorna Almonds Windmill's excellent biography. (The mass of material and all the changes of scene are powerfully knit in her vigorous and apposite style, and her own military background must have been a great help.) George and I had many friends and many places in common; I only learnt how many as a result of reading this biography.

When he founded and commanded the SBS I was astounded to learn that the base for his flotilla and his buccaneers had been the old Crusader Castle of Athlit, Le Château des Pèlerins, bang on the sea at Haifa, under Mount Carmel. It had been my military billet too, the year before, with a gathering of Cretans listening to my totally ignorant discourses on the German and Italian weapons we hoped to capture one day. Later, I was interested to learn more of the background as to how Jellicoe and Ian Patterson pedalled at full speed into the heart of Athens while the tail of the German army was hastening out at the other end of the city. His name is rightly honoured in Greece, with which he has kept an abiding link. This was notably corroborated after the war by General Christodoulos

Tsigantes, the legendary commander of the Greek Hieros Lochos, or Sacred Squadron which, in the last phase of the war, he led victoriously all the way from the Middle East to Rimini. General Tsigantes died in England during the Colonels' dictatorship, asking George for the hospitality of his village churchyard in the Wiltshire downs. When the dictatorship fell, his remains were translated to free Greece. His name and dates, and a quotation from Homer, are inscribed in Greek on the headstone above the empty grave. Between them runs the famous epitaph from Thucidides.

General Tsigantes

1898–1970

When great men die

The whole earth is their sepulchre

Now that he was at last visible, George's face, with its piercing eyes, the prominent bridge to his nose, his jutting chin and his cheerful laugh, gave him the look of a young Roman centurion of boundless vigour and capacity and, as the post war years advanced, the features, without loss of youth, kept in step, advancing to legate, proconsul, consul and almost imperator. In real life it went even faster; he was a brigadier at twenty-six and adorned with a whole chime of gongs. Just as after demobilization, when he eventually plunged into diplomacy, he soon filled an important post in Washington, at the very moment when diplomats were flitting east in a covey, and later became Deputy Secretary General of the Baghdad Pact. Stepping into politics, he quickly advanced to First Lord of the Admiralty and Conservative Leader of the House of Lords. He has a first-rate brain, passionate application to whatever he takes on, diligence, flair and tireless energy. Thank God, all this is balanced by an equally impetuous verve in the pursuit of the good things in life, the enjoyment of friendship, in skiing and in alertness for random pleasure. We all know how, years ago, this landed him in the soup for something which anywhere else in the world would have been brushed aside. But he was a member of the Government. One fellow minister had got into serious trouble with someone who might have been a danger, and had evaded the truth. Another had erred through clinical pluralism. Rather than bring down more trouble on

ix

his side, perhaps subconsciously prompted by the spectre of William of Wykeham, he unnecessarily but honourably and quixotically resigned, stepping forever off the ladder of advancement. The author wonders what heights he might have reached if he had remained in office. So do I.

In point of fact, that interim merely switched his gifts in a different direction, which carried him to the presidencies of the Royal Geographical Society and of the SAS Regimental Association and several other undertakings of honour and influence: to the summit, in fact, of anything he undertook. It was natural that he should subsequently become involved in helping to launch the commercial cloak and dagger company, Hakluyt.

Looking at what I have just written, I see that I have left out an important aspect of his idiosyncrasy. It is a mixture of directness, charm, the lure of adventure, an entire lack of pomp, a complete openness of character, a strong comic sense and, touch wood, luck. He was luckiest of all with his wife, Philippa, a marvellous compound of good looks, kindness and unpremeditated style, humour equal to George's and a total originality of mind.

We have sometimes exchanged houses, so I know all the charms of their stretch of the West Country. George's house – something out of Jane Austen in a fold of Samuel Palmer landscape, full of books and gramophone records, and often overrun with descendants – is a deserved blessing. The great hurricane of two decades ago blew down a whole avenue and a spinney of beech on a steep meadow opposite the front windows, and the bareness was much lamented. But now, in what seems no time at all, new trees have shot up, and – as if by a miracle – to the same height as their predecessors, and the chestnut mare and her foal can once more graze in their shade. In the southern Peloponnese, by contrast, there is a fearsome jutting rock thirty feet above our inlet which is widely known as Jellicoe's Leap.

In either place, it is no longer the explosions of sixty years ago that herald nightfall but the friendly popping of corks.

Patrick Leigh Fermor, DSO, CB
in the Peloponnese
April 2005

Acknowledgements

I am greatly indebted to the many people who helped me to research and write this book. To all the people I interviewed, some of whom also provided photographs, dug out papers and old correspondence and took the trouble to read my drafts, I am truly grateful. Above all, I would like to thank them for their enthusiastic support for what most said was a rather daunting project, and for their personal encouragement to me. Their names are in the notes on sources and are too numerous to mention individually here.

A few must receive a special mention: Paddy Leigh Fermor for the foreword; Andrew Gibson-Watt for his painstaking and generous advice on the whole text and expert opinion on the military chapters; Leonard Dickson for his expert advice on the Royal Air Force aspects; James Irvine for his help with extracts from the Dobrski papers; Michael Wheeler Booth, Michael Davies and Michael Pownall for their unstinting help and expert advice on the parliamentary part of the story; and Janet Morgan, Chapman Pincher and Jack Sibard who gave me copies of their own books relevant to, respectively, the attempt to reform the House of Lords, the Cambridge spies and the raid on Crete.

I acknowledge with thanks the assistance of the National Archives (TNA), formerly the Public Record Office (PRO) – records held by them appear courtesy of Her Majesty's Stationery Office – and the assistance of the House of Lords Library and the House of Lords Public Record Office whose staff patiently helped me to track down the right documents. I am also grateful to the SAS Association for their help and cooperation.

Most of all, I would like to thank George and Philippa for their enormous help, their elephantine memories and their great kindness and immensely generous hospitality over three years from St George's Day 2002 until April 2005. I have greatly valued their friendship and support. The work was already fascinating but they made it fun too and I have had the unique experience of re-living the life of a most remarkable person.

As always, my literary agent, Duncan McAra, has been efficient and effective on my behalf. I am grateful to my family for their patience and forbearance while I have been living Jellicoe for the last three years and to Ian Fletcher for his ceaseless encouragement. The last word of thanks must go to Peter de la Billière, whose enthusiastic support convinced me that I should write George's story.

Preface

From my earliest childhood, I was always aware of the name 'Jellicoe'. But unlike Paddy Leigh Fermor, in his kind foreword to this book, I did not know it in the context of the sailor hero, Admiral Jellicoe, and the Battle of Jutland. Through my father – 'Gentleman Jim' Almonds – one of the first men in the SAS and a member of David Stirling's 'L' Detachment – my knowledge of the name was in connection with the admiral's son in the context of the Coldstream Guards and the SAS. Of course, my father had forbidden me, and my brother and sister, ever to mention the SAS or even to admit that we knew anyone in it. But the Jellicoe stories gradually leaked out.

My mother was the first to talk. (She was the only member of the family who had never had to sign the Official Secrets Act.) In September 1942, Jellicoe had a knee problem so he missed the disastrous third SAS raid on Benghazi, code-named Op BIGAMY, during which my father was captured and went – for a time – 'into the bag'. During Jellicoe's recuperation in England he wrote on 24 November one of those difficult letters that it falls to young officers to write when one of their soldiers is killed or missing. He sent not just a brief dutiful note to my mother but a six-page letter full of hope and confidence about the outcome of the war. It brought her untold comfort for the next three years until my father made good his second escape from an Italian POW camp and got clean away back to England.

Much later on, when there was no longer any point in pretending that the SAS didn't exist, my father would talk of annual Allied Special Forces reunions in Paris. Jellicoe and Stirling were always there. They could sometimes be seen the next morning wearing dark glasses to hide signs of the previous night's carousing. Stirling, who always helped his men out when they needed it (he set Dave Kershaw up with a fish and chip shop after the war) was not beyond borrowing money from those he thought had done well enough. He put my father, who would unquestioningly stump up with the odd £20 when required, in the latter category.

Even later still, Jellicoe used to attend meetings of the SAS Regimental Association Executive Committee, chaired by the Vice President, John Slim. My brother, John Almonds, who had served in the SAS and was also on the committee, told me about a discussion on membership, when it was mooted that another ex-SAS peer should be invited onto it.

'Would that not be a Laird too many?' asked Tanky Smith, the Scots ex-SAS Secretary to the Association, his vivid blue eyes darting from Jellicoe to Slim and back again. There was then ribald speculation around the table as to whether the potential member was in fact a 'proper' lord (that is, whether he held his title in his own right or had a courtesy one). His possible election had nothing to do with that – as it happened he was a proper lord – but it showed that the exceptional qualities demanded by the SAS were still well represented among hereditary peers in the post-war years.

I was thrilled to be able to research and write this story – and proud that Lord Jellicoe chose to entrust the task to me. As both an ex-army officer and civil servant, I have at least been able to understand these two cultures in which Jellicoe spent almost all of his professional life. My problem has been how to scope such a huge project and capture the sprawling figure of Jellicoe in all his roles, guises and modes. My second has been that, like all SAS 'imprinted' at an early age by Stirling, he never talks about himself. This sometimes required me to employ interrogation methods that would do credit to a war crimes tribunal. He bore it well and always graciously, was amazingly trusting and open and never sought to interfere with my more critical assessments. Fortunately, in addition to what is in the public domain, I have been able to get others, who were well placed to do so, to talk to me about him. Like many before me who have worked closely with him, I have found it a pleasure and a privilege; hard work but also huge fun.

I only hope I have done my subject justice.

Lorna Almonds Windmill
South Battersea
St George's Day, 2005

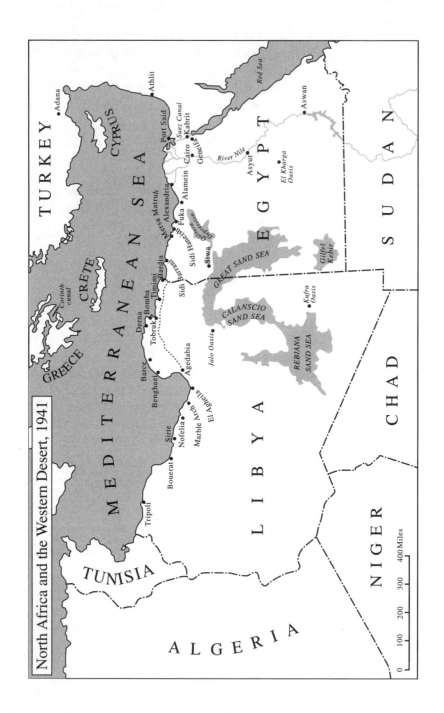

North Africa and the Western Desert, 1941

TURKEY

CYPRUS

• Adana

• Athlit

GREECE

CRETE

Corinth canal

MEDITERRANEAN SEA

Port Said
Suez Canal
Kabrit
Cairo
Geneifa
Alexandria
Mersa Matruh
Fuka
Alamein
Sidi Haneish
Siwa
Dabaa
Daba
Qattara Depression
Bardia
Sidi Barrani
Timimi
Derna
Bomba
Tobruk
Barce
Benghazi
El Agheila
Agedabia
Jalo Oasis
Sirte
Nofelia
Marble Arch
Bouerat
Tripoli

TUNISIA

ALGERIA

LIBYA

Red Sea

Aswan

River Nile

Asyut
El Kharga Oasis

EGYPT

SUDAN

GREAT SAND SEA

CALANSCIO SAND SEA

Gilf el Kebir

Kufra Oasis

REBIANA SAND SEA

CHAD

NIGER

0   100   200   300   400 Miles

xvi

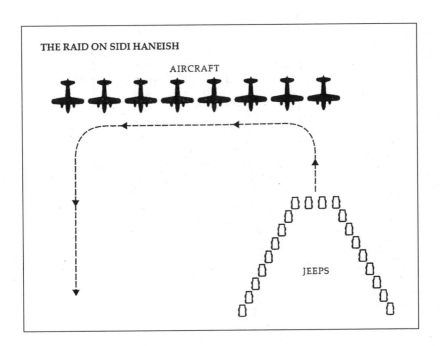

The Raid on Crete

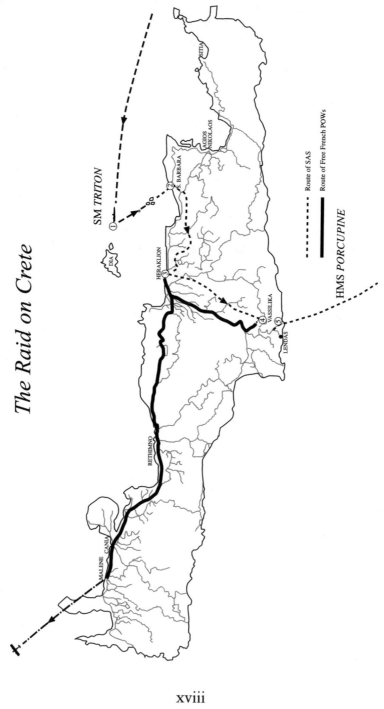

SM *TRITON*

DIA

SITIA

AGIOS NIKOLAOS

S. BARBARA

HERAKLION

VASSILIKA

LENDAS

RETHIMNO

MALENE

CANIA

HMS *PORCUPINE*

Route of SAS

Route of Free French POWs

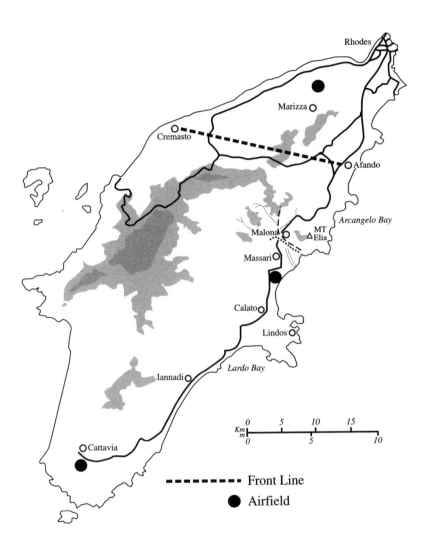

Rhodes

Marizza ○

Cremasto ○

Afando ○

Arcangelo Bay

Malona ○   MT
             △ Elia

Massari ○

Calato ○

Lindos ○

Iannadi ○

Lardo Bay

```
        0      5      10     15
Km
m ┣━━━━━┿━━━━━┿━━━━━┿━━━━━┫
        0            5            10
```

Cattavia ○

– – – – – – – Front Line

● Airfield

Island of Rhodes

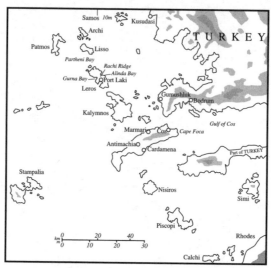

Dodecanese Islands 1943

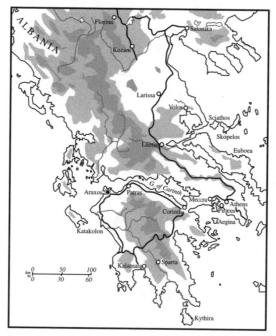

Greece 1944

Italy 1942-1943

Ancona

Porto San Giórgio

Ascoli Piceno

Gran Sasso d'Italia

Aquila

I T A L I A

Pescara

Ortona

Rome

ABRUZZI

GUSTAV LINE

Termoli

Cassino

R. Garigliano

Campobasso

Fóggia

VIKTOR LINE

Benevento

Naples

Castellammare

Salerno

Bari

Altamura

*A D R I A T I C
S E A*

*T Y R R H E N I A N
S E A*

Taranto

0 10 20 30 40 50 miles

xxi

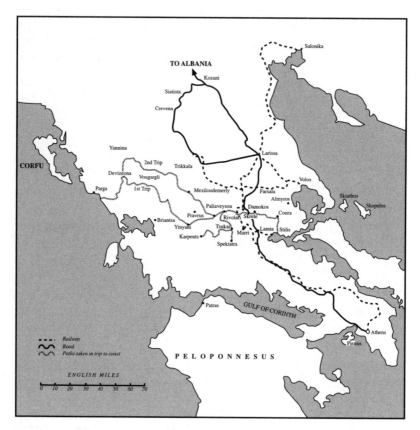

Greece

Map illustrating routes taken on foot from Lamia to Parga. Road used by retreating Germans and deviation via Trikkala taken by Jellicoe's force to cut them off at Kozani.

Part One

Soldier

(September 1939 – December 1944)

Chapter One

A Young Man's Fancy

The Western desert, 21 January 1942. Cool damp night air, smelling faintly of the sea, wafted inland from the Mediterranean. Rommel's second offensive was imminent.[1] Where the coast road to Tripoli runs very close to the sea, a powerfully-built young Guards officer with crisply curling hair and a confident walk was leading a small patrol westwards out through sand dunes between the sea and the road. He wanted to see what the Germans were up to. He was George Jellicoe – son of the First World War Admiral[2] and, since his father's death, the Second Earl Jellicoe.[3] He had a genial, usually smiling, face and a Churchillian approach to alcohol. He was with the 3rd Battalion 22 Guards Brigade, on the right (sea) flank of the Eighth Army.

When the patrol could go no further toward the Germans by truck because of the dunes, they left the vehicle and continued on foot. Floating over the moist, clumpy sand came the distant sound of labouring engines and heavy rumbling. Jellicoe went to the top of a dune to see where it was coming from. Men and vehicles were advancing about half a mile away. The German attack had started.[4]

The patrol hastily retraced their steps to the vehicle, to find it gone. They moved rapidly east, walking all day and night. Next morning, they found a well. Jellicoe went forward with one man but as they got close to the well, they came under heavy fire. Jellicoe was shot, the bullet passing down through his right shoulder and emerging half way down the side of his chest.

1

He was rather concerned about other matters and carried on. Twenty-four hours later, they met a section of an armoured car regiment who ran them back to Benghazi. By then, 22 Guards Brigade had withdrawn back to just west of Tobruk.[5]

Jellicoe was bandaged up and rejoined his company a few days later. Unsurprisingly given the desert conditions, his wound went bad. The medics sorted it out at No. 8 General British Military Hospital in Alexandria with the help of a pretty nurse called Dollar Bugle, whose patients called her 'Penny Whistle'.[6] Jellicoe went on sick leave to Beirut. There he caught malaria and was soon back in hospital. Lying beneath the slowly turning fans, he contemplated his war.

In spring 1936, as a young man of eighteen, he had skied at St Moritz with his sister Prudy and spent the evenings improving his French. Even then he had been up for the dangerous, taking part in the terrifying Cresta Run, where his key competitor was another novice, Joe Kennedy, son of the American Ambassador, Joseph Kennedy and elder brother of Jack, the future President of the United States. In early April, Jellicoe skipped his last term at Winchester and accompanied by his mother and Prudy, spent an extended gap year in Germany. He aspired to a career in the diplomatic service and wanted to learn German.

While they were staying in a hotel in Berlin, his friend, the young Prince Friedrich of Prussia, 'Fritzi', the youngest son of the Crown Prince and grandson of the Kaiser, came to see them.[7] They knew each other from the Kaiser's sailing days at Cowes. Fritzi's family lived at the Cecilienhof in Potsdam (where the Potsdam Conference was later held), described by Chips Channon as 'a dreadful Lutyens sort of house, ugly and bogus Tudor, built just before the war, only redeemed by the fact that it overlooked a lake'. There, on 10 August, Channon found the young Lord Jellicoe swimming with Princess Cécile, Fritzi's younger sister.[8]

Fritzi was eager to do all he could to help further Jellicoe's German. He said it was too silly for Jellicoe to lodge in Berlin and invited him to stay at Cecilienhof.[9] That summer, they returned briefly to St Lawrence, the Jellicoes' home on the Isle of Wight, for Cowes week (Fritzi was also keen on Prudy) before sailing back from Southampton to Bremerhaven. With two young American women they met on the boat, they lunched in Bremen with some friends of Fritzi's family before returning to Berlin and the second week of the Olympic Games. One black American athlete, Jesse Owens, annoyed Hitler by beating all the blond Aryan competitors and winning four gold medals. But the man who really infuriated the Führer was the German long jumper, Luz Long, who befriended Owens and was the real hero of those games.[10]

At a ball at the Cecilienhof, Jellicoe danced with Mussolini's daughter, Countess Edda Ciano. Her husband was Mussolini's Foreign Secretary even as the axis between Germany and Italy was being forged. The Countess was very attractive and Jellicoe was enjoying himself. Eventually she said,

'I think you like burning your fingers, George.'

'Yes,' he replied.

When the band struck up again, he grabbed her by her slim waist and, despite some resistance, propelled her onto the floor. Then he noticed that no one else was dancing – the band was playing the Italian national anthem. Later that summer he lost his heart to Christa von Tippelskirche, a friend of Princess Cécile. Christa was pretty, with lovely long legs, and very intelligent.[11]

With a friend of the Hohenzollern family, Goffie von Furstenberg, Jellicoe travelled to the Dutch border, then south to the Rhineland and on to the Black Forest. In southern Germany, they joined the party of the Crown Princess of Prussia, visiting Munich, Nuremberg and Bamberg, with its beautiful cathedral. There he began to worry about the possibility of war. Goffie tried to allay his fears.

'George,' he said reassuringly, 'I don't think you need worry. The senior officers of the *Wehrmacht* will not allow anything stupid to happen.'[12]

October 1936. Jellicoe went up to Trinity College Cambridge. On 12 May 1937, aged nineteen and wearing picture-book knee breeches, a frothy cravat and a long, frogged jacket with lanyards on his right shoulder, he was page to King George VI at his coronation. It was an amazing sight, being the only occasion on which coronets are worn. That night, in contrast to the august

3

proceedings of the day, he discovered the delights of night-clubs. Women did not yet feature much in his life. Apart from a passing, innocent relationship with Pixie Pease, the sister of his friend Peter Pease, his life at Cambridge was romantically uncomplicated. But his mother had matrimonial aspirations for him and kept photographs of the Princesses Elizabeth and Margaret strategically positioned around the house.

Not having brothers, Jellicoe's male friends meant a lot to him. Tim Marten, an old school friend, had gone to Oxford after leaving Winchester College in 1934. Other friends included Billy Cavendish (Lord Hartington), the eldest son of the Duke of Devonshire and future son-in-law of the American Ambassador Joseph Kennedy, and his brother Andrew. His closest friends were Mark Howard and his two younger brothers, whose family owned Castle Howard in Yorkshire; David Jacobson, who had been top scholar at Eton; and Pease. Reserved and self-effacing, Pease was a committed Christian. Over six feet tall, his biographer later described him as 'the best looking man I have ever seen'.[13]

Having been so well taught at Winchester by Harold Walker, Jellicoe's first two years at Cambridge were easy. He was chairman of the main lunch club, the Pitt Club, and joined the more select Athenaeum. In 1938 Carol Mather looked out from his lodgings at 27 Trinity Street and saw Jellicoe dropping champagne bottles out of the window of the Athenaeum after a rowdy late-night party.[14] There was sport too. He enjoyed golf on the nine-hole course out towards Newmarket, playing with Archie Wavell at Stoneham, and sometimes on the East Anglian golf courses with Willie Whitelaw, David Jacobson and Mark Howard, achieving a low handicap. He also played tennis and real tennis.

Cambridge saw a great flowering of Jellicoe's wider intellectual and artistic interests. He became lifelong friends with his tutor, Steven Runciman.[15] Communist idealism was flourishing at Trinity, from which the Cambridge spies had fledged a few years earlier, but Jellicoe was too rigorous a thinker to be seduced by it. In 1938, he spent two months in Paris chez Monsieur Martin who was recommended by the Foreign Office to aspirants wanting to improve their French.[16] Jellicoe was well read, devouring works in English, French and German, and maintaining a detailed reading list in his diary. During his final year at Cambridge, he took Florentine history as a special subject, went to Florence in the Easter holidays and enjoyed the city but did no work. At the last moment, he switched his special subject to the origins of the Great War but did not attend a single lecture. He continued ski racing and the Cresta Run, where Joe Kennedy remained his principal rival. They were fairly equally matched – in both skill and nerve. Jellicoe suffered no injuries but his mother, watching as he hurtled over Battledoor and Shuttlecock, slipped and had a terrible fall.[17]

On his birthday, 4 April 1939, Jellicoe wrote in his diary, '21 for my sins'. At the height of the debutante era and as a highly eligible bachelor he was invited to all the coming out[18] dances, including those at the US Embassy and Court Balls at Buckingham Palace. It meant little to him, being typified by diary entries such as 'Kemsley's bloody dance'[19] and 'Somebody's dance – quite fearful – at Claridges'.[20] However, he developed a real but critical taste for music, noting on 1 May, 'First night of the opera. *Bartered Bride*. Very badly done'.[21]

On 29 May, he took the first part of the Tripos in modern European history, noting that he had written a 'tolerable answer'. Next day, he sat the examination on political thought, which he thought a 'fearful bungle'. The special subject followed (the Great War) which was 'messy'. By Thursday it was all over and he was free for a weekend of golf at Walton, *Figaro* at Glyndebourne and *Don Giovanni* at Covent Garden. He got a First in Part I of the History Tripos for Modern European history and an Upper Second in the Florentine history, but still gained a BA First Class Honours in the Historical Tripos overall. On 25 July, he took his seat in the House of Lords.[22] After taking the oath, he sat on the cross-benches. The Hansard entry says simply 'The Earl Jellicoe – Sat first in Parliament after the death of his father'. He had never been in the House with his father, who had attended rarely.[23]

The rest of that leisurely summer was overshadowed by impending war. In mid August Jellicoe went to Gartmore in Scotland to stay with one of his uncles on his mother's side and spent a pleasant and energetic '12th' bagging thirty brace of grouse. On 21 August, he arrived at Castle Howard with his mother. His diary records 'Mark was amusing in his possessive casualness' as he showed Lady Jellicoe around. Mark's sister, Christian, joined them with Debo Mitford and Billy and Andrew Cavendish.[24] Jellicoe was accompanied by an impressive reading list.[25]

He was first down to breakfast next morning. The Russo-German Pact had exploded like a thunderbolt in the headlines of the *Yorkshire Post*.

'This means war,' pronounced a fellow houseguest and everyone was alarmed. Jellicoe was loath to believe it.[26]

'Perhaps,' he wrote on 31 August, 'the news of the appointment of a sort of Military Cabinet in Germany forebodes ill. Joe[27] is being called up.' There was worse to come. Jellicoe heard a wireless announcement: 'There have been some developments during the night in the international situation.' This was the prelude to the invasion of Poland. 'It's obviously the end of the tether – the curtain raiser to the last trump,' he noted.[28]

Back in London, he set off for the House of Lords but went instead to the Commons, which promised more immediate drama. The Kennedy brothers, Joe and Jack, were in the Strangers' Gallery. They all looked down on the muted gathering below. The Prime Minister, Neville Chamberlain, was grave, slightly broken and rather pathetic but delivered a calm, determined speech.[29]

3 September 1939. Jellicoe arrived early at the Lords to dump his luggage. On going to the tape-machine, the first thing he saw was the eleven o'clock statement. From the Peers' Gallery in the House of Commons, he heard war declared, then returned to the Lords sports room and listened to the Prime Minister's broadcast. There was a general air of stiff upper lip. He sauntered out into the warm September sun for a walk before the House met at noon.

Strolling up and down in front of the Palace of Westminster, he heard the sinister wailing of an air-raid siren. He told a perplexed girl what it was and lent his gas mask to an elderly woman. Everyone crowded into the ARP[30] shelter under Parliament Square where Jellicoe helped put two sandbags in place. An amusing American correspondent said they were closeted with the Polish Ambassador. Some people heard guns. Jellicoe thought the air raid was probably a rude German answer to the polite British declaration of war. In the House, after prayers, came more warnings and more confusion.

In the Commons, he saw Joe and Jack Kennedy again. Chamberlain was as pathetic as ever but Churchill had a great phrase, 'our hearts are at peace', up his sleeve.[31]

Jellicoe stayed at Claridges, where he talked to Wavell and Jacobson about the situation. Their mood was sombre. Yet they could not help admiring the beauty of the barrage balloons. At 3 am, Jellicoe was awoken by the tinkle of Claridges' telephone. Gradually the awful warning impinged itself onto his sleepy consciousness. Another air raid. They were invited down to the cellars. Panicking slightly, Jellicoe dressed and hurried downstairs, but forgot his gas mask. To his great shame, one of the staff went back to fetch it for him. This bothered him because he thought this time they were in for it. But an American suggestion that they should play a round game and the obvious care the women had taken over their makeup soon restored his morale. This time, he too thought he heard guns, but it was only doors slamming.[32] After breakfast, he dispatched some facetious letters to the War Office and Cambridge, filled some sandbags for Claridges and enjoyed the sun in Green Park. Girls with gas masks slung round their shoulders interrupted his contemplation of the ducks. Later that night, he went back to St Lawrence to find a vast mob of aunts and went to bed depressed.[33]

He read Rauschwig's *Revolution of Destruction*, on modern Germany. One sentence caught his attention: 'The creative will now emerging is of a harshness ... that Europe has not seen for centuries.' It seemed to Jellicoe that harshness was the kernel of the Nazi system. Even more so, it was the basis of its technique, combined with elastic opportunism. Hitler was not only a supreme tactician. He was also a crazy mystic. He and Germany therefore probably had a strength that many underestimated.[34]

People continued to talk of a short war. Jellicoe thought this could only be blind, wishful, optimism. 'I anticipate a five-year plus war,' he wrote. He could not foresee British strategy when

Poland was lost, thinking that this would force Britain onto the offensive, whereas a defensive stance was much more to the country's advantage. The West looked impregnable, yet ultimately, the struggle would descend into one of national will. He noted Churchill on war: 'If on land hopes had been dupes, fears at sea had also been liars.'[35]

As he lay on the beach at St Lawrence, waiting for call-up, losing consciousness in the sun, the war faded away and became even more unreal. It made him keener to read, to listen to music, to coordinate what intellect he had and be more introspective. Yet so far, the war was absurdly vague. He confided to his diary: 'Blackout claptrap; innocuous newspapers; doctored wireless; war talks; women war fuss; Red Cross turmoil; and all the rest of it. I'm bored of this war already.'[36]

Fortunately, there were other diverting attractions. He dined with friends at L'Escargot and, after an extremely tipsy evening, the finishing touch being a magnum of claret and vermouth, found himself for no apparent reason on the bonnet of his Packard in the middle of Regent Street. The next morning he had trouble locating the car, which was just behind Claridges. After a hair-raising drive back from London to the Isle of Wight, he missed the ferry, which was tiresome, as he had never driven faster or more dangerously.[37]

18 September. He drove over to Cambridge where, after some embarrassment, he was passed medically fit to get killed. He recorded in his diary the names of nine young men, two of whom later married his sisters, Norah and Prudy, and underneath, 'I would be very sad if any of the above got himself killed.'[38] Sunny September days at St Lawrence were filled with beach walks, tennis, golf and trips up to London to dine or go to the opera with friends. He read avidly. And he wrote, pouring out to the diary his philosophy of life:

> I love tolerance ... [but] there has never seemed to me much point in getting in a state (religious, political, or personal) about *anything*.[39] That limits the depth of one's feelings. One may not be able to plumb life this way – but scratching at its surface can be great fun. Should one aim higher than that?[40]

8

The interlude of idle days before training to kill became precious, bittersweet. It was the most marvellous social time; he saw many of the great houses of Britain and friends and families he loved. Still his unconscious stirred him. One night he woke in a luxurious bedroom and for the first time realized that some poor person had to empty the chamber pot under his bed.[41] The weather was paradoxically beautiful. The garden at St Lawrence was heavy with autumn, the turf firm and full, the roses' scent strong and satisfying while apples swelled on the trees. Yet from somewhere, insistently, the drone of an aeroplane pulled him back to reality. Time was a little too insistent, like the second movement of Beethoven's Seventh Symphony, to which he listened as he wrote up the diary. That evening, the shore was in animal spirits. A buffeting wind thrashed the sea into long, harsh, regular waves. A ship or two were all over the place. The sun kept coming through strongly at intervals, casting a sparkle over the whole scene.[42]

The next day, Jellicoe heard he had three weeks before call up. They would be mortgaged but precious. He reckoned on about four months at the Royal Military Academy Sandhurst, which would be bloody, and then another month or two with the battalion. 27 October. He was called up and posted to 161 Officer Cadet Training Unit, in the first wartime intake at Sandhurst.[43] It was as expected:

> The usual Sandhurst round. Gas instruction in the morning – the rears frozen up after breakfast (mealy porridge, fried bread and elongated fishcake, doped tea, two pats of butter, marmalade) – mechanical engineering and coffee and buns at break, kit inspection – [at the] disposal of Platoon Commanders.[44]

But Jellicoe caught pneumonia, which ended his few months at Sandhurst. While he was convalescing, he heard that volunteer officers and officer cadets were needed for 5 (Special Reserve) [Ski] Battalion of the Scots Guards for intended operations in Northern Scandinavia in support of the Finns. The new battalion wanted experienced skiers to undertake two weeks' winter warfare skiing in Chamonix. Jellicoe was definitely up for this and on 16 February transferred to the Ski Battalion – the 'Snowballers'. The Commanding Officer of this remarkable and hastily assembled unit was a Coldstreamer, Jimmy Coats, MC, an expert skier and Cresta Run competitor.[45] Coats had three weeks to pull together men, stores, equipment, weapons and expertise into a force capable of fighting on skis.[46]

They underwent initial fitness and weapon training in February at Bordon Camp in Hampshire.[47] There, Jellicoe found Carol Mather and David Stirling.[48] Stirling, like others, had dropped to the ranks in order to get in.[49] Jellicoe knew many of them already and most knew him by his name, unofficially commemorated by the 'Jellicoe Express', a train that ran up and down to the west coast of Scotland with men going to and from their Naval duty stations.[50]

Leaving a trail of empty champagne bottles beside the railway track, the Snowballers went off by train for ski training at Chamonix with the French Chasseurs Alpins.[51] At Southampton, they crossed the Channel in the *Ulster Prince* with a destroyer escort to Dieppe and continued by train to Chamonix. The fighting skiers then settled down to cross-country ski training, sledging, winter warfare and survival instruction. Living conditions were primitive but they were young, fit and in Haute Savoie where there were French girls (and some English), instead of at Sandhurst doing Orderly Officer Cadet duties.[52]

Returning from Chamonix, they re-crossed the Channel, went by train to Scotland and boarded a ship at Glasgow bound for Norway. But it was not to be. After one night on board, an armistice was declared between Finland and Russia, making their presence in Scandinavia no longer necessary.[53]

23 March. Jellicoe was commissioned as a second lieutenant in the Coldstream Guards,[54] and posted to the Coldstream Holding Battalion at Regents Park.[55] By May, the battle for France was raging and he hated being there instead of in action. Bored by day, he began to slip away at night to the Bag o' Nails so-called nightclub. Some very entertaining women frequented this establishment and to one of these he soon surrendered his virginity. Having discovered this new pastime, he got back to

barracks later and later. One night, he was so late that he was confined to barracks for fourteen days. When in June he heard of the formation of 8 Guards Commando, he jumped at the chance to escape from Regents Park.

The Commando were being raised by Colonel Bob Laycock, a pre-war officer of the Royal Horse Guards, in response to Churchill's memorandum of 3 June calling for raiding units to tie down German forces on the coasts of occupied Europe.[56] During the selection interview, Laycock asked why Jellicoe wanted to join the Commando. He hesitated and Laycock posited, 'I suppose you want to have a crack at the Boche?' to which Jellicoe quickly affirmed 'Yes', was accepted and joined 8 Guards Commando on 2 August.[57] It consisted of volunteers from the Coldstream, Scots Guards and Royal Horse Guards, together with some Royal Marines and Light Infantry. Jellicoe was one of two subalterns in 2 Troop, under Squadron Commander Captain Mervyn Griffith-Jones. The other was Second Lieutenant Ian Collins, son of the publishing family and international tennis player. The troop sergeants were 'Gentleman Jim' Almonds and Pat Riley.[58]

8 Commando trained at Burnham-on-Crouch on the Essex coast where there was ample scope for escape and evasion, night exercises, water training and personal survival tests, in addition to the normal Guards fitness and endurance training. 2 Troop set up their HQ in a pub called the Welcome Sailor. At twenty-one, Jellicoe already had a way of talking to his men that carried conviction and a sense of humour.[59] On one occasion, he set the troop an exercise to develop the survival skills they would need on the run in enemy territory. He dispatched them with a list of items they were to procure by nightfall, by fair means or foul: a bowler hat; a cockerel and a hen; a bicycle; a motor vehicle; and other bizarre items. This did not amuse the longsuffering local populace and as men with bundles reappeared at the pub-cum HQ, other men had to stand guard over them. The booty was then returned to its rightful owners.[60]

As winter closed in, 8 Commando deployed to Scotland where the rugged terrain of Inverary and Loch Fyne was perfect for more arduous training. They forded the Douglas Water and at Largs

11

carried out an attack and defence on the moors and an assault on the Big Cumbrie. On the Isle of Arran and Holy Island they practised cliff climbing and carried out a mock battle at Brodick. HMS *Glenroy*, a newly refurbished Landing Ship Infantry, then arrived to take them to the Middle East.[61]

On 28 January 1941, 8 Guards Commando, 11 Scottish Commando with some Royal Horse Artillery and Marines, boarded HMS *Glenroy* as part of Layforce, the newly formed Commando Brigade under Colonel Bob Laycock. At 1700 hours on 30 January, Admiral Sir Roger Keyes, gave a farewell address to the combined Commandos.[62] They put to sea next day, in weather so appalling that the forward gun positions had to be abandoned. Many of the men and crew (but not Jellicoe) were seasick. The decks could not be used and they had to amuse themselves as best they could. David Stirling spent so much time asleep in his cabin (when he was not gambling or playing chemin de fer) that he was nicknamed the giant sloth.[63]

Second Lieutenant Randolph Churchill, 4th Hussars, the Prime Minister's son, was appointed Admin Officer for the voyage. He and Evelyn Waugh took turns to keep the War Diary. For two aspiring writers, their entries could not have been more perfunctory. Much of Jellicoe's time was spent gambling and by the time they reached the Red Sea he had lost two or three years' income. But he won it all back again with a seven against a six in a game against his future second father-in-law, Philip Dunne.[64] Randolph Churchill lost even more.[65]

The ship settled into a disciplined routine of weapon training and kit inspections. As the days lengthened, 'darken ship' times were published in daily Part I Orders posted on the mess decks. Smoking was allowed for twenty minutes after that time, before the Navy then piped 'Out pipes'. They could not be too careful. There was no comprehensive convoy system throughout the Atlantic and German aircraft and submarines had a range from their recently acquired bases in France and Norway which exceeded that protected by any of the Allied escort zones.

19 February. HMS *Glenroy* docked at Cape Town. After the confines of the ship, Jellicoe and Stirling set off with boots and packs to tackle the hills.[66] 8 Commando was warmly welcomed

and Jellicoe went to pay his respects to Smuts.[67] On 2 March, they passed the island of Socotra and entered the Gulf of Aden. After the Red Sea, the sight of wrecks reminding them of the possible presence of mines, they quickly reached their final destination: Geneifa on the Great Bitter Lake.

There followed four frustrating months during which there was nothing really for 8 Commando to do. The intention had been for them to attack Rhodes but that had been overtaken by Rommel's offensive. Instead, they were transported around the north coast of Africa to take part in various engagements with the enemy, most of which did not happen because of bad weather or because the odds against them were too overwhelming. They kept busy with camp duties, weapon training and practising for raids on aerodromes and harbours. They began to train in collapsible paddleboats from HMS *Aphis*, an 'insect class' gunboat.[68]

27 May. 8 Commando set off in *Aphis* to attack an aerodrome at Gazala, thirty miles west of Tobruk. It supported the German and Italian HQ for the siege of Tobruk and was therefore strategically important.[69] *Aphis* was soon dive-bombed by Stuka aircraft. They dropped out of the sky with a menacing, long, descending drone and came perilously close before depositing their bombs at the last moment. In the sharp action that followed, one Stuka was hit by the ship's Bredas and exploded in midair. Three more were shot down into the sea.

During a brief lull in this, Jellicoe's first taste of action, someone took a photograph of him thoroughly enjoying the engagement. Wearing a Mae West and round-rimmed sunglasses, he looks like a young man from a much later era.[70] Bombing had disabled the *Aphis* and she limped slowly back to Alexandria. But Layforce's days were numbered. A vain attempt to reinforce Crete against the German attack in May 1941 was not enough to prevent the disbandment of the Commando force. Its men were needed to reinforce the newly forming Eighth Army. On 1 June, the news was official. Some men went to the Far East, others to desert patrol special service units and the rest back to their battalions. Jellicoe decided to join the 3rd Battalion, Coldstream Guards.

While Jellicoe and Mather waited for posting orders in Alexandria, they decided to have their own crack at the Gazala airfield. Perhaps they and two men could succeed where 100 had not. They needed a means of getting to the airfield and the agreement of General Morshead, Commander of Tobruk.

After helping themselves to stores, explosives, Tommy guns and ammunition, they let the authorities know they were going in and caught the nightly destroyer to Tobruk. It deposited them and slid silently away, leaving them with their pathetic bundles of kit on the deserted quayside. Dawn began to break, revealing the ghostly masts of Allied ships sunk in the harbour. The Port Commandant, an obliging Royal Engineers Major, invited them to share his headquarters, a dilapidated shack conveniently close to the Royal Navy. At night, they slept, or tried to, at the empty shell of the Albergo Tobruk hotel.[71]

The Jellicoe name quickly opened the door to General Morshead. He suggested they tell the Royal Navy what they wanted. A very fast light landing boat, the *Eureka,* would be ideal for taking them to the target and possibly taking them off afterwards. Following a briefing from the friendly 18 King Edward's Own Indian Cavalry Regiment, who were holding positions to the extreme west of Tobruk next to the sea, Jellicoe and Mather memorized the view of the German lines and no man's land. If they could not be taken off by sea, they would need to get back through the German lines, avoiding mines and snipers in the process.[72]

In late June they made two or three unsuccessful attempts in the *Eureka* but were never able to make a proper landfall. The difficult coastline also made recovery by sea almost impossible. Even if they made it back through the German lines, they would have had great difficulty getting through the lines of the 18 Indian Cavalry since the Indians might not have realized who they were.[73] On their return to Alexandria, Jellicoe and Mather were loath to return their guns, explosives and ammo to the 'Q' stores. But Layforce was breaking up so they couldn't hang on to them. They therefore stashed them away in the attic of the Alexandria flat of an employee of Mather's family firm.[74]

18 July 1941. Jellicoe reported to the 3rd Battalion, Coldstream Guards on the Libyan frontier. Life was completely different from Regents Park. The officer commanding his company, John Loyd, was an excellent leader and commander.[75] Jellicoe spent six enjoyable months leading desert patrols, before the Battalion's prominent role in 22 Guards Brigade. But the Allies had extended themselves dangerously, advancing some 300 miles westwards to Agedabia in a few weeks, their long supply lines making them vulnerable to attack.. . .

The fans still turned slowly overhead. Jellicoe's sickbay reverie was suddenly interrupted by the horrifying realization that the hospital was an Australian establishment staffed entirely by male nurses. He never got out of hospital quicker.

In the Long Bar of Shepheard's Hotel in Cairo, he ran into David Stirling who was already famous for the SAS's successes. He was looking for a second in command and offered Jellicoe the job. He was amazed but keen, as long as his battalion was prepared to release him. He was sorry to leave the Coldstream but could not resist the chance to join the elite force.[76] Stirling was already angling to take over the Special Boat Section (SBS).

30 April 1942. Jellicoe was posted[77] to 'L' Detachment, the supposed detachment of a fictitious 1 SAS Brigade.[78]

The desert and his destiny awaited.

15

Chapter Two

The Admiral's Son

George Jellicoe led his first raid at the age of seven. In summer 1925, three boys played in a large house at St Lawrence Hall, Ventnor, on the Isle of Wight. In the fashion of the day, they wore white sailor suits with navy blue and white-edged collars and white toggled lanyards. But these boys had more than the average claim to naval attire. George, Viscount Brocas of Southampton, was the only son of Admiral of the Fleet Earl Jellicoe of Scapa. The other boys were the sons of a Royal Navy friend of Lord Jellicoe's, Commander Frank Marten who had also served at Jutland. The elder, Tim Marten,[1] was nine and his brother, Toby, seven.

Towards lunchtime, young Brocas – George – suddenly said, 'Come on! Let's go and eat the nectarines in the peach house.' The three diminutive mariners quickly invaded it. The Marten boys ate three or four ripe fruits while George managed four or five. They then went in for a nursery lunch.

That evening, a distressed head gardener came to see Lady Jellicoe.

'Ma'am, I'm afraid the nectarines that were just ripening in time for the visit of King George and Queen Mary have disappeared.' Lady Jellicoe was furious, believing that the Marten boys were leading George astray. The next day, the Martens' chauffeur arrived to take Tim and Toby with their nanny home to Cheltenham.[2]

George Patrick John Rushworth Jellicoe was born, weighing 14 lb, at Hatfield on 4 April 1918, where his parents lived for a year after his father resigned from his post as First Sea Lord at Christmas 1917. The King, who had been in the Royal Navy and knew Jellicoe very well, had made known that he would like to be godfather.[3] So it was that the baby came to be named after his monarch.

His father had married late in life. When George, the Jellicoes' sixth and last child, was born, his sailor-hero father, John Rushworth Jellicoe, was fifty-nine. His wife, Florence Gwendoline, daughter of Sir Charles Cayzer, a Victorian ship-owner, was thirty-nine. George's character was to be influenced by the Victorian values of his parents.

John Jellicoe was a Naval officer of outstanding ability, equally effective in command at sea or as a staff officer on land. But he had been held responsible as the admiral in charge when the mightiest, most modern Navy in the world had failed to achieve a Trafalgar-esque victory against the German High Seas Fleet at Jutland in 1916. After a bloody but inconclusive engagement in the North Sea on 31 May, the German Navy had given the British the slip.

Some said that Jellicoe had been overcautious, but most men in his position would have been circumspect. He was the 'only man who could lose the war in an afternoon'.[4] The defeat of the British Grand Fleet would have amounted to the removal of Britain's main deterrent, leaving the way open to a German invasion. On the other hand, it is arguable that during the long Victorian peace, the Royal Navy had forgotten most of the successful tactical doctrine of Nelson's time and had become dominated by 'Regulators'.[5] Whatever view one takes, it is a fact that no other Naval commander, not even Nelson, has ever had to bear the kind of responsibility that Jellicoe bore at Jutland.[6]

On 31 May 1916, the British Grand Fleet clashed with the German High Seas Fleet. The outcome has been controversial ever since. The Germans had come out to tempt the British Fleet into a submarine trap by raiding the East Coast. Aided by superior intelligence, the Royal Navy was waiting. The battlecruiser fleet (led by the adventurer Admiral Beatty) met its German equivalent on the afternoon of the 31st. After losing two out of five battlecruisers to superior German gunnery and sighting the rest of the German fleet, Beatty – sensible at last – fled north, leading the Germans onto the guns of the Grand Fleet.

Jellicoe manoeuvred his ships superbly, gaining the advantage of the fading light. Seeing the Grand Fleet, the Germans ran before them, although another British battlecruiser blew up. Jellicoe placed his fleet between the Germans and their escape routes. But the German fleet slipped through the rear of the British line at night, turning one by one in a way that was unusual and unexpected, and escaped.

Strategically, the Battle of Jutland was a British success. Although the German fleet won every significant tactical engagement in the battle, Jellicoe kept Britain strategically dominant. This position remained unchallenged for the rest of the war. After that encounter, the German Fleet dared not risk another.

The Jellicoe family had long been associated with Southampton. The name Jellicoe possibly derives from the French 'joli coeur'.[7] One had married the heiress of the French Basque Brocas family,[8] whose English origins had begun in the time of English rule in Aquitaine and Gascony. There were de Brocas at Crécy and the Siege of Calais.[9] At least one died in defence of English shores and another, Sir Bernard Brocas, was attainted and executed for remaining faithful to Richard II.[10]

John Jellicoe was born in Southampton in 1859. His father, Henry, a commodore in the Merchant Service, commanded his own ship at twenty-one. In 1842, Henry was mentioned in House of Commons questions in connection with his heroic exploit as a seventeen year-old midshipman on *The Clyde,* a merchant steamer, at St Kitts. The Governor had come aboard uninvited and Jellicoe was ordered to put him ashore at the nearest landing place. The Governor wanted to be taken further and an altercation ensued. 'Gentlemen, I must land you here,' said Jellicoe, to which the Governor responded 'You shall not!', seized the tiller and pushed Jellicoe overboard. He climbed back aboard and one of his crew told the Governor 'If you touch him again I will shove my oar down your throat!' Jellicoe then put the Governor firmly ashore. He received much positive publicity, before going on to a successful career.[11]

On his mother's side were several Royal Navy officers, including two admirals, one of whom was Second Sea Lord at the time of Trafalgar and another who had been a surgeon RN. From his earliest days, Jellicoe wanted to go to sea.[12] His outstanding intellect was recognized when the village school-master told his mother, 'I don't think you realize what a clever son you have. He has just solved a problem in half an hour which took a friend of mine over a week ... '.[13] In 1874, Jellicoe passed out of Britannia,[14] the forerunner to the Dartmouth Royal Naval College, top of his term.

By 1897, Captain John Jellicoe RN, flag captain to the C.-in-C. of the Far Eastern Fleet, had met Florence Gwendoline Cayzer, daughter of Sir Charles Cayzer, who had founded the Clan Line shipping company in Perthshire. Gwendoline was pretty, intelligent and rich, with a mind of her own, which she was not afraid to use. Jellicoe was mature, successful and charismatic, his reputation already enhanced by his survival from the loss of HMS *Victoria*, in 1893. After colliding with another ship, the unfortunate vessel sank, drowning the C.-in-C., Vice Admiral Sir George Tryon, a noted naval modernizer.[15] That year, Jellicoe went to China but maintained a correspondence with Gwendoline.

In June 1901, he became involved in what he called 'the Boxer business'. Under Admiral Seymour, Jellicoe was Chief of Staff of the Boxer Rebellion Expedition, whose aim was to relieve the besieged British and other Western Legations in Peking. About thirty miles from the city, in addition to Boxer resistance, the international force ran into difficulty when the Chinese Dowager Tz'u-his Empress set the Imperial armies on them. They retreated to Tientsin and while clearing a village Jellicoe was shot in the lung, leaving it impaired for the rest of his life.[16] Gravely injured and presumed dying, he made a will and sent it home with a picture of him being carried into Tientsin on a stretcher with Admiral Seymour walking beside him.[17] Quite unintentionally, Jellicoe had stolen the scene.

On returning to England in 1901, he was appointed Assistant Controller of the Navy to Sir William May, the Third Sea Lord,

Controller of the Navy and a member of the Board of the Admiralty. Jellicoe's duties included naval construction and he visited the Clyde shipyards and renewed his acquaintance with the Cayzers.[18] While accompanying them on board a Clan Line ship during her acceptance trials and skylarking with some friends, Jellicoe fell, sprained his ankle and was nursed for a week at the Cayzers' house. Later in life he wrote:

> During this week, I came to the conclusion that my future happiness depended on my persuading Gwendoline to marry me. I proposed on 9 February and to my joy was accepted. We were married at Holy Trinity, Sloane Street on 1 July and my married life was one of the most perfect happiness ... Our love grew if possible stronger and stronger as the years passed and she was besides a most loving mother to our dear children. I do not think that many men could have been so fortunate in their married life as I was.[19]

Gwendoline's father, Charles Cayzer, of Cornish extraction, was founder and major shareholder of a shipping dynasty which included the Clan Line, the country's largest ocean-going fleet.[20] He had started with nothing but died a millionaire in 1916.[21] This supreme example of enterprise and endurance gave the grandson he never met a respect for hard won achievement and an openness to new ideas.

The Jellicoes moved to a large flat over Harrods, a retailer from which Lady Jellicoe never liked to be too distant. Here their first daughter, Gwendoline was born in 1903. Jellicoe took command of the armoured cruiser HMS *Drake* and departed for the West Indies. Family and Royal Naval relations were reinforced by the marriage of Gwendoline's sister Constance to Captain Charles Madden, later Chief of Staff to Jellicoe when he became Admiral of the Grand Fleet.

In 1904, Jellicoe was recalled from his command to serve at the Admiralty on a special committee set up by Admiral Sir John Fisher to consider a new design of warship, known as 'Dreadnoughts'. These formidable battleships aimed to combine the greatest number of heavy and long-range guns that could possibly be carried (except for the lighter armaments necessary for outer torpedo-boat defence) instead of the usual mixture of heavy and medium-calibre armaments. After serving on the Dreadnought Committee, Jellicoe became Director of Naval Ordnance, with responsibility for procurement of the vital heavy gun mountings. Fisher wanted the Dreadnoughts ready for sea trials a year from laying the keel – an almost impossible timetable.

The next ten years were marked by a period of rapid professional and domestic change for Jellicoe. But he made time to play as well as work – at a furious pace. When golfing, he would charge full-tilt between one hole and the next, on one occasion causing his opponent to protest, 'I say Jellicoe. I thought this was a round of golf, not a steeplechase!'[22]

In 1905, a second daughter, Betty was born. In October 1907, King Edward VII knighted Jellicoe on the occasion of the review of the Home Fleet at Cowes and appointed him Second-in-Command of the Atlantic Fleet. In Quebec in 1908, during the Tercentenary celebrations, Jellicoe was presented to the Prince of Wales on board HMS *Exmouth*. The dreadnought HMS *Indomitable* acquitted herself well, prompting the Prince to give Jellicoe the royal photograph in a magnificent silver frame.[23]

A third daughter, Myrtle, was born. Jellicoe was appointed Controller of the Navy. A fourth daughter, Norah, was born in 1910 but in the same year five-year-old Betty died suddenly of mastoids in the ear.

At the end of 1910, Winston Churchill, First Lord of the Admiralty, persuaded Jellicoe to accept command of the Atlantic Fleet. It was part of Fisher's plan to groom him for command of the Grand Fleet in the anticipated war. In October he had written to Arthur Balfour:

My absorbing thought for six years has been the one point you mention, to push young men to the high commands who will think in submarines and thirteen and a half inch guns! Such a one – the first fruits of ceaseless opportunity – goes as Commander-in-Chief of the Atlantic Fleet next month – Sir John Jellicoe. Phenomenally young and junior.

He will be Nelson at Cape St Vincent until he becomes 'Boss' at Trafalgar when Armageddon comes along in 1915 or thereabouts....[24]

The future commander needed experience commanding a fleet of Dreadnoughts. The nation expected another Trafalgar.

On 22 June 1911, Sir John and Lady Jellicoe attended the King's coronation and his review of the fleets at Spithead. The Cayzers owned St Lawrence Hall, on the Isle of Wight and during Cowes week Jellicoe met Prince Henry of Prussia and raced in the Kaiser's yacht, *Meteor*. In December, Churchill invited Jellicoe to take command of the Second Division of the Home Fleet but Jellicoe wanted to remain in Gibraltar. After many years' service with the Royal Navy abroad, he preferred a station where his family could accompany him. But Churchill would have none of it and Jellicoe was told he had no option. This did not get their relationship off to a very good start.

Jellicoe's standing was then enhanced by another strange turn of fate. Just after three o'clock in the morning on a stormy grey 13 December 1911, the P&O steamer *Delhi* was wrecked off the west coast of Morocco. The ship ran aground just south of Cape Spartel. But this was no ordinary passenger vessel. On board were the Princess Royal and her family. Jellicoe was woken at 0315 hours in his residence at the Villa Plata and given the news. He immediately took charge of the situation. He coordinated a brilliant rescue, planning ahead, issuing orders, and thinking of every detail. He ordered the *Duke of Edinburgh, London* and *Weymouth* to get up steam and instructed Rear Admiral Craddock to shift his flag to the *Duke of Edinburgh* and put to sea. Meanwhile extra wire hawsers and grass ropes were sent from other ships to the *Duke of Edinburgh* and *London*. Jellicoe then put to sea himself in HMS *Prince of Wales* to effect the rescue. Before leaving, he wrote to the Governor asking for military rocket apparatus to be sent to Tangier in *Weymouth*, in case he had difficulty in approaching *Delhi* from seaward, and wired the minister at Tangier to ensure full cooperation should he need to use it.[25] He also asked for a lifeboat and dockyard tugs, offering a crew for the lifeboat from *Prince of Wales*.

Despite very heavy seas and bad weather, *Duke of Edinburgh* reached the wrecked ship at 0900 hours and with some difficulty and danger sent her cutters, helped by boats from the French cruiser *Friant*, to get the royal party and other survivors to safety.

Jellicoe was the man of the moment. The King sent a telegram to the Fleet and Queen Alexandra sent a long personal message, full of thanks. These were the more heartfelt because the *Delhi* had been completely lost. Jellicoe's fame spread. By the end of the First World War he was a household name, with his picture on everything from cigarette cards to tea mugs. A fifth and last daughter, Prudence, known as Prudy, was born in 1913.[26]

In August 1918, four months after George was born, Jellicoe became Viscount Jellicoe of Scapa. In 1919, he toured the world to review the Commonwealth Navies but it was New Zealand, with its mountains, lakes and glaciers and opportunities for shooting, fishing, tennis and cricket that captured his heart. He was offered the Governor Generalship of either Australia or New Zealand and chose the land of the long white cloud. The Jellicoes went by sea to New Zealand and little George had his second birthday in the Panama Canal.

George's able, forthright mother and four surviving older sisters provided strong female role models. He adored, and was adored by, all of his sisters and grew up to appreciate capable women and expect that they would love him. He was particularly close to Prudy, who was nearest to him in age. His intimacy with his sisters enabled him to grow up without being in awe of women. But because he looked up to them he also did not believe that women were inferior to men. He related to them on their own terms.

From his mother came candour and commonsense, without her occasional lapses of diplomacy. From his father, George inherited an easy capacity for making friends, a sense of fun, humility and prudence.[27] From both parents, he inherited an appreciation of the good things in life, a prodigious appetite for hard work and the ability to be a survivor.

Government House in Wellington had huge lawns and gardens, with ample space for exploring. On summer evenings, the whole family would play hide-and-seek up and down its long corridors.

There, George sustained his first wounds by falling off the garden swing, cutting his forehead, and collecting a scar from a car accident when his mother was at the wheel. So he grew up with the usual ups and downs of childhood in a loving and disciplined environment. As the last child and the long-awaited son and heir, there must have been some risk of him being spoiled. But there is no evidence that his loving older sisters indulged him while his mother was rather strict. Some found her fearsome but to her family and especially to him she was great fun. They holidayed at Ninety Mile beach in the North Island, where George learned to swim. His mother was an accomplished horsewoman and he went hunting with her and his sisters.

George seems to have grown up secure, self-effacing and extremely open. As the Governor General's only son, he must have been a symbol of hope to New Zealanders, who had lost so many sons to the Great War.[28] His sisters were not the only girls around. With his mother, he judged a beauty competition of little girls – an opportunity not open to many small boys. He joined the Wolf Cubs, but since there was no Wolf Cub pack in the vicinity,[29] he was attached to the Brownies – an event, he told me with some glee that changed his life.[30]

Before leaving New Zealand in 1924, the Jellicoes toured the South Island. After crossing on the ferry from Wellington to Picton, they took a steam train down the east coast to Christchurch. As they were approaching the city, six year-old George watched his father completing his morning ablutions. While chatting, Jellicoe was rinsing his false teeth, swirling them round in a glass of water. He then tossed the water out of the window, only to discover that he had jettisoned his dentures as well. On arrival in Christchurch, a great gathering of local dignitaries, supported by Guides and Brownies, was waiting to meet them. The Guides and Brownies were immediately dispatched back up the track to find the Governor General's teeth, which they did.[31]

With many fond farewells and crowds waving from the harbour quay, the Jellicoes left Wellington.[32] But George never forgot his New Zealand childhood. Passing through the Suez Canal, the Jellicoes stayed in Cairo at the Mena House Hotel, where young George was troubled by bedwetting.

24

On being created an Earl in 1925, John Jellicoe chose Viscount Brocas of Southampton as his second title, by which George then became known. In London, the family lived in Exhibition Road, Kensington, where a nanny would take the seven-year-old to swim in the Serpentine. They moved to 90 Portland Place and then to 19 Prince's Gardens (Lady Jellicoe was wont to move house frequently). Summers were spent at St Lawrence Hall where the King and Queen came to stay during Cowes Week.

At eight, George went off to preparatory school at St Peter's Court at Broadstairs in Kent. Although in the bottom form, he was soon leader of a group of rather bullying little boys. But when it emerged that Brocas occasionally wet his bed, there was a *changement d'alliances* and he was the one persecuted.[33]

At St Peter's Court, George was well taught and had plentiful opportunities for sport. He became junior and senior boxing champion and was mad keen on rugby, playing scrum half for the school fifteen during his last two years. He was joint Head Boy for his last year. He spent holidays with his parents and sisters on the Isle of Wight. St Lawrence Hall was an attractive, late nineteenth century property, purchased by George's shipowner grandfather and left to Gwendoline. It was large, with beautiful gardens that ran down a slope towards the road and the sea. All the Jellicoes had rooms there until the beginning of the Second World War when Lady Jellicoe found it too difficult to get up and down to it from London.[34] George enjoyed the gardens, swimming in the sea, golfing and sailing. His only regret on leaving St Peter's Court was that he had not continued with Greek or piano lessons.

Although George was destined for the Royal Navy, Lord Jellicoe thought that the breadth of a public school education at Winchester would be better for his son than the more focused regimes of Osborne and Dartmouth.[35] In 1931 George achieved a good pass there. He went into Freddies House and was the smallest boy at Winchester. He was no slouch academically and moved rapidly up the school, specializing in science, since this seemed most useful for his intended naval career. The fact that it was not his forte was brought home to him when he went to look at a set of exam results on the College notice board. He began looking, modestly enough, in the centre. There was no sign of his name. He looked upwards, but it was not there. Then he looked downwards. Finally, at the very bottom, he saw 'Brocas' with three marks out of 150.

He switched to languages and history and the inspiring tuition of Harold Walker, with very much better results, winning the Vere Herbert-Smith history prize.[36] His housemaster, R. L. G. Irving, the distinguished mountaineer who coached the later conqueror of Mount Everest, Sir Edmund Hillary, invited him to go climbing in Scotland. But George was rather terrified of mountaineering and always declined.

Already he had a large capacity for work and play. By January 1933, he had reached Senior Part 3 and top of his form, having collected both the junior and senior history prizes. He reached the rank of corporal in the OTC and coxed the college four in rowing. That year, he learned to ski in St Moritz and continued the following year in Verbier. In 1935, at Murren in Switzerland, he was part of the Winchester College ski team that won the British Schools Championship.[37] He was also a school prefect.[38] Even though he was not called Jellicoe, people knew him by his famous father; a fact of life for George and his sisters. He always felt proud when someone mentioned him.

Winchester did not really mean much to George until his last couple of years there when he had more freedom to go sailing at weekends. He had many friends. Tim Marten was in the year above him; Edward Bird[39] was a year or two older than him, as was another firm friend, Archie John Wavell. The two travelled together to Paris and the Ardennes. Wavell's sister Pamela was the first girl that the young Viscount Brocas kissed.[40]

George's social life was edifying. Lady Jellicoe was always late for everything and Jellicoe used to say that he could take the whole Home Fleet to sea in less time than it took his wife to get ready to go out.[41] When King George V and Queen Mary visited the Jellicoes at St Lawrence in the summer of 1935, Fritzi joined them. He quickly became rather keen on Prudy.

Summer days were filled with parties and sports. They played tennis with Borotra, the French and Wimbledon tennis champion. George sailed with his father at Bembridge Sailing Club in J Class boats and occasionally in the schooner, *Westward*, which belonged to a South African millionaire. There was riding – the Jellicoes followed the Isle of Wight foxhounds in winter – swimming, shooting, golf and sailing. The family kept a fourteen-foot dinghy, *Winnie the Pooh*, on the River Hamble and George, with his father or sometimes his cousin, Elizabeth Madden, used to sail it over to Bembridge and back, calling at a few pubs before cycling back to Winchester.

There was, however, one small cloud on George's horizon. That summer, he wrote to his father to say that he was sorry but he did not, after all, want to go into the Royal Navy. His father wrote back to say that he should not worry about this but that they should chat about it when he next had an exeat. George cycled from Winchester to Southampton and took the ferry to Cowes where his father met him. They drove to the Shanklin Golf Club and played a round before having lunch in the Club House. Having talked over his son's disinclination to join the Navy, Jellicoe said, 'Let's not worry about it now. Next time we meet, we'll talk about what you'd like to do instead. And now let's have another round of golf' – an inordinately understanding response from the Admiral who had commanded the Grand Fleet at the battle of Jutland.[42] But the son never told his father the real reason for not wanting to go to sea – his absolute dread of wetting a hammock.[43]

Another, much more ominous, cloud appeared. On 20 November, George's housemaster told him that his father was very ill. He had stood too long in the cold on a very bitter Remembrance Day and his 'good' lung was infected. George took the next train to London and hurried to their home in Wilton Crescent. Lord Jellicoe was in bed, very pale and feeling quite ill. He apologized for not being in better form. They talked about a recent shared day's shooting and George's scholarship exam to Cambridge in two weeks' time. Then his father said, 'Let's have another chat tomorrow, when I'm feeling a bit better'.[44]

George went out for a stroll down the Brompton Road. Suddenly, he felt an overwhelming urge to return. Tearing back up the road to the house, he rang the doorbell. The butler, an old friend of the family, opened the door with tears in his eyes.

George knew at once that his father had died. The new Earl Jellicoe was seventeen years old. He had had the most marvellous father and it was a terrible blow for them to be separated, just at the time when he was getting to know him as a man. They had begun to talk about his father's impressions of the war, though he had never talked of his own role in it.[45]

Before the funeral, the family went to stay with the Madden family.[46] John Jellicoe was buried in St Paul's Cathedral with the full honours of a grateful nation. The Prince of Wales, later King Edward VIII, the Duke of York, later King George VI, Admiral Earl Beatty, who had risen from his sickbed to attend, and Fritzi were among the chief mourners on the slow journey from the Admiralty to St Paul's. George had recently been with them all and the King on board HMS *Britannia* during Cowes week and was ten days away from sitting his Cambridge history scholarship exam. He achieved an Exhibition, despite not doing any further work from the day his father died.[47]

Shortly after the funeral and his return to Winchester, Jellicoe wrote from Morshead's, to his cousin Elizabeth Madden, who had recently suffered bereavement herself.

All the dons see one – stare – and then don't know what to do ... whenever they offer their condolences I am almost reduced to tears. It is the same with my friends. I am longing to let myself go, but always they must talk about some trivial thing ... I thought that when I got back here I would be able to slip back into my ordinary life. I thought that the sadness of Daddy's death would pass and only the love and pride remain. But it isn't so ... I don't seem to be able to think of anything but Daddy; every little letter of his, every gift he has given me, of the places where I have walked and talked with him ... Moreover, although I am immensely proud of him (for who could fail to be after Monday?) his achievement and his goodness seem almost overwhelming. There is more sadness than pride, whilst I am ever cursing myself for not repaying *all* the love he gave me, for not knowing him as well as he knew me. It is all the sadder since in the last few months he has never helped me more, whilst I have never known him

28

better. It looked as if I would be able to bridge the gap of years. And then he died ... However long I live, he will always be with me, if not in spirit, at least in memory. He is a foundation on which to build; his thoughts, his ideals are an example for me and although I stray and am afraid, his memory will be a comfort and a conscience.[48]

The sudden end of a boy's relationship with his father is tragic at any time but for an only son so close to a father who had provided total stability and security, and a famous father at that, it was particularly traumatic.

The dangers and temptations of the world lay ahead.

Chapter Three

The SAS Submarine

In April 1942, Jellicoe reported to the do-it-yourself headquarters of Stirling's newly founded 'L' Detachment, SAS Regiment at Kabrit, north-east of Suez on the edge of the Great Bitter Lake. Everything from the tents and basic furniture to the vehicles and training equipment had been 'borrowed' from other unsuspecting Allied units. By April 1942 however, 'L' Detachment was very much in business carrying out raids on Axis airfields, roads and installations deep inside enemy territory.

Jellicoe had a rather unpropitious introduction to the SAS. He was shown into a tent for the night having been told 'the chap is away at the moment'. No sooner had he installed himself and was comfortably dozing off when he was rudely awakened by the unexpected re-entry of the tent's owner, Paddy Mayne. Mayne, the huge Irishman whose brilliant leadership was to win him three DSOs and command of 1 SAS Regiment, was not one to mess about with pleasantries and seldom had Jellicoe found himself more rapidly expelled. In everyday life however, Mayne turned out to be very easy to get along with. He had an extraordinary tactical ability, which superbly complemented Stirling's strategic vision, and a quite unbelievable courage.[1]

Jellicoe had already seen something of David Stirling's ability during Commando training in Scotland. He had risen easily to the challenges of escape and evasion exercises over the rough Scottish countryside of Inverary and the Isle of Arran, in which he showed both exceptional mental agility and emotional reserves as well as a prodigious capacity for physical endurance. In the abortive Middle East 8 Guards Commando raids and on HMS *Aphis*, Jellicoe had also been able to watch Stirling in action and observe his preparations. It was then that Jellicoe had begun to appreciate the Scotsman's astonishing rapport with those with whom he dealt. His immense courage was matched by an incredible, persuasive power over people. Despite his youth and relatively junior status, he could, for example, see just about anybody he wanted at any time, getting the ear of senior officers and talking them into supporting his schemes. He was just as adept at talking his way out when things backfired, often not because of him.[2]

Stirling also had the capacity to be several jumps ahead of everyone else in his thinking. It was always inspiring to see him at Kabrit but in truth he was as much in Cairo as in the unit that he had founded. Already greatly admired, by that time virtually anyone in the SAS would have followed him anywhere. Throughout 1941 and until January 1943 when he was captured,[3] whether at Kabrit, at his brother Peter's flat in Cairo right opposite the British Embassy[4], or in the desert, his amazing, inspired leadership was there just the same. As founder and leader he had incredible power and magnetism. He knew everyone serving under his command. They knew that he himself would do twice what he was asking of them. He was, above all, creative and a doer. In particular, he was passionate about training and perhaps the first proponent of the adage 'train hard, fight easy' or, in the case of the SAS, 'fight easier'.[5]

From May 1942, for about a year, Jellicoe was Second-in-Command of the SAS – not that Stirling ever took much notice of that sort of thing. With the job went things that Stirling did not want to do himself, including administration, such as it was. Jellicoe's first contribution to the SAS therefore involved working out stores and rations indents and mileage, and solving other essential but not particularly riveting problems. Stirling was good at delegation. He knew when and what to delegate and how to pick the right man for the job. He then didn't interfere unless there was some need to vary the orders through changed circumstances.[6]

The SAS had not long since lost a key collaborator of Stirling's, Jock Lewes, a young Welsh Guards officer whom Jellicoe had known during Layforce days. Lewes had been killed during an SAS raid on Nofelia on New Year's Eve, 1941.[7] Though Jellicoe was not close to Lewes, there was no doubting his courage or ability, his considerable contribution to SAS training and his exceedingly useful 'Lewes bomb'. He too had been a brilliant tactician. Jellicoe admired Lewes in those early days because his role was vitally important to the development and early success of the SAS. It helped them stay in business long enough to prove themselves. But David Stirling was undoubtedly *the* Founder and although he himself later acknowledged that he had had co-founders, those who suggest that there was another, *real* Founder are very much mistaken.[8]

News of Stirling's growing band of expert saboteurs soon attracted other volunteers. Mather joined 'L' Detachment and revelled in the tough life. Even good administration could not prevent the inevitable privations of desert raids. As Stephen Hastings said, if the food ran out they would live off their fingernails. For a man who appreciated the finer things of life, Jellicoe seems to have been able to rough it without losing his sense of humour. He was always even tempered and invariably saw the funny side of events.[9]

Stirling also gave Jellicoe responsibility for liaison with the squadron of Free French parachutists who had joined the SAS at Kabrit. Their leader, Commandant[10] Georges Bergé, was a tough, resilient character from Gascony. Jellicoe acted as their guide to British naval and military habits, counsellor and friend. His fluent French made him perfect for the assignment. Stirling, typically, was drawing fully on all available skills.[11]

The Free French were a small unit but, as Jellicoe was to say years later, 'they were very, very free and very, very French'.[12] They had already served with distinction in South Africa, Palestine, Libya and Syria, before arriving in Kabrit in January 1942, following an agreement between Stirling and Bergé that they should join forces. The Free French were all trained parachutists but needed to be fully integrated into the SAS. This task fell to Jellicoe and he designed joint fitness and endurance training for the French and British SAS men and special courses in demolition and weapon training.[13]

From the outset, and showing his extraordinary foresight, Stirling was keen that the SAS be prepared to mount raids by sea. He made clear that the French would be involved in this too. At the beginning of June, Bergé duly presented the rank and file of the Free French unit to Jellicoe. They knew he was the son of the admiral who had faced the Kaiser's Navy at the Battle of Jutland in 1916. It therefore seemed entirely appropriate to them that he should be the one to teach them silent rowing on the Little Bitter Lake.[14]

The French were also greatly struck by the fact that, in contrast to themselves, Jellicoe was always smartly turned out in his 'so British' uniform, as they called it even when speaking French. It was a huge delight to them that Jellicoe operated in French. This removed many potential difficulties and helped bind the two nationalities together into one effective team.

To test the joint operational capability of the integrated squadron, Jellicoe mounted a mock raid on the aerodrome at Heliopolis. Jellicoe, Bergé and the rest of the French then made the requisite number of jumps together.[15] Jellicoe loathed parachuting, particularly at night. One of the Free French, Jack (not Jacques) Sibard, made his last drop in a stick with Randolph Churchill, who was jumping for the first time. As each parachutist descended towards the earth, the dangling man looked down on the upturned faces of a huge crowd of reporters and cameramen who rushed over towards him shouting through megaphones, 'Are you Churchill?' Churchill was in fact the last to jump, which meant that all the press mobbed him as soon as he landed.[16] Since Stirling had made Churchill responsible for contacts with the media, this is probably exactly what both had had in mind.

By May 1942, the trained and integrated men were badged[17] and ready for action. This took the form of a daring raid on Heraklion airfield in the north of Crete. The mountainous island, 260 kilometres long, 103 kilometres wide and only 112 kilometres south-east of mainland Greece, had fallen to the Germans the year before as the German Army swept all before it throughout mainland Europe.[18]

33

The aim of the raid was to reduce the strength of German air attacks on a supply convoy from Alexandria destined for Malta. The island was on the point of collapse and Churchill was adamant that vitally needed supplies should get through. The SAS raiders were to land by sea and blow up German bombers – particularly Junkers 88s – at Heraklion.

The assault, timed for the night of 12 June, was planned to coincide with SBS raids on other Cretan airfields at Maleme, Kastelli Pediados and Tymbaki. But it was typical of Stirling that he inserted himself into high-level operational planning and earmarked for the SAS the key target of Heraklion. For good measure, seven other German and Italian air bases in Cyrenaica were also to be attacked by the SAS, with all assaults coinciding with the passage of a Malta convoy, Operation VIGOROUS. On leaving Alexandria, it would face heavy enemy naval and aerial bombardment to the south-west of Crete.

The Cretan operation needed considerable detailed planning. Stirling left this entirely to Bergé and Jellicoe, just as he left the planning of SBS raids very much to its commander, Mike Kealy.[19] The raid would involve the Royal Navy, the Greek Navy and a Greek submarine. David Sutherland, a young SBS officer, was to carry out the raid on the Tymbaki airfield, so it had been necessary to tie in with his plans too. Jellicoe was also responsible for close liaison with Naval HQ, since it was easier for him to handle this. But Bergé was very much in command, with Jellicoe as his adviser. So they planned the raid together.

In front of a large tent at Kabrit, which served as officers' mess, instruction room and meeting room, Bergé formed up his thirty men to handpick those for the raid. The selection process was swift. 'Mouhot, Sibard, Leostic, stay with me,' he barked. The rest he stood down. Bergé had chosen Sergeant Jacques Mouhot and Riflemen Parachutists Jack Sibard, originally a seaman in the French merchant navy, and Pierre Leostic, who was only seventeen.[20]

Jellicoe, Bergé and his three men moved to Alexandria to begin preparations. Out on a night water-training scheme, they ran into some of Jellicoe's Greek girlfriends. They were rather curious as to what he was up to but he did not enlighten them.

34

5 June. Night fell in Alexandria. In great secrecy *Triton*, a submarine of the Free Greek Navy under command of Captain Kontogiannis, took on board the five SAS operatives and their equipment. Lieutenant Costas Petrakis, a Cretan, of the Royal Hellenic Army, had joined the party and was to be their guide.

Before embarking, the group carried out water training in inflatable dinghies. This preparation was important since the inflatables were frail and not very manoeuvrable. Jellicoe took one with Mouhot and Petrakis. Bergé, Sibard and Leostic took another from which they towed one with equipment, weapons and bombs. Each man carried a 30-kilo burden containing dry rations, water, explosives, detonators in separate oilskin bags and twenty-five plastic bombs. This weight was in addition to his weapons: a Colt 45, a Beretta machine gun, modified by Bergé to be more compact, an American dagger, two hand grenades, plastic bombs, compass, maps, aerial photographs and various small gadgets.[21]

The submarine, *Triton*, had a fine Greek commander and an excellent crew. However, being a fairly basic French vessel built in the early 1920s, she was not very comfortable. The cramped conditions were exacerbated by the fact that the submarine was never meant for passengers. With several nationalities on board, differences of language and culture also had to be overcome.

Despite these difficulties, Kontogiannis and his crew made the SAS very welcome, willingly engaging in three-way hot bunking so that each man could get about eight hours' sleep out of twenty-four. *Triton*'s dives lasted for up to eighteen hours and life on board was strict. There could be no unnecessary noise and smoking was not allowed when the submarine dived. When they surfaced, before the hatch was opened, the officer of the watch advised everyone to rest with mouth open to reduce pressure on the ears.[22]

The SAS spent their time memorizing the mountainous and inhospitable Cretan terrain and mastering details like the password for local agents, 'I am Captain Manolis'. A rendezvous had been arranged for their return at the village of Krotos on the south side of the island and at Gallos further to the west.

After five days at sea, *Triton* surfaced off the north coast of Crete. Jellicoe's first sight of the island and of Greece was through the periscope of the submarine: a long dark mass seen only intermittently through the waterline lapping across the viewfinder.[23] *Triton* dived again to about a dozen metres to await 'H' hour. Suddenly, the British petty officer listening to the sonar gestured to the officer in charge aft. The klaxon blared and the watertight doors closed, dividing the occupants of the submarine into three groups.[24]

The SAS were in the middle of the vessel, listening for the slightest noise while the *Triton* sank deeper and deeper. The dial on the depth counter showed twenty metres, thirty metres and forty metres before steadying at forty-two metres. The pressure on the men's eardrums was enormous. The crew remained motionless at action stations. *Triton* was operating on her enormous batteries. In the almost complete silence, everyone could hear the drumming propeller screws of ships passing overhead. The submarine rested, suspended, dragging gently in a bottom current. Silence reigned. Interminable hours passed. Eventually, the petty officer gave the signal to surface and 'up periscope'. It had been a close run thing. The prospect of being depth-charged in a tube of steel had gone away.[25]

In the early hours of 10 June, *Triton* dropped the SAS three miles out from the small beach at Karteros. This was much further than they had anticipated and they were faced with a long haul in with their paddles. Commando water training was beginning to pay off. As in training, Jellicoe, Petrakis and Mouhot were in one boat, towing one with the stores and explosives. Sibard and Leostic paddled another, with Bergé at the helm, which also towed a loaded boat. Then the dinghies began to leak.[26] Jellicoe, always immaculate when going into action, immediately took off his gold-trimmed, peaked hat and started baling.

After some hours, the sound of waves breaking on a beach told the raiders that they had reached the small creek of San Barbara. There was no reception party so it was important to conceal all trace of their arrival. After unloading the inflatables and filling them with large stones, Jellicoe and Mouhot undressed, swam out with them several hundred yards from the shore and stabbed them, sending them gurgling to the bottom.[27] The party was about twenty-five miles from their target and so left the beach, in single file, not even stopping to check for mines. They passed a shepherd who greeted them amiably with a 'Yassou!', as if the sight of sinister SAS men on a Cretan beach at three o'clock in the morning was totally unremarkable.[28]

By now, the operation was well behind schedule. In addition to the longer than expected trip, they had too much heavy equipment. Their landfall was also further east than they had planned and the terrain hillier and rougher than they had been led to believe. It was impossible to reach a lying up point close to the airfield that night so they stopped to rest. Some friendly Cretan peasants, who never failed to spot anyone turning up like this, soon found them. Even the occupying Germans knew that the civilian population of Crete always gave all possible assistance to what later became known as 'the sabotage organization of Captain Jellicoe'.[29]

On the night of 12/13 June, the party moved off and got up close to the barbed wire surrounding the airfield. Then they almost ran into a German patrol. The situation was hopeless: they could have overcome the patrol but their cover would have been blown. So the attackers withdrew to the south-west to lie up through the day at a vantage point from which they could watch the airfield. Fifty or sixty Ju88 bombers were parked around the runways. Bergé and Jellicoe then made a recce for a spot to get onto the airfield.[30] It was the night of 13/14 June.[31]

While they were cutting their way through the barbed wire, another enemy patrol appeared. Jellicoe thought they had not been seen, but the last German in the column challenged them. With astonishing inspiration, Mouhot instantly rolled onto his back and began to snore loudly. The snores were so reverberatingly realistic and the Germans so clearly disgusted by the apparently drunken Cretan peasants that without more ado, they moved on. Mouhot's action saved the day because if the SAS had engaged the enemy, the raiding opportunity would have been lost.[32] Thus the lack of curiosity and diligence of two German patrols gave the SAS their chance. The Germans were good soldiers but bad sentries.[33]

Much encouraged, the raiders cut their way onto the airfield. Annoyingly, the German patrol returned. But then came a second piece of good luck: two Beaufighters attacked the airfield. This unexpected diversionary cover enabled the SAS to get to one of the two clumps of aircraft, where they set about placing bombs on twenty-two aircraft, including one Fieseler Fi156 Storch, a highly efficient, slow-flying reconnaissance aircraft, and some petrol dumps.

While Mouhot and Sibard were fixing their Lewes bombs to the wings of the aircraft (nineteen Ju88s, one Me109, one Do17 and the Fieseler Storch), each with a two-hour time pencil fuse, Jellicoe with his *flegme britannique* (British cool) said to Bergé, in French, 'Commandant, I'm just going off to see if there is anything else to be done'. Some time later, he reappeared, having planted more bombs on the engines of some still-crated aircraft and on several trucks.[34]

The first bomb went off. The whole airfield was suddenly wide awake. The intruders now could not tackle any more aircraft, as they had planned. But how to get out of the airfield? A German patrol was marching out of the west gate and without any hesitation Bergé led the party forward. The SAS moved out, fell in smartly behind the patrol and at the appropriate moment outside the perimeter fence neatly peeled off into the darkness. They had not even been noticed. At that moment, there was a final explosion and a huge conflagration, the sound magnified by the closeness of the hills. The whole bomb depot had gone up. Bergé was delighted. They had done plenty of damage and Jellicoe immediately congratulated their leader. Hardly pausing to comment, Bergé responded, 'Mouhot, Sibard and Leostic – and you too Jellicoe – you're all going to get the Croix de Guerre. And Sibard you're promoted to corporal as from today.'[35] In addition to the aircraft, which included seventeen serviceable Ju88s, they had destroyed two aero engines, two trucks and the bomb dump.[36]

It was still dark. The party quickly put as much distance as possible between themselves and the airfield, heading, as they thought, south with Bergé leading. Before long, Jellicoe drew Sibard's attention to the Pole Star in the sky up ahead of them.

The Frenchman quickly understood that Bergé was leading them north. Since this would have been rather a disaster, Sibard casually queried with his Commandant whether they were in fact going in the right direction, whereupon Bergé, somewhat piqued, said, 'All right then, you take the lead if you're so clever'. But instead, he called a halt to get their bearings while Petrakis went off to seek news.[37] He returned a couple of hours later with a Cretan couple, a demobilized army officer and his wife, who brought a stew of courgettes and snails. The food went straight down.[38]

The news was that the Germans had shot fifty Cretans at Gazi, about five kilometres west of Heraklion.[39] They included twenty hostages, among them Tito Georgiadis, a former Governor-General of Crete, a seventy-year-old priest and some Jews in the prisons.[40] This dreadful news gave the party fresh motivation, as if any were needed, to get across the island to the arranged rendezvous on the south coast near Krotos, east of Tymbaki. There, they were to be taken off in a small trawler commanded by Lieutenant Commander John Campbell RNVR.[41]

They continued due south and on the night of 15/16 June, reached the edge of the little mountain village of Karkadiotissa. At dawn, Petrakis again went for news and returned with an old shepherd who had killed one of his sheep for them – a great personal sacrifice – which was quickly devoured. Two young Cretans, who promised to go with them and guide them to the rendezvous, joined them at this feast.

Nightfall, 16/17 June. They ran into a problem. The two Cretans, who by now knew their intended route, changed their minds and said they would go no further. This meant the raiders would leave behind two people who could betray them. Bergé was furious. In his view, they had to be killed and pulling out his Colt 45, he gestured towards the two men who threw themselves on their knees. It was a terrible moment. To kill in cold blood two men with whom they had just shared a meal was unthinkable. With Petrakis translating, it was finally agreed that they would, after all, continue to act as guides. Petrakis went with one of them to the village to tell the families of both that they were not going home that night. The other was held and would be killed in twenty minutes if his friend did not return. Petrakis and the Cretan returned and the matter was resolved, the allies in the party reminding themselves that Cretans were moreover a people of honour who could be trusted.[42]

They continued south, moving by night and resting up during the day. The terrain was hilly and in the dark they made slow going. During the nights of 16 to 18 June, they crossed the valley east of Tymbaki and lay up in a steep valley in the hills.

Dawn, 19 June. Bergé and Petrakis returned from Apessokari, the village where the latter's sisters lived, with a veritable feast: chicken, cheese, cucumber and bread. A quickly improvised spit soon had the chickens turning, while Jellicoe crushed black olives with his bare hands and spread the oil over the gradually bronzing birds. Meanwhile, Mouhot and Leostic were kept busy gathering more wood to feed the novel Franco-British cooker. After the lavish meal, they turned in under the pale but still starry Cretan sky.[43]

Lying up there, within a couple of hours of the rendezvous, they were again discovered. The Cretan who found them offered to bring food and drink. But Bergé was suspicious. He asked Petrakis who this man was, since he did not like the cut of his jib. Petrakis could not really say because he had left his village some years before and the man was a relative newcomer.[44]

At 1500 hours, Sibard woke Bergé as prearranged. He had asked Sibard to go and make contact with their rendezvous at Krotos. To Sibard's surprise, Bergé then changed his mind. He wanted Jellicoe, whom he perceived as having status, and Petrakis, who was a local, to go instead. The two men set off but after reaching the rendezvous and confirming their disembarkation plans with the Greeks, Petrakis's feet gave up. Jellicoe made his way back alone to find Bergé.[45]

Returning to their valley, Jellicoe could find no sign of his French comrades. He searched the valley from top to bottom. Puzzled, he searched the two valleys to the west and east of it. Then he withdrew. At dawn, he searched the original valley again. In the daylight, he was certain that it was the right one. Then he found his comrades' belongings, arranged suspiciously neatly. Such tidiness was most uncharacteristic. Something was very wrong. Some young Cretans appeared, curious to see what had happened. Though Jellicoe could not understand them, they intimated in no uncertain terms that he should leave as fast as he could. The Cretan had, after all, turned out to be that rarest of rare birds, a Cretan Quisling.

The French had indeed been betrayed. At about 1900 hours, as they had been preparing to move off, Bergé had suddenly shouted, 'Look out! We're surrounded!' The four men were trapped in a culvert with the mountain towering around them. They made a square and tried to take shelter behind a high bluff, with Bergé and Mouhot to the west and Sibard and Leostic facing 180 degrees to the east. A troop of Germans approached. They had clearly been well informed.[46]

Bergé immediately opened fire and a German crumpled. Another German shouted orders as the enemy took cover among the scrub. There was a confusion of rifle fire and grenades. Bullets ricocheted off rocks and it was difficult for the Frenchmen to know where to aim. Then Leostic yelled, 'Let's go south! There's nobody there.' But Sibard had seen a German firing from that direction.

'No! Pierrot! No!' he screamed. But it was too late. Leostic had launched himself southwards and within a second there was a short burst of machine-gun fire. After a moment's silence, Sibard could hear his comrade moaning, 'Maman, Maman'. The German fired again. The crescendo of gunshots was followed by an even more awful silence. The young French soldier lay dead. He was just seventeen.[47]

Being out of ammunition and hopelessly outnumbered, the French decided to surrender. At their shouts, the enemy held their fire. After a last attempt at evasion, the three Frenchmen were eventually captured. The Germans lost no time in interrogating their prisoners.

'There are six of you. Where are the others?' they demanded and, more menacingly, 'You General de Gaulle soldiers. You terrorists. You kaput.' Fortunately for the new POWs, it was the German air force at Heraklion, rather than the Gestapo, who interrogated them. The *Luftwaffe* did this thoroughly but engaged in no foul play or torture. On 2 July, the captives were flown out to Italy.[48]

Meanwhile, Jellicoe had returned to the rendezvous. A few mornings later, walking along the beach, he was spotted in the binoculars of David Sutherland, who identified him by his khaki shorts and shirt and his jaunty walk. Sutherland's raid on Tymbaki had been aborted because the airfield was empty. The two men lay up for two nights in a cave where they suffered the most appalling fleabites.[49]

23 June. John Campbell in HMS *Porcupine* arrived at night to pick up Jellicoe, Sutherland and the remaining SBS men to take them back to Mersa Matruh.[50] As they were being ferried out to the ship, they passed an Englishman being brought to the island. It was Paddy Leigh Fermor, operating with the Special Operations Executive (SOE) out of Cairo,[51] on his way in to begin a singularly successful partnership with the Cretan resistance.[52] He and Jellicoe could not see each other but exchanged names by shouting.

'I'm Paddy Leigh Fermor. Who are you?' the new arrival bellowed across the wine-dark sea.

'George Jellicoe,' Jellicoe shouted back. 'Good luck!'[53]

Leigh Fermor and his radio operator were the only men landing from *Porcupine*. As they went ashore, a crowd of guerrillas waited to be taken off but there was simply no room on the boat for them.[54]

The SAS and SBS raids together had destroyed twenty-six aircraft, fifteen to twenty trucks and considerable quantities of POL, bombs and other munitions.[55] Despite this destruction, the convoy from Alexandria to Malta was forced to return to port after sustaining several losses. But ships from the convoy from Gibraltar got through.[56] The attacks also contributed to the substantial overall harassment of the Axis forces. Rommel later wrote 'Stirling's SAS did me great harm'.[57]

These achievements were, however, tinged with sadness. In the case of Heraklion, the loss of Bergé and his compatriots was keenly felt, both personally and strategically by the SAS. But the dangers and challenges they had faced together had forged a firm friendship. For their part, the French had noted Jellicoe for his ability and courage.[58]

25 June. Back at Kabrit, Jellicoe found David Stirling talking ambitiously of leading a large group of SAS around the Qattara

Depression to establish a new base, well behind the German lines at El Alamein. This would avoid a long and dangerous trek through enemy lines for each raid. Instead, they could remain at large inside enemy territory and retire to their hideout to rest up between raids. In Jellicoe's absence, Mayne had convinced Stirling that the SAS should also have their own jeeps, in order to save walking the last miles to and from their targets and to ensure quick getaways. Stirling quickly procured fifteen jeeps with two Vickers 'K' guns and twenty 3-ton lorries.[59]

'L' Detachment aimed to attack the enemy's landing grounds from El Daba to Sidi Barrani and the road between El Daba and the Halfaya Pass, known to the soldiers as 'Hellfire'. They were to be supported by the Long Range Desert Group (LRDG), another private army that operated in patrols using fast all-metal trucks to mount road watches and gather data about enemy traffic[60]. Stirling had enough supplies to set up the base, from which he could opportunistically raid airfields in the Tobruk, Derna and Martuba areas.[61]

The arrival of the jeeps was a defining moment in SAS history. At a special briefing on 2 July in Peter Stirling's flat, Jellicoe was delighted to see Stephen Hastings. Hastings had been with 22 Guards Brigade north of Agedabia but when he and a brother officer heard that Stirling was recruiting for 'L' Detachment they had both volunteered and been accepted.[62]

At the briefing, Jellicoe was in one corner of the room with a whole lot of Top Secret maps (he was keen on maps) outlining the salient features of the terrain and the proposed route. In another corner, a whole lot of girls were having a drink before going to the races in Gezira.[63] The briefing had been delayed because Mo, Stirling's Sofragi servant, had unwittingly hidden the maps earlier that morning in a fruitless attempt to tidy the bachelor abode of the Stirling brothers. Here Jellicoe met Hermione Ranfurly, who later published her remarkable wartime diaries.[64]

Tobruk had fallen on 21 June and by the end of the month the Allies had retreated to the El Alamein line. However a counter-attack was on the cards. Stirling was keen for the SAS to play a major role. He needed to go and talk to General Sir Claude Auchinleck at MEHQ and asked Jellicoe if he would bring up the new trucks and jeeps (acquired from a US consignment bound for the Eighth Army). Jellicoe had four days in which to prepare and move out. Fifteen jeeps needed adaptation to take special equipment (since the SAS had not hitherto been motorized) and twenty 3-ton lorries had to be loaded. He was at pains to point this out in his report, recording that drivers and maintenance crews had to work for seventy-two hours non-stop as their departure hour approached.[65]

At last, the large convoy set off northwards, accompanied by LRDG Patrols G.1, G.2 and Y.2 to help with navigation and carry out their own observations. As planned, Stirling drove down from Cairo and met Jellicoe and Mayne south of Alexandria. From there, the large convoy, consisting of most of the SAS who were not involved in training at Kabrit, drove westwards towards the fearsome Qattara Depression, south of the ends of the two sets of Allied and enemy battle lines which ran south from the Mediterranean coast.

The Depression was a vast sunken area of plain several hundred feet deep with salt lakes and quicksands surrounded by towering, jagged escarpments. Its supposed impenetrability was the reason why it formed the southern end of the El Alamein line. As the convoy made its way through the Depression, they were at constant risk of air attack, from both enemy and Allied aircraft, and mechanical failures. The vehicles thudded up and down over scorching, rocky gullies and fissures.

Sixty miles from the Mediterranean and 150 miles behind enemy lines they found a series of ridges, just west of the Mersa Matruh to Siwa Oasis track. Here Stirling chose a spot with caves and wadis as their rendezvous, or 'laager', in which they could camouflage the jeeps during the day. From this ideally located base, deep in enemy territory, they would spend the next two months carrying out raids in different directions. Despite the heat and flies, Jellicoe wanted to be there. It was time for business.

Jellicoe, Hastings and Mather, who had also joined the SAS, went out in jeeps, each with two gunners, to attack the coast road between Fuka and Galal, behind the German lines.[66] They were to shoot up German transport and generally make a nuisance of themselves. This was Rommel's only supply line and since it was in use round the clock it promised to be a worthwhile target. A second party led by Lieutenant Robin Gurdon of the LRDG, was to move into position and be ready to attack two landing grounds at Sidi Barrani.[67] These two raids had the furthest to go and were therefore forced to do some of their approach in daylight. A third party was to attack three landing grounds in the Fuka area. Meanwhile, the enemy was flying a regular patrol up and down the deep escarpment of the North African littoral, close to the sea at Halfya.

The 'three musketeers', each with two men in their vehicles, drove fifty miles or so. As they were approaching the great escarpment towards evening, Jellicoe signalled to the others to halt. He pointed to some scrub about half a mile away in which they could take cover. As they set off, they sighted enemy aircraft – Italian Macchi fighters – coming in over the edge of the escarpment.[68]

The fighters struck suddenly. The SAS men immediately scattered but were barely a dozen or so yards away from each other when the enemy opened fire. Jellicoe's jeep got some bullets through the radiator but he immediately drove it into a small crevice in a wadi, jumped out and threw some camouflage over it. By the time the aircraft had run out of ammunition and had flown off, Hastings' and Mather's jeeps were burning like torches, but no one was injured.[69]

As they surveyed the remaining jeep, the planes reappeared with a vengeance. This time, the nine men managed to get 100 yards from the burning vehicles and hide among the desert scrub before the shooting began. As darkness fell, the enemy flew off, no doubt intending to send out search patrols in the morning. The SAS were knocked out as far as the raid was concerned but still had to get back to base.

The enemy had not seen Jellicoe's jeep and soon there were nine of them on it with seventy miles to go. Amid the smoking ruins, Jellicoe sat with his feet on the bonnet singing 'I wish I was a bee'. The radiator was so badly damaged that it kept running out of water yet the trusty jeep still functioned. Using plastic explosive from their Lewes bombs to plug holes in the radiator, they were mightily relieved when the jeep's engine started without blowing up. Since water was precious and the radiator often boiled over, they took it in turns to pee into it. The one surviving jeep made it to within a few miles of the rendezvous before it seized up and stopped. Nine lives had been saved to fight again another day.[70] Not everyone was so lucky. The same aircraft got the other patrols, killing Robin Gurdon, whom Stirling viewed as a possible future commander of the SAS.

Three weeks later, Stirling and Jellicoe made the hazardous trip through the Qattara Depression back to Cairo for supplies, returning with fresh vehicles and reinforcements. The stage was set for a major raid, unique in the history of the SAS, on the airfield near Sidi Haneish, about thirty miles south-east of Mersa Matruh. It involved a totally new approach, whereby sixteen jeeps in columns would carry out a mass attack in full moonlight. Stirling would lead in the centre, with Jellicoe and Mayne leading the columns on either side. Since each jeep had two machine guns, such massed firepower would enable the attackers to shoot their way through the perimeter fence.[71]

The reason for this further change of tactics was that Stirling wanted to outwit the enemy's latest methods of aerodrome defence. On moonlit nights, the Germans had started to scatter their aircraft over several landing grounds to minimize the effects of RAF bombing and make sabotage more difficult. Stirling's new approach would in future keep the enemy guessing about where attacks might come from, forcing the Axis forces to deploy larger numbers of men in defensive positions.[72]

25 July. The SAS practised their new method of night attack, with live ammunition, about 100 miles behind the enemy's front line. It was critical that they kept no more than ten yards apart so that Stirling could keep control by means of Very lights fired from a pistol. Next day, it took four hours to cross the desert to the target in bright moonlight. The journey itself was not without incident; there were six punctures and one LRDG truck hit a mine. During the last mile, at a speed of about four or five miles per hour, a few jeeps fell into anti-tank traps.

There was no question of bothering about concealment. When they reached the landing ground, they lined up at the perimeter fence and sprayed the parked enemy aircraft with their sixty Vickers K – a twin gun in front and a twin in the rear – to keep the enemy's head down. Every jeep blazed away and the noise was deafening. Several aircraft burst into flames. The enemy did not react until the raiders fired into their huts. Rather belatedly, Stirling then fired his Very pistol to signal the attack, bathing the whole scene in an eerie green light. Tracer and incendiary bullets added to the effect, revealing the positions of more aircraft. The columns then advanced at a relatively slow speed of one or two miles an hour while the occupants of the jeeps painstakingly, one by one, shot up around thirty planes.

Stirling led in the centre with Jellicoe on his right and Mayne on his left. The two flankers, Hastings and Mather, followed slightly behind. Hastings's jeep was hit but he and his men were unharmed. Just as the demolition of the first line of aircraft was completed, the Germans opened up with a 20-mm Breda. Until then, the enemy's fire had not been very accurate. More gunfire hit Hastings's jeep, went through his legs without hitting him, and through the engine. Still the jeep carried on. Stirling, as cool as a cucumber, then stopped and asked, 'Are you alright?' Hastings was fine but covered in oil. The valiant jeep then collapsed and its occupants had to find themselves seats in the other vehicles, with about nine of them clinging to each one.[73]

The columns returned the fire. Then, wheeling round and keeping perfect dressing, as only the Brigade of Guards can, they turned to deal with the next parked line of aircraft. The previous night's practice had paid off and the manoeuvre was successful, with Stirling adding a lighter touch of command and control by sounding a hunting horn.[74]

The second group of aircraft received the same treatment as the first, with the enemy still unable to prevent it. Only the approaching dawn forced Stirling to desist. At this point a fog conveniently descended and the SAS left the scene. The enraged Germans then mounted a non-stop search for the attackers, including flying an hourly patrol of six Ju87s up and down the main track. They discovered one of the French parties and attacked the LRDG's T.1. Patrol which managed to escape. The rest returned to base unscathed in the following two days.

From this time on, the Germans were forced to dig in all around their airfields. This meant that the SAS could neither walk in nor mount a mass attack without encountering stiff opposition. This was extremely uneconomic for the enemy, keeping men tied down who were sorely needed elsewhere.[75]

On the way back from the raid, the SAS split up to avoid easy detection. Two or three vehicles were lying up together when a Fieseler Storch flew low overhead and then landed nearby. Two men got out, probably to have a pee or take a look round. One of the British jeeps got to it first, cutting off the occupants' return. They were the German pilot and another officer. The latter immediately shot up his hands, shouting that he was a doctor, probably thinking that the information would reduce his chances of being shot.[76] Both were taken prisoner.[77]

Jellicoe was having problems with a knee. Malcolm James Pleydell, the SAS's own doctor,[78] had been at the rendezvous throughout so Jellicoe had two medical opinions on his condition. The German doctor, Baron von Luterotti, turned out to be the son of the family that Jellicoe and Fritzi had met in Bremen before the war.

The doctors had different diagnoses but, as it turned out, they were both right. There were two things wrong with the knee; a torn internal collateral ligament and a damaged cartilage. The two doctors were, however, of one mind about treatment; Jellicoe should rest the leg. He ignored this advice and the outraged knee seized up completely.[79]

That was the end of action for Jellicoe that summer. Back at Kabrit, he went off to hospital in Cairo, where an operation on his knee was completely successful. In late November he recuperated in England, staying with his mother in Sunningdale. Apart from the joy of having her son back again, Lady Jellicoe still maintained high matrimonial hopes for him and the pictures of the Princesses Elizabeth and Margaret remained prominently displayed.[80] But Jellicoe was more interested in seeing friends, catching up on his reading and going to the opera.

While he was still convalescing in England, Bill Stirling, who was standing in as Second in Command of the SAS, invited Jellicoe up to the Stirling family home at Keir in Scotland. Goose shooting at night, Jellicoe met a fellow guest who was a young Dane. It was Anders Lassen, already well known from his bold raids in West Africa and on the Normandy coast. The holder of an MC at the age of twenty-two, he was a mixture of courage, compassion and ruthlessness.

Jellicoe's first impressions were of an engaging personality and a deep, driving force. This was partly Danish pride and patriotism and partly a profound hatred of Hitler's Germany. But Lassen's fierce animosity towards Nazism and a naturally belligerent war-loving element in his character were balanced by an immense kindness towards the victims of Axis aggression.

5 November 1942. Jellicoe's name appeared among the War Office entries published in the Supplement to the *London Gazette*. The King had been graciously pleased to approve an award of the DSO in recognition of gallant and distinguished service in the Middle East to Lieutenant (Acting Captain) The Earl Jellicoe (124546) Coldstream Guards (Sunningdale). This was for his part in the raid on Heraklion, described in the 'MOST SECRET' commendation signed by the C.-in-C. Middle East Forces, General Alexander:

> His cool and resolute leadership, skill and courage through-out this very hazardous operation were mainly responsible for the high measure of success achieved. He ... placed charges on the enemy aircraft and brought off the survivors after the four Free French members of the party had been betrayed and killed or captured.[81]

Back at Kabrit, Stirling was again looking for a Second in Command. He wanted Jellicoe to take command of a new unit that he was forming from the remnants of the Special Boat Section. Looking ahead, the creator of the SAS saw that raids would need to be mounted across the islands of the Eastern Mediterranean to attack the soft underbelly of Europe. It was a potential opportunity for the SAS – if it could operate by sea.

Jellicoe was to turn the Special Boat Section into the Special Boat *Squadron* and carry it into what became the Raiding Forces: 'the last inheritors of the great Elizabethan spirit', the seadogs of the Aegean.[82]

Chapter Four

Commander of the SBS

New Year, 1943. Jellicoe was about to make one of the most important transformations of his life; from front line soldier to serious mid-ranking commander who made the decisions about who to shoot.

Still in the UK, he mixed business with pleasure. He visited a number of units which might take part in special forces activities. After a dinner at White's Club with Evelyn Waugh and Bill Stirling, they went on to a Soho nightclub. Jellicoe went off to chat to some female dancers and, on returning to his seat, found a great commotion taking place. Waugh had accidentally tripped up a couple of men and when the ensuing argument descended into a fracas, they succeeded in heaving Waugh and Jellicoe from the establishment.

As they were ejected, a police patrol marched past, whereupon Waugh promptly stopped them and lodged a complaint about their assailants. The police took all four men to the police station where Waugh declared his intention to prosecute. Jellicoe was due to leave early the next morning to observe a raid on the Normandy coast. As he sobered up, he attempted to dissuade his friend from taking any further action. But without success. Waugh insisted on pressing charges so eventually Jellicoe said, 'Look. I'm going to withdraw from this' and extricated himself from the affair. Returning from the raid, he drove from Poole to Sunningdale where he found his mother in a state of high dudgeon about an item in the newspaper about the nightclub incident. The club had the same name as the local Boy Scout unit and Lady Jellicoe thought her son had been arrested for going to a Scout club.

One morning, while staying at Brooks's, Jellicoe received a message from 10 Downing Street inviting him to lunch. He duly presented himself and found he was eating alone with the Prime Minister and Clementine Churchill. They asked about the raid on Crete, which had clearly been the reason for the invitation. Jellicoe obligingly launched into the story but soon realized that he had not got going quickly enough. His illustrious leader was quietly dozing off.[1]

Not long afterwards, he went to the Four Hundred Club in Leicester Square with Mary Churchill, Patricia Mountbatten and a friend called Alastair Forbes. Jellicoe seemed already a bit under the weather. He was not making as many jokes as usual and danced, rather badly, being hampered by his knee trouble, with both ladies. He did not normally have a problem holding his drink but on this occasion he was suddenly copiously sick over both of them. They must have forgiven him because a few days later he was invited to Chequers for the weekend and driven down by one of Mary's sisters.[2] Churchill and Jellicoe's father had not always seen eye-to-eye but that seems not to have prevented a rapport developing between the Prime Minister and the Admiral's son.

Jellicoe also went to Whitehall to brief Lord Mountbatten, Chief of Combined Operations,[3] on the SAS raids. After listening to Jellicoe's explanation that one of the main problems with mounting coastal raids was the lack of proper rubber boats, Mountbatten suggested he put the problem to the great scientist and zoologist, Solly Zuckerman. He was advising on bomb blast effects and how such knowledge could help to develop strategy.[4]

Zuckerman was keenly interested and eager to help. 'I hadn't expected him to listen to me,' Jellicoe said later. 'But he did. I took to him at once.'[5] Zuckerman invited Jellicoe to design a suitable boat but he felt unqualified to do so. So they found some young engineers who did a very thorough job. Long after the need for rubber boats had passed, 'the Jellicoe inflatable intruder' was filling the locks and harbours of Alexandria, Haifa and Beirut.[6]

Just before he was due to return to Egypt, Jellicoe received a message from Stirling asking him to accompany the Greek Sacred Squadron, the 'Hieros Lochos', up to the front to join the Eighth Army at Tripoli. Mountbatten said the quickest way to get back to Egypt was to go to Gibraltar and then 'thumb a lift' in one of the many US aircraft going through to the Middle East. In a few days, Jellicoe was in Cairo.[7]

The Greek Sacred Squadron was made up of officers and men of the Royal Hellenic Army and others who had escaped from occupied Greece. Its influence grew as it recruited Greeks from many countries, including Egypt, the Sudan and elsewhere in Africa. Its history inspired awe. It had come into being only twice since antiquity and then only when the freedom of Greece was threatened. Its first incarnation in 370 BC only ended when every last man died fighting to save Thebes from the Spartans. The second squadron ended with similar heroism fighting the Turks in 1821.[8]

The third equally famous squadron had been founded on 12 September 1942 by a larger-than-life character, Christodoulos Tsigantes. He and his brother had taken part in the Venizelos revolt in 1935.[9] The Greek Navy had supported Venizelos on his home island of Crete. But the army had not and the revolt failed. The two brothers were tried and sentenced to death, which was later commuted to long-term imprisonment. In the middle of Constitution Square in Athens, they were stripped of all rank and medals. However, the punishment was further reduced and Tsigantes was in Romania at the time of the German invasion of Greece. He escaped to Ethiopia and then Egypt to found the squadron, which he brought into the Special Forces under Stirling's overall command on 1 January 1943.

It was on the long slog from Kabrit though the Western Desert to Tripoli, just after the El Alamein advance, that Jellicoe first got to know and like Tsigantes. A large, bearded, powerful figure, he was most often seen in a dark duffle jacket, peaked forage cap and dark glasses, a cigarette between his fingers. He exuded confidence. A man of high intelligence, culture, humour and overall good sense, he had a particular gift for leadership.[10] Jellicoe was not alone in this assessment. David Sutherland also found

52

Tsigantes incredibly bright and a strategic thinker in the early days when Greece was in disarray.[11]

A fierce spirit of patriotism, courage and self-sacrifice animated the Greek Sacred Squadron and it was clear that Tsigantes appreciated the rare quality of his officers and men. He in turn had become a rallying point for free Greeks. Jellicoe's relationship with Tsigantes was to parallel the bond of friendship and trust that he had known with Bergé. Both men gained high standing in their own countries and Jellicoe's friendships with them meant as much to him as any other relationship in his life.[12]

When Jellicoe and Tsigantes reached Tripoli, they learned that Stirling had been captured on 27 January.[13] Jellicoe went straight back to Kabrit where a certain amount of confusion reigned. Stirling had never been one to commit his ideas to paper, partly because he was thinking them one step ahead even as raids were in operation and partly because he strained every nerve to avoid any paperwork whatsoever. So he was the only man who knew what was happening where. With their leader's sudden absence, a giant spanner was thrown into the SAS works. Strategic plans were unknown and, following the absence of Jellicoe, administration had also become almost nonexistent. Something had to be done.

By late spring 1943, the campaign in North Africa was over. On 1 April, HQ Middle East divided the SAS, which by now had grown immensely larger than the original 'L' Detachment, in two. The logic was to do so under the two men who had led the columns to the left and right of David Stirling at the raid on Sidi Haneish; Mayne and Jellicoe. By February, the Allies were occupying all of Tunisia so the role of the larger portion of the SAS was to operate westwards to support the Eighth Army there. This force became the Special Raiding Squadron under Paddy Mayne.[14] Its first major operation was the invasion of Sicily, followed by the attack on the Italian mainland.

The smaller part of what had been the SAS was to deploy eastwards throughout the Mediterranean. Since this necessarily involved operating over water, it would be called the Special Boat Squadron. At the age of twenty-four, the newly promoted Major the Earl Jellicoe became its first commander.[15] Even by the standards of the Second World War, Jellicoe was extremely young to become an officer of field rank. Neither the depletion of sufficiently senior officers through casualties nor personal connections could have enabled it to happen but only the combination of intelligence, courage and sound judgment that he had displayed in the desert, in the raid on Crete and at Sidi Haneish.

The Special Boat Squadron (SBS) had a strategic role. Churchill wanted control of Rhodes, its airfields and the Aegean by way of an eventual Dodecanese campaign that would persuade Turkey to join the Allies. The SBS would be key in achieving that aim. It still aimed to attack traditional SAS targets, including airfields, roads, railways, bridges, munitions dumps, communications and other installations, while its men would still occasionally deploy by parachute. And it would operate as part of a new arm called the Raiding Forces Middle East under its no-nonsense commander, Colonel Turnbull, controlled from its own headquarters in Azzib.[16]

The Raiding Forces consisted of the SBS, the Long Range Desert Group (LRDG), the Special Forces Malta Command (SFMC) and the Greek Sacred Squadron. From 1943 until 1945, the Raiding Forces operated in tandem with the Levant Schooner Flotilla, consisting in turn of the Royal Hellenic Navy, the Royal Navy and the Royal Marines. This was joint, and indeed international, Services cooperation, long before the concept of joint Services was formalized in post-war Britain or the EU's Common Foreign and Security Policy was dreamed up in Brussels.

In addition to the men from the SAS, the SBS was formed from the remnants of the Special Boat *Section*, which owed its origins to Captain Roger Courtney. He had formed the first Folboat Section in 1940, which operated using the small collapsible paddle craft named after its manufacturer. After training for beach reconnaissance in the Isle of Arran that winter, Courtney had conceived the idea of also using his new, small force for clandestine raiding. The section joined Layforce just before it embarked for the Middle East.[17]

Courtney and his men trained near their base at Kabrit on the Great Bitter Lake and became No. 1 Special Boat *Section* (SBS). Operationally, they were deployed to Alexandria and attached to the 1st Submarine Flotilla, where they added considerable value to raids against enemy shipping throughout the Mediterranean and the Aegean.

By December 1941, following a spectacularly unsuccessful raid in November to capture Rommel from his house in Tobruk, Courtney became ill and returned to the UK.[18] His successor, Captain Mike Kealy, tried hard to avoid the empire-building clutches of David Stirling but by June 1942 the two units had become close enough for Stirling to assume command of their combined successful raids on Crete.[19] By November, Kealy was back in England and the SBS was down to a strength of thirty-five, including its only two surviving officers; David Sutherland, with whom Jellicoe had shared the attentions of one million fleas in the cave on Crete, and Tom Langton. It was ripe for takeover by the SAS.

Jellicoe's first concern on taking up post was the resources at his disposal, the most important of these being the men. In theory, the squadron had a total strength of around 250 but the numbers of trained and experienced operatives were sadly depleted due to casualties, ill health and normal postings turnover. Fortunately, Sutherland was still there but Jellicoe's immediate priority was to rebuild the unit's depleted numbers with the best men he could get.[20] Another part of his personal transition came to the fore. Jellicoe's networking began to come into its own.

He lost no time in getting in touch with Bob Laycock, by now Chief of Combined Operations UK, to ask him for two outstanding officers. The first was the Dane, Anders Lassen, whose track record and personal qualities had so impressed Jellicoe a few months before at Keir. The other was Philip Pinckney, who did not stay long because he was soon needed in Italy to blow up the Brenner Pass railway tunnel. The next steps were to establish a proper base, begin training and acquire, SAS-style, the necessary stores, equipments and boats, to open for business.[21]

With whatever vehicles and resources they could lay their hands on at Kabrit (most went westwards with the larger portion of men joining Mayne), the new SBS set off in convoy in April 1943 to move up to Athlit, on the coast about six miles south of Haifa in what was then Palestine. Near Athlit was a beautiful bay, at the northern end of which stood a fine, ruined Crusader castle. The training-ground potential of the surrounding terrain was the main factor in selecting that precise spot but the Crusader castle certainly added tone.[22]

Another valuable acquisition was Fitzroy Maclean. Indeed, his capture was something of a coup for Jellicoe. Lieutenant Sir Hew Fitzroy Maclean, to give him his full title, was destined to become the 15th Hereditary Keeper and Captain of Dunconnel. He was courageously able and immensely popular with the soldiers. After living dangerously as a diplomat in Stalinist Russia, Maclean had got himself adopted as an MP because it was the only way in wartime he could get out of the Diplomatic Service and enlist as a private in the Cameron Highlanders. He had joined Stirling in spring 1942 and during the first raid on Benghazi in March had demonstrated his usefulness. When challenged by a Somali Italian sentry on the Benghazi waterfront, Maclean had had the nerve to pretend to lose his temper and bawl the chap out in Italian. It had worked and the humiliated *caporale* had stalked off in disgust.[23] Maclean was indeed a catch.

Maclean and his men arrived back from Iran, where they had been on a major operation, reporting directly to the Commander-in-Chief, General 'Jumbo' Maitland Wilson. While there, they had selected and trained a small SAS-type force to operate behind enemy lines in Iran if the Germans invaded. This activity had resulted in Operation PONGO and the capture and abduction of an Iranian General, Zahedi, who was suspected of colluding with the Germans.[24] Maclean immediately joined the SBS at Athlit. Following a few weeks of water training with the canoes and rubber dinghies, he and his detachment moved north up to the coast of Lebanon to Zahle, beyond Beirut, to complete their mountain warfare training. By now he and his men were itching for action. It was common knowledge that the Eighth Army were likely to land on Sicily soon.[25]

Jellicoe thus had three detachments, lettered according to the names of their commanders: 'L' Detachment under Tom Langton, 'M' Detachment under Fitzroy Maclean and 'S' Detachment under David Sutherland. Each had two platoons divided into five sections or patrols commanded by officers. A number of other men who were signallers, medics, clerks, drivers and cooks made up Jellicoe's headquarters and became a small fighting patrol for his own use. By comparison with the rest of the army, an officer for each patrol might seem slightly excessive (normally a young subaltern officer has command of a platoon, with a number of NCOs responsible for each section). This was because SBS patrols often operated alone, calling for the sort of strategic decisions that needed to be taken by an officer.

Sutherland and Jellicoe had been subalterns together in 'L' Detachment at Kabrit. When off duty, as is the subaltern's wont, they had often gone into Cairo and Alexandria to enjoy pleasant evenings in the company of beautiful Greek girls in the officers' clubs there. But at Athlit, Jellicoe soon became known for being on the tough side. Sutherland thought Jellicoe 'knew a great deal about how to get into, and out of, trouble'. His style was low key but 'What the Lord said, you did'. They all trusted 'the Lord', as he was known.[26] These things might well be said about David Stirling himself, who had made an impact on Jellicoe when he was still at an impressionable age.

Sutherland himself was known for his courage. He and Marine Duggan had been the sole survivors of twelve who had carried out a successful raid on Rhodes the previous September, in the aftermath of which, rather than be taken prisoner, they had swum exhausted and starving straight out to sea. They were eventually picked up by the submarine HMS *Traveller*, but it had been a close run thing. Sutherland was nicknamed 'Dinky' because whatever hardship they suffered, he was always smartly dressed.[27]

Having acquired Lassen, who was under David Sutherland's command, Jellicoe discovered some unusual facets to his character. Shortly after the Dane arrived, he and Jellicoe had a night out together. It took them forty-five minutes to drive into Tel Aviv. They did the usual round of nightclubs and ended up having a chat in one of them, which must have become quite serious. The next thing Jellicoe knew was that he was picking himself up off the floor. Lassen had taken exception to something that his commander had said and had hit him quite hard. The newcomer had clearly been on a short fuse. But Lassen was too valuable to lose and so Jellicoe patched things up with him and they drove back to Athlit.[28] This was a lenient line to take on the serious offence of striking a superior officer but Jellicoe knew when pragmatism should triumph over the rulebook. One wonders too whether Lassen's behaviour had – even if sub-consciously – been influenced by Paddy Mayne's famous striking of his commanding officer, from which situation Stirling had extricated him from 11 Scottish Commando to join the SAS.[29]

Sutherland thought himself extremely lucky to have Lassen under his command. The Dane was totally fearless, stunningly good looking and gave the impression of being every inch a Viking. He was born to be effective; this seemed to Sutherland to be in the Danish blood. Lassen was deadly with weapons. He was also fiery-tempered, highly intelligent and quick-witted.[30] Perhaps it was the raiding quality of life that attracted men like Mayne and Lassen to the SAS and SBS.

The base at Athlit was highly organized. All the necessary equipments and training were arranged in parallel; parachute training took place with the Royal Air Force Squadron at Damascus, while boat training at sea, explosives and demolition training and fitness training in the hills were all local. As always, the men had to undergo parachute training together. It was particularly important to do this to weld the remnant of the Special Boat Section and the men who had served under David Stirling into a new, unified fighting force.[31]

John Verney, Jellicoe's adjutant wrote an evocative description of what it was like for the men living in the camp.

> A lovely spring, an ecstasy of fitness and sense of mission. . . . Days and nights spent swimming across the bay, in naked races along the sands, in landing canoes and dinghies on the rocks watched only by a few tattered Arabs living with goats and chickens amid the ruins of the Crusader castle ... The latrines were buckets emptied by the people of the Kibbutz. From a distance, and against the evening sky, the buckets looked like truncated columns of a ruined Greek temple, for the contractor who had supplied them had failed to provide any kind of shelter or partition. Most of the pirates didn't mind. The site alone, with its view across the Mediterranean, was worth a visit.[32]

Leigh Fermor was there for a couple of months in 1941 to 1942, weapon-training the Cretans. At night, the sea washed into the great banqueting hall where they slept, swirling round the legs of their camp beds without, by some miracle, wetting them.[33]

The new SBS commander was a disciplinarian when it came to seeing that what had to be done was done. The Guards' training really showed.[34] SBS selection was particularly important. Just as in the SAS, the only discipline was self-discipline, with the final sanction of being 'RTU'd' (returned to unit). There was simply no time to discipline any man who didn't perform well under his own steam. Stirling's culture lived on.

Every member of the Squadron, whatever his rank, also needed a formidable range of personal and intellectual qualities. He had to be physically fit with, above all, the endurance to make it back from a raid, however exhausted. He had to be able to carry an 80 lb burden for twenty miles over tough and mountainous terrain and live off the land, eating various noisome grubs, insects, roots and hopefully the right edible plants in order not only to survive but be fit to fight. He had to be able to exist for weeks on end with hardly any human contact or, by contrast, put up with continuous close confinement with a comrade when hiding after a raid.[35]

One other personal quality was needed. All felt that it was impossible to survive without keen intelligence. This feature of SAS selection was made even more explicit in the Special Boat Section. Courtney had kept a notice on his door which read, 'Are you tough? Then push off. I want buggers with intelligence.'[36] In addition, having the courage to do what they did seemed to be connected to the moment in which they lived. They were excited by success; they were on the right side and they were winning. An atmosphere of high expectation and energy pervaded the camp.[37]

The first operation, ALBUMEN, was the summer raid on Crete, led by Sutherland. He knew the island well and he was experienced. He took with him three officers to lead the raid on each target. The purpose of the attack was, as before, to destroy enemy aircraft which might otherwise be used to attack enemy shipping taking part in the invasion of Sicily. The three Cretan airfields were Heraklion, the responsibility of Lieutenant

Lamonby; Kastelli, which would receive the attentions of Anders Lassen; and Tymbaki, to be attacked by Lieutenant Ronnie Rowe.[38] The parties landed by motor launch on the night of 23 June 1943. The raids were scheduled for 4 July.

After five nights of slow and torturous progress over the rocky gullies and canyons of Crete, they approached their targets. Heraklion proved to have been downgraded by the Germans and had few aircraft so Lamonby and his party instead blew up 150 to 200 tons of aviation fuel at a nearby petrol dump. This made quite a bonfire and they retreated back to the beach.

Lassen's party were treated to even more vicarious thrills. The eight Stukas and five Ju88s on Kastelli airfield were in two different corners so Lassen divided his force in two to cause diversions while just two men set off to deal with the aircraft. This tactic worked well. While five aircraft were blown up, Lassen pretended to be German, bluffed his way into a German guardroom and shot four sentries. He and one man escaped to the hills. But instead of lying up through exhaustion after days without sleep, Lassen was waiting when the Germans came looking for him and gave them the slip. After three days in a cave without food or water, he and his comrade made it back to the rendezvous. There they found that once again Tymbaki had proved empty of aircraft and Rowe had returned disappointed with no kills to his name.[39] After a fortnight on Mount Isla, Rowe's guide had defected. On climbing down, the patrol had run into a German patrol, killing two and capturing two.[40]

Nothing comes easy. Within a few months, Jellicoe lost two key people. In July, having been on standby for a raid on Crete, Maclean was very disappointed when he and his detachment were stood down at the last minute because the Germans had changed their dispositions. He let HM Ambassador at Cairo know about his exasperation and intimated that he would not say no to a job with SOE. Within a few days, he found himself summoned to London to report to the Prime Minister. On return, Maclean went to see Jellicoe and said apologetically, 'I'm terribly sorry George; I've just been asked to report to London as Churchill wants me.'[41] He parachuted into Yugoslavia under orders to assess and work with the resistance group that operated most effectively against the Germans.[42] The Diplomatic Service then recruited Maclean to act as their key liaison person with President Tito of Yugoslavia.

Jellicoe's equanimity in releasing Maclean without a murmur marked another stage in the former's maturity as a commander and potential diplomat. Maclean had decided to go but Jellicoe made no attempt to dissuade him. The future 'Lawrence of Yugoslavia' was to act as personal go-between for Churchill and Tito and operate in commando-style raids with Tito's partisans behind enemy lines in the last, highly dangerous stages of the German occupation of Yugoslavia. Jellicoe knew where the greater good lay and, knowing that nothing could have prevented Maclean from going, was wise enough not to make a fuss.

Unfortunately, another loss soon followed; Langton's health gave out. Fortunately, Jellicoe managed to recruit some outstandingly good replacements. He signed up Ian Lapraik to replace Maclean and John Verney to replace Langton. Lapraik, a Cameron Highlander and commando, came with the excellent credentials of having run a commando training school on Malta.[43] He was to stay with Jellicoe during the days of his raiding from one end of the Aegean to the other. Verney was a writer and artist by background but had taken to the raiding lifestyle. Gradually, Jellicoe became closer to Verney than anyone else in the unit. He also came to rely very much on Walter Milner-Barrie, an older officer with experience of serving with the Greek forces and Tsigantes.[44]

Despite being based in Athlit, Jellicoe spent quite a lot of his time in and around Beirut, which was the centre of naval operations. The SBS used the surrounding area to train not only for marine operations but also for mountain warfare (Jellicoe also happened to like Beirut). In winter, he also went into the mountains to ski. All of this must have done some good because he went on to become the ski champion of the Lebanon. He also liked a party. There was ample local wine in addition to what spirits the SBS men could lay their hands on from more official sources. The barman in the Hotel Saint Georges, a sort of Claridges of Beirut, probably knew more about what the SBS were up to than HQ Middle East.[45]

In June 1943, Jellicoe was asked to develop a plan for a July SBS attack on the German and Italian airfields in Sardinia, called Operation HAWTHORN. The SBS were keen, partly because they liked destroying enemy aircraft but above all because they wanted to give the impression just before the Sicilian invasion that Sardinia was the real target. The objective was the Sardinian airfields and the operation was entrusted to L Detachment SBS, by now commanded by John Verney. Jellicoe flew to Algeria to set up the training at Philippeville, while Verney and Edward Imbert-Terry, another Coldstreamer, followed on later to help plan the raid.[46]

On arrival in Algiers, Jellicoe ran into the Pole, Peniakoff, known as Popski. A kindred spirit of Stirling's, Popski had also created his own small but expert specialist force, 'Popski's private army'.[47] It operated with great versatility by combining intelligence gathering and raiding. Popski had acquitted himself well in an LRDG raid on Barce the previous September, timed to coincide with the ill-fated third SAS raid on Benghazi. Popski's high intelligence and leadership impressed Jellicoe. Popski was also personally very credible and could carry conviction in the most unlikely circumstances.[48]

Neither commander had anywhere to stay. They found what they thought was some suitable accommodation, only to discover two nights later that it was a brothel, at which they beat a hasty retreat. A few days later, Randolph Churchill joined them but soon had to drop out because of ill health.[49]

While Jellicoe was still camped among the cork trees near Algiers, Paddy Leigh Fermor invited him to join a daring snatch raid on Crete to capture the German Divisional Commander, General Müller, notorious for his hated reprisal massacres. The plan was to hold up Müller's car and dodge the Germans' patrols by force-marching him over snow-covered Mount Ida. Much as Jellicoe relished the prospect, he could not absent himself from his own hair-raising activities but instead sent a covering force, led by Lieutenant Bob Bury, a bookish, young Etonian who had been training gigantic wild Kurds at Narkover on Mount Carmel near Athlit. In fact, Leigh Fermor's action was some time in the planning and did not take place until April 1944. By that time

General Kreipe had replaced Müller but the action went forward and was crowned with success.[50]

Within a week of the planned Sardinia operation, Jellicoe was asked to report to HQ in Algiers. Here he was dismayed to be told that he could not take part in the raid because he knew the full plans for the Sicily attack, Operation HUSKY, which was about to be launched on 10 July. Jellicoe thought this was not to be supported and appealed to Field Marshal Alexander. But it was no use. His pleadings fell on deaf ears. Alexander was not inclined to risk Jellicoe being captured by the enemy and then, under torture, spilling the beans. He was forbidden to go and John Verney was given command of the raid.[51]

It did not get off to a good start. During the outbound journey in the Royal Navy submarine, it became clear that about half of the ten or so men were unwell. Their training area on the Algerian coast had been malarial and they had indeed contracted malaria. While their illness was discovered on the journey in the submarine, the fact that it was malaria was not recognized. The fit half of the party were therefore put ashore while the rest turned back, including Verney and Imbert-Terry, since it was by then too late for their party to make their landing under cover of darkness.

After the briefest of brief stays near Algiers, Verney and Imbert-Terry's small party of five were dropped by parachute on Sardinia on 7 July. They landed safely and made a forced night-march to the airfields before lying up under cover the next day and completing their detailed preparations. They went in that night and, encountering no sentries or resistance from the by now rather lackadaisical Italians, carried out a successful raid. After destroying a number of aircraft, bomb dumps and stores depots, they then had to cross the north-west part of Sardinia southwards to the rendezvous with the other detachments. They never met up with the earlier party, none of whom made it. Though they must have got close, they were either captured or killed.[52]

With Jellicoe on board, the submarine skirted the east coast of Sardinia and waited to pick up the returning men. But it was a sad and fruitless vigil. Gradually, it became clear that there was no one to take off. The four or five men never appeared. Jellicoe finally had to make the agonizing decision to give up the watch, not knowing whether swimmers were still in the water desperately waiting to be picked up. Verney and Imbert-Terry were also missing – they escaped two months later at the time of the Italian Armistice and marched south until they reached the Allies. The fact that three of his French friends had also been captured and one killed on Crete made the disaster even worse.[53] Despite this terrible discouragement, Jellicoe went back to carry on commanding the SBS.

By late July 1943, it was clear that the SBS's strikes at the enemy were having a wider effect than just the damage they inflicted on the targets. The Axis forces were obliged to divert men from active service to act as sentries on vulnerable ports and airfields. Lieutenant D. I. Harrison, who was serving with Paddy Mayne in the Raiding Squadron, took part in the raid on Sicily. As their Landing Craft Assault (Light) came within range of Crete, they searched the sky for the first worrying signs of German reconnaissance aircraft. But Jellicoe's men were busy keeping the German aircraft on the ground. Not one enemy aircraft was seen during the whole approach to Sicily, even though the Germans must have known that the huge convoy was on the way.[54]

In the space of barely a few months, Jellicoe had brought the SBS to a state of readiness where it was poised to strike further afield at enemy-occupied islands in the eastern Mediterranean. He had turned a dog-eared platoon into an effective fighting squadron that was to become the Special Boat *Regiment,* with three raiding squadrons and an HQ squadron.

Together with the rest of the Raiding Forces and the Levant Schooner Flotilla they were to terrorize the enemy throughout the Aegean.

Chapter Five

Two Lords A-Leaping

Like his father, Jellicoe was a man to whom things happened. The next turn of events in his life flowed from the Italian Armistice. On 8 September 1943, the Italians capitulated to the Allies but Germany fought on. Secret terms for the Italian surrender had in fact been agreed on 3 September. The deal was that Italy would be treated as leniently as it deserved by the part it would play in the continuing war against Germany. Although Italy was now neutral, the terms of the armistice required that Italian forces surrender their weapons to Allied forces, that POWs be released and not allowed to fall into German hands and that all Italian and Italian-held territories be made available to the Allies for the continued prosecution of the war. Italian neutrality, however, was short-lived and on 10 September Italy declared war on Germany.

Jellicoe had been back at Athlit for about six weeks when, on 7 September, he went to Beirut for the day to plan a number of operations in the Dodecanese Islands in the Aegean, close to the south-west coast of Turkey.[1] That evening, he was having dinner in the Hotel Saint Georges with a former SAS comrade, who was with a lady, when a military policeman came to the table with a message for him. He was to report at once to the Raiding Forces HQ at Azzib, north of Haifa. Reluctantly, because the Hotel Saint Georges was very pleasant, Jellicoe got his driver to take him down to Azzib. There he was told that a plane had been sent from Cairo to Haifa to take him at dawn to MEHQ in Cairo. He drove back to Athlit, had two hours' sleep, packed and reported to Haifa where the aircraft and pilot were standing by.[2]

At Cairo, another waiting car drove him straight to Grey Pillars, the complex of buildings which housed MEHQ, where he found a major planning meeting taking place. About twenty men were sitting around a large table. Since the discussions were well under way, and nobody stopped to recap for the late arrival, it took Jellicoe a few moments to grasp what it was all about.

He learned that an armistice had been agreed with Italy that evening and the Allies were very keen that a special mission should get to Rhodes as soon as possible to contact the Italian Governor of the Dodecanese, Admiral Campioni. The islands were Italian but had Greek populations, having been ceded to Italy as part of the peace settlement just after the First World War.[3] The Admiral was also responsible for all the Italian forces in the Aegean. In line with the terms of the armistice, he needed to be persuaded to hold the Dodecanese using his available troops, until the Allies could take over. The island had three strategically important airfields.

Jellicoe soon gathered from the discussion that there appeared to be about 35,000 Italians and 5,000 Germans on Rhodes under command of the German General Klemann. The British Commander-in-Chief, General Sir Henry Maitland 'Jumbo' Wilson, had been ordered to send a mission to Rhodes to try to persuade the Italian Commander-in-Chief of the Aegean to come over to the Allied side with his 35,000 troops. If Campioni intended to follow the orders of his political master, the new Prime Minister Marshal Badoglio, he might be able to hold the Germans at bay for a few days. But his political disposition and that of his men was unknown. The plan being mooted was for a party led by Colonel Turnbull, Commander of Raiding Forces Middle East, to leave Egypt by sea and proceed via Castelorizzo, a small island east of Rhodes and very near the Turkish coast. Turnbull would then land secretly just inland of Trianda, some ten miles south-west of Rhodes town. However, they would not reach Rhodes until 11 September. Turnbull was away so he was not even at the meeting to have a say.[4]

After about twenty minutes, Jellicoe could contain his puzzlement no longer. 'Why,' he asked when a suitable opportunity for an intervention presented itself, 'Why on earth have we not been alerted before?' He was not only perplexed but also rather angry. The SBS had clearly only been told at the last minute. However, it occurred to him that the lack of communication on the subject was probably because of last minute pressure from Churchill who could see an opportunity for another front to push up into the 'soft underbelly of Europe'.

'I am very surprised to learn this,' Jellicoe continued, having got their attention. 'You have been saying that Admiral Campioni will be contacted by the SOE agent but it has now emerged that his radio has been out of action for the past month. It seems that the obvious thing is to drop a small party of men in straightaway. They should go tonight and report back to both MEHQ and Colonel Turnbull.'

There was a short, expectant silence.

'Are you on for this?' said one of them.

'Yes, of course,' Jellicoe replied. Then someone else from across the table, a major in his early forties, said.

'Do you speak Italian?'

'No,' Jellicoe had to admit.

'I do,' said his interlocutor, 'and I should be glad to come with you.'

'Are you parachute trained?' countered Jellicoe.

'Oh yes,' replied the officer.

'Fine,' said Jellicoe and the deal was done. He was still silently fuming that he had not been informed before and had therefore appeared on the scene so late in the day.[5] Nevertheless, he had taken control of the meeting, replaced the plan under discussion with an idea of his own and inserted himself as the key player into an exciting and dangerous special operation.

The voice across the table turned out to be that of Count Julian Dobrski, a secret Agent of the Special Operations Executive (SOE), the tough dirty tricks branch of the secret services.[6] It had been set up by Winston Churchill in 1940 to 'set Europe ablaze' by working and fighting with the secret resistances of countries occupied by Axis forces. SOE was a complex organization, with a worldwide network of contacts employing some quite exceptionally brave and multi-talented people. The Raiding Forces had always had close contact with SOE, while not necessarily going along with everything they said.

Dobrski, who was known by his alias of 'Major Dolbey', was half Polish and half Italian but spoke perfect BBC wireless announcer English. He had a slight accent which was not easy to place. His father was a Polish Count, while his Italian mother was still living in Italy during the war. He was six feet tall with dark brown eyes and hair and had a slim but strong build.[7]

They needed a wireless operator and somebody said that Sergeant Kesterton, Royal Corps of Signals, was the man for the job, making them a party of three. He would be carrying and using codes, making him a key player as without him whatever the officers achieved would be virtually useless unless secretly and successfully transmitted.

Two days before the meeting, on 6 September, Dolbey had noted in his secret record, 'The last messages from Mallaby[8] [in Rome] were too much in keeping with what I know of the man to be a plant – and if the messages were genuine, we should be getting near a separate armistice with Italy.' Dolbey felt very much that if the Italians were to capitulate suddenly, the Allies would face a chaotic situation in Yugoslavia, Greece and the Aegean. After 'morning prayers', he had spoken to Keble, the brigadier who was his boss and chief of staff for SOE in Cairo. He agreed that they should use more than their usual caution with their Italian contacts on Samos.[9]

The next day, an excited Keble had called Dolbey in. He had just learned that the Italian armistice had been signed.[10] Without advancing any precise reasons as to why, Keble was keen that SOE should take part in a possible operation on Rhodes. Dolbey, however, thought that with subversive operations in the whole of Italy to worry about, Rhodes was arguably less important. Moreover, SOE only had four Italian-speaking officers with knowledge of Aegean affairs and two wireless telegraphy (W/T) operators trained in secret transmissions. The SOE network of agents in the Aegean was mostly outside the Dodecanese Islands. Of the four officers, Randolph Churchill was none too fit. Another was too temperamental, leaving the choice between Dobrski and a younger colleague. It was decided that 'knowledge of the Italian character and ... secret organizations in Greece and the Aegean was more important than youth or dash' so Dolbey got the job. He was to act as interpreter and adviser on secret intelligence and political issues. 'The planning up to now,' he noted, 'cannot be called brilliant or imaginative.' Thus at 10 am on 8 September, the SOE and Turnbull's team had met at Grey Pillars to finalize plans, which were then fundamentally changed by Jellicoe's intervention.[11]

A 'dispatch flight' for Jellicoe, Dolbey and Kesterton had been arranged from Cairo West that evening. Dropping agents in the right place was an exacting game. Consideration of the route, drop zone, run-in, bearing, intelligence on enemy aircraft, flak, weather and a hundred other critical factors had been going on all afternoon. There were no radar systems or radio aids in that part of the Mediterranean. Moreover, radio silence had to be maintained. The human skills of the navigator and pilot would be crucial.

It was too late for a moonlight drop so the operation, code-named RODEL, was timed for between dawn and sunrise on 9 September. Apparently, they were to land on a golf course just near the town. Other SOE missions were also departing, in which Dolbey was involved. This led, he recorded, to 'a state of organized chaos which must be an all time record, even for Rustum Buildings (the SOE HQ). Three missions have to be equipped and fitted with gold and diamonds, W/T codes, escape devices, weapons, dropping equipment etc. and my section, which will be ticking over with four officers out of five gone, needs a spring clean before folding up.'[12]

At 9 pm exactly, the affectionately named 'Stiffs' personnel carrier arrived with Kesterton and Jellicoe. Jellicoe had in his possession a five-page letter from Jumbo Wilson to Admiral Campioni. It was written on blue grey Foreign Office notepaper meant to last for 100 years. The party then left Cairo by the Mena Road at about the time that people in the city were heading out of town for dinner at the Auberge des Pyramides. The late summer moon was haloed in a midnight blue, starry sky.[13]

On arrival at Cairo West, they learned that the DZ had been changed to eight kilometres south of Rhodes town. Too bad. Dolbey had been looking for a soft landing on the greens. On the tarmac, in the shadow of the powerful aircraft [14] that would take them to their destination, they struggled into their ill-fitting parachute harnesses. Then came the classical hitch of every SOE operation. No dispatcher. This greatly exercised Dolbey who said he would rather jump naked and barefoot than without the comfort of knowing that there was, at the ready, a big boot to kick him out. This hitch was resolved and then followed by the usual palaver of sorting out equipment and repacking containers. It began to look as if they would be making a breakfast landing on Rhodes. [15]

At 2.30 am the three men lay, trying to rest and not to think, in the fuselage of the Liberator as it took off over Cairo. Below, 'the black shape of the pyramids and the thousand twinkling lights of Cairo slid away into the night. Soon, when the moon sank behind the western dunes and the darkness was swept away by the ghostly desert breeze which heralds sunrise, they would be flying over the gold and red rocks set in the deep blue of the Aegean Sea.' As he fell asleep, Dolbey dreamed of 'shining dots and dashes flashing across the Mediterranean, over Crete and Malta, over Italy and France and across the Channel to England. In London, a bored cypherene was decoding "RODEL airborne" while a sleepy duty officer pencilled the message's priority and distribution on the message sheet.' [16]

It went wrong. By 5.30 am they should have been over Rhodes but low cloud almost completely covered the sea and islands, obscuring everything. The aircraft circled repeatedly. Occasionally they caught glimpses of the Turkish coast. At 6.30, it was broad daylight and the sea of cloud remained. Had the enemy heard the sound of their engines? The problem was that the aircraft had just flown down at very short notice from near Damascus and the crew had not had time to brief themselves properly. Consequently, as Jellicoe said, 'They couldn't find the bloody island!' If they dropped now, would there be a full reception committee waiting? 'If we stay much longer,' noted Dolbey, 'we shall have fighters on our tail; it is somewhat surprising that none has come up to investigate the bumble bee flight of our lonely aeroplane.' [17]

The pilot decided to return to base. Just after 6.30 they turned south-eastwards. Back they flew to Cairo West, whereupon Jellicoe made straight for Shepheard's Hotel. [18]

At 7 pm the next evening, having changed their parachutes for ones that fitted and with improved W/T communications, they flew out again from Cairo West, still with the same crew and dispatcher. The Operation RODEL men checked their harnesses and agreed that Jellicoe would drop first, then Dolbey and then Kesterton, Dolbey noting cheerfully in his account, 'It will give them a chance to pick up my remains for a Christian burial'. If the three were separated on landing, it was agreed that they would each make for Campioni and attempt to do the business. [19]

This second flight again took nearly three hours as the three passengers sat uncomfortably in the noisy fuselage. For the crew, the ever-present fear of a lone *Luftwaffe* night-fighter was tangible but they had to find that all-important landfall on Rhodes. As they crossed the coast, a call from the navigator alerted the dispatcher to get the passengers ready, hook up the static lines and get the first chap into position. The aircraft banked slowly and the engine noise changed as the pilot pulled back the throttles to get the exact speed and height. In the nose, the navigator peered out desperately looking for the DZ while maintaining a steady stream of instructions to the pilot, 'Left, left, right; steady, steady, right, steady ...'.

At 10.40 pm, they were over the target. The red light came on and the dispatcher opened the hatch. The cool night air and smell of the earth below rushed in. Dolbey's note captured the moment: 'Jellicoe is in position, facing the red light, legs straight down the hole. I look over his shoulder to the ground below. It was an awesome sight – a lunar landscape of hilly, broken-up country, which fills my heart with dismay'. [20] Just before Jellicoe jumped, Dolbey said, 'Sorry George. I told you a lie. I've never been trained to parachute.' [21]

At 11.50 p.m., the red light turned to green.

'Go!' shouted the dispatcher. The first Lord leapt.

'Jellicoe is off,' Dolbey's note continued, 'according to the book and as if on parade. I follow, fumbling somehow out of the hole, less happy than ever as I can see by now that they have opened fire

71

on Jellicoe as soon as his parachute opened. A headlong eternity of nightmares and doubts as I fall downward. Two seconds later I am floating. The night could be romantic ... the rush of the scented, aromatic breeze, the moon grinning over the low horizon, the sea of Odysseus so near ... if it were not for the popping of noises down below, for the odd bluish-yellow spurts of flame and the occasional unpleasant whine of a bullet which seems all too near ...'[22] The second Lord had not, after all, had to be pushed.

'Troops gone,' reported the dispatcher laconically to the already banking pilot and navigator.

A strong wind was blowing and the three parachutists were scattered. They had moreover landed considerably further south than had been intended. Dolbey thought he saw Jellicoe land on some hilly high ground about 200 yards from the DZ while Kesterton was still floating to earth about 100 yards away.[23] In fact, they were both much further away. They had been shot at as they were descending and the fire continued after they hit the ground. Jellicoe and Kesterton soon met up. Dolbey was nowhere to be seen.

He, being a completely untrained parachutist, had been struggling to stop the swing of his parachute and was vainly trying to face the wind as the ground rushed up to hit him. It was a hard, rough landing on the main coast road. His parachute immediately dragged him, face down, into a rough field. This discomfort was increased by the fact that he disliked intensely the idea of the splendid white marker of the parachute which showed his progress to unknown marksmen.[24]

After a further twenty-five yards of being dragged across rough and stony ground, Dolbey managed to unhook the harness and watched with relief as the balloon of white silk floated away in best Scottish ghost style into the darkness. It was only when he tried to get up that he realized he had broken his right leg. Having landed very badly on the metalled road, he had broken his femur. It was a compound fracture and the bone was sticking out through the skin up near his thigh.[25]

After a painful crawl, with bullets still spattering by, he dragged himself into a ditch alongside the road. He could hear

72

general, fairly intensive firing, of which most was directed towards where he thought Jellicoe and Kesterton had landed. The firing continued, with mortars joining in, and he began to wonder why so much ordnance was being expended on three parachutists. Had the Germans taken over? Were the Italians rebelling against their King and Badoglio? Or had they all joined forces?[26]

Another hour passed. The firing diminished and he heard voices shouting in Italian about 100 yards away. Realizing that he would get nowhere with a broken leg and would be picked up when dawn came, Dolbey began a shouted conversation in Italian. He explained that he was a British officer and wanted to see their CO. The firing stopped. An armoured car and a lorry, with steel protective sheeting tied to its sides, appeared, inching up the road. The first vehicle came level and would have missed him if he had not called to the soldiers on board. He was ordered to stand up but when he told them that he had broken his leg there was an ominous silence. He did not like it. They were clearly a trigger-happy bunch. Eventually, four soldiers got out of the lorry and helped him onto the road.[27]

The officer in charge of the party, a Captain Brunetti, listened carefully to Dolbey's account. They were all very curious but became friendlier when he said that his aim was to see that the terms of the armistice were enforced. 'One corporal has suddenly discovered that we are allies and that some obvious sign of hospitable welcome is overdue. Cigarettes, brandy and two blankets on which to rest my bad leg appear. I am slapped on the back by each in turn and assured by an admiring chorus that I deserve *la Medaglia d'Oro*.' Then he turned to business.[28]

He asked them where the Germans were, a not unreasonable question under the circumstances. They replied that the enemy were only 500 metres away and they (the Italians) had already killed hundreds of the sons of bitches. Dolbey listened with one ear to their heroic deeds while simultaneously trying to work out the coefficient to apply to the Italian half kilometre. 'Two or three seems conservative, especially in view of the din that they are making on this moonlit road.'[29]

'Why did you fire at us?' he asked them. They were rather shamefaced. They had been told that a German parachute

73

battalion was about to descend on them. When they saw above them a huge, sinister 'bomber' with strange red and green lights and then the white puffs of deployed parachutes they had fired in self-defence. Moreover, they all insisted, they supposed that Germans had then returned their fire.[30] The Operation RODEL contingent had landed in no man's land and the Italians' estimate had been right. Had it been a few hundred yards even further to the south, they would have become German POWs (or, due to rather better German marksmanship, they would already be dead). Dolbey asked them whether the Italians on the island were for the King or Mussolini. They all, to a man, assured him that the only Fascists on Rhodes were one or two black sheep.[31]

Having heard enough, Dolbey told Captain Brunetti that he must rejoin the other two members of his party. He began to shout in English in the direction of where he thought Jellicoe and Kesterton had landed that they should come out of hiding. Nothing happened. The Italians seemed disappointed at this obvious lack of cooperation. Brunetti agreed to leave some soldiers behind to make contact with Jellicoe and Kesterton and bring them in with their containers of radio and equipment. Dolbey spent a few minutes instructing the two Italian four-man search parties how to shout 'Jellicoe, Dolbey of Rustum, say you are OK'. At this point, he noted, 'the scene begins to be rather humorous with the Italians desperately trying to master an English accent'.[32]

Meanwhile, in order to shelter from the continuing fire, Jellicoe and Kesterton had hidden behind a mound.[33] Gradually, it became clear that the men firing were closing in on them. Jellicoe was very worried that Jumbo Wilson's letter might fall into enemy hands. The ground around them was rocky and unbreakable. There was only one thing to do. He took out the letter and ate it. The Foreign Office paper was particularly difficult to chew and rather indigestible; he was glad that it was not a very long missive. No sooner had he consumed it than the soldiers appeared. They turned out to be Italian, possibly one of Dolbey's language-trained search parties, whose newly acquired English phrase had however been insufficiently accurate to register with Jellicoe, if indeed he had even been within earshot. The Italians realized

74

who the SBS men were and took them by truck into Rhodes to meet Campioni.[34]

Some distance away, Dolbey had been rather painfully inserted into the armoured car, which had then set off with Brunetti towards the nearest Italian headquarters. On the way, he learned that the Italian Regimental Colonel was a hardliner who was likely to give the mission a hostile reception. The headquarters turned out to be a small farm near Calitea. The Colonel was marching about, shouting orders amid a scene of utter pandemonium. Soldiers blundered in all directions without, it seemed to Dolbey, any particular purpose like ants whose nest had been trodden upon. The Colonel was in an inexplicable fury, swearing at everybody but venting most of it upon the hapless Brunetti. One of his apoplectic utterances included a command that Dolbey should be placed on a stretcher and put in a room next to his office.[35]

Ten minutes later, nothing had happened and the injured man was still lying outside the farmhouse in the dimly waning moonlight, the complete failure to carry out his orders no doubt explaining the Colonel's apparently uncontrollable temper. Dolbey still had not been able to get his message across to the Colonel. Suddenly, Brunetti appeared and in the best Italian opera *sotto voce* whispered into Dolbey's ear that ... the Colonel did not see anything urgent in his mission and ... had enough troubles as it was without having to make special arrangements to send him off to Rhodes right away. At this, Dolbey launched once again into the importance of his mission, his status as envoy of the British Commander, the fact that the British fleet was waiting just around the corner and above all into what would happen to him, the Colonel, and anyone else around if he was not allowed to contact the Governor immediately.[36]

This threat produced the offer of a ride in a motorcycle sidecar, which duly arrived, pushed by hand, into which he was again painfully inserted. The motorcycle started up and they set off for Rhodes town. Progress was slow. Lorries and a few armoured cars were moving in each direction, while soldiers seemed to straggle along every roadside. The motorcycle sidecar was obliged to stop many times while the sergeant accompanying the injured agent bragged about his mission and Dolbey wearily fended off more cigarettes, brandy and blankets. At 1.15 am on 10 September, they passed through the massive stone walls of the castle of the Knights of St John, a beautiful marble palace where Campioni had set up his HQ.[37]

Mercifully for Dolbey, on being carried into the hall a doctor appeared and after examining his leg pronounced that the only damage was the broken bone.[38] An ADC then materialized and arranged for the SOE agent to be taken at once to see Campioni. Four sailors carried his stretcher up to the first floor and into the magnificent mediaeval reception hall of the Knights Crusader. The huge room and sudden intensity of the lights made Dolbey feel as if he had suddenly walked onto the stage of the last act of a Verdi opera. Staff officers in brilliant uniforms, capes of many colours, golden epaulettes and glistening swords moved around as his stretcher was carefully grounded by the side of a red, velvet-covered armchair.[39]

Admiral Campioni was a small man, in his late fifties. After a slow start, in which he was clearly suspicious of an officer who until the day before had been the enemy, he became more cordial. Dolbey's first objective was to ensure that the Operation RODEL party was reunited and their containers and radio set recovered. Campioni at once ordered search parties to be sent out. Dolbey then again repeated the purpose of the mission. The Allied Command aimed to occupy Rhodes and Scarpanto, the island between Rhodes and Crete, and an expeditionary force would probably land by about 15 September. General Wilson therefore requested that Campioni hold the Rhodes airfield or at least Marizza in the north.[40]

Campioni appeared, not surprisingly, agreeable to this rather optimistic scenario, but swiftly updated Dolbey on events. The Germans controlled all armed forces and all communications on the island and had already taken all the aerodromes, overcoming some remaining Italian resistance in the process. The extra twenty-four hours afforded them by the delay to Operation RODEL had indeed cost the Allies dear.

Querying only one or two points, Campioni agreed an outline plan. The Italians would warn the Commanding Officer of the garrison on Castelorizzo of the impending arrival by sea of Colonel Turnbull and his men while Turnbull would be told that it was safe to set off for Simi, to the north of Rhodes. Simultaneously, the British Commander-in-Chief Middle East would be radioed to the effect that the Italian garrison on Rhodes had been cut in two, east to west, along a fighting line from Cremasto to Afando.[41] Italian command and control of approximately 35,000 Italians south of it had been lost, reducing the Italian forces under direct command to about 6,000. There was no sign of the *Luftwaffe*. Italian troops north of the line were in good heart and still fighting. Campioni said he hoped to hold this position until 15 September, provided that the Allies could provide diversionary attacks in the south of the island to divide the Germans and encourage Italian troops. Active naval and aerial presence in the area around the Cattavia airfield in the south might be enough to do the trick.[42]

At this point, Jellicoe and Kesterton arrived with Brunetti. They found Dolbey in excruciating pain, his broken femur sticking out of his leg, but doing business. He immediately switched over to interpreting for Jellicoe who resumed command.

'Jellicoe looks fit . . . and well fed,' Dolbey noted, 'as he explains to the Governor that fearing he had been dropped in the German lines he has eaten the letter of General Sir Maitland Wilson. The Governor is somewhat upset. He explains that he finds himself in a rather awkward position because he does not know yet officially that an armistice is signed. He says that of course he does not doubt our word, but he feels that some official information should be sent to him. We agree that this request should be added to our [radio] message.'[43]

There is no doubt that despite the ingestion of Jumbo Wilson's letter, Jellicoe's arrival greatly encouraged Campioni. The Admiral was in the unenviable position of having been forced to agree to a demand from Klemann to keep all Italian troops where they were (he had no transport with which to move them anyway) and he had lost control of the island's airfields. His apparent readiness to agree a plan with Dolbey was probably at least partly feigned since it cost him nothing to cooperate if the Allies did not then produce the necessary forces to deal effectively with the Germans. However, with the appearance of Jellicoe, 'it seemed to him that the British would hardly commit a real English milord to a project they did not intend substantially to underwrite ...'.[44] (Little did he know how matter of fact was the way in which the British Army dealt with titled officers.)

Dolbey, being by now full of pain and brandy and relieved that Jellicoe was once again in charge, asked if he could fall out. He was carried to a palatial bedroom upstairs, while Jellicoe continued discussions with Campioni. It was decided that Dolbey should be taken by boat to Simi and flown to Cyprus in a seaplane later that day, taking with him a message from Jellicoe to be delivered orally to GHQ. This was to suggest that since the Governor did not seem very energetic and his staff being rather of the yes type of officer, the deployment of about 200 men, of the Special Forces and LRDG, should be sent to force the hand of the Governor and stiffen the backbones of the Italian forces in the south.[45]

Despite Dolbey's earlier optimism, Jellicoe was quite clear in his own mind that if it was even a starter for Campioni to come in on the Allied side and resist the Germans, he would want much greater assurances about back-up. The Germans were occupying the centre of the island. Campioni had the 35,000 troops south of the front line but could not communicate with them. The other 6,000 Italians were spread across the north of the island, mostly without transport, equipment and supplies. For them to be asked, suddenly, to change sides would be extremely difficult to manage. However, Jellicoe was desperate to take and hold for the Allies at least one of the three airfields. After some discussion, Campioni eventually said that if the Allies could promise very quick and powerful reinforcements he would come over to the Allied cause from his presently neutral position.[46]

Jellicoe had a short sleep in the Italian HQ. He had to be very careful because the Germans were in the vicinity. Indeed, at one point when he was speaking to Admiral Campioni, he was aware that they were in the adjacent room. He also had to be careful because although he and Kesterton had weapons and equipment, none of the containers had been found. These held the radio needed to communicate with the Commander-in-Chief. It was a race against time to send the message and get clear before the German enemy discovered the British presence on the island.[47]

By now, it was getting close to daybreak. Seeing their predicament, Campioni arranged for Jellicoe to send HQ Cairo a coded radio message via the Italian radio stations in Rhodes and Leros. In it, Jellicoe delivered a SITREP on Campioni's position. He made clear that there was a real chance of the Italians coming over to the Allied side, subject to sufficient support being made available to Campioni very quickly. Kesterton, who sent the message out in code, pronounced that it was likely to have been received.

Of the several containers dropped, it was a real piece of good fortune that about four hours later, an Italian patrol reported in with the container with a W/T set. It was brought straight up to Dolbey's room and an Italian engineer swiftly erected an antenna. From then on they had more or less constant communications with Cairo.

The response to Jellicoe's message, deciphered by Kesterton, was disappointing. All that Cairo was able to promise was a brigade in about six days' time, but with no guarantee that it would be assault loaded, and up to some 200 Special Forces a few days before that. By way of encouragement, the message from Cairo emphasized that several SBS detachments had already arrived at Castelorizzo. Jellicoe relayed all this to Campioni but was unable to promise the other early substantial reinforcements that the Italian was looking for. Jellicoe kept up the dialogue throughout the day and did his utmost to persuade the Italian to come over onto the Allies' side. He hoped in particular that the assurance of having a body of Special Forces would tip the balance, since he was keen that at least one of the airfields in the north, where the Italians had been resisting the Germans quite effectively, should be held. [48]

But, after nearly twenty-four hours of fruitless but amicable negotiation, Campioni decided that this was not enough for him and he would not join the Allies. Though Jellicoe had achieved his aim of carrying Jumbo Wilson's message to the Italian, the Allies' hasty strategic planning does not seem to have anticipated what might be required to guarantee his cooperation. Under the circumstances, the Admiral was probably right in his decision, since there is always a considerable risk for anyone changing sides.[49]

On the evening of 10 September, Campioni woke Jellicoe from his first proper sleep for days to tell him that the Germans were advancing on Rhodes and that he had signalled Turnbull to tell him not to come to Rhodes but to make straight for Simi or Castelorizzo. The Admiral then suggested that Jellicoe and Kesterton should get away under cover of darkness in a motor torpedo boat (MTB) that he would provide, taking with them his own Chief of Staff, Colonel Fanetza. Jellicoe extracted more and set off for Castelorizzo not only with Fanetza but also with maps of the Rhodes defences and most importantly information about the Aegean minefields. The US had made clear that they wished to focus on the advance in Italy, leaving the islands in the Aegean still available for use by the enemy.[50] The airfields, particularly the one on Kos, and the naval base on Leros, were therefore of strategic importance.

At 11 pm that night, while he was waiting for his seaplane on Simi, Dolbey was woken by an Italian delegate, Mr Raffaeli, waving a telegram from Rome. The King of Italy had abdicated in favour of the Crown Prince. Italy had promptly declared war on Germany, leaving a jubilant Raffaeli pronouncing 'Now we are Allies'.[51] When Dolbey finally got to hospital on Cyprus, the landing of an enemy seaplane having been sufficiently well coordinated to avoid it being shot down by enthusiastic Allies, he refused to be operated on until he had first delivered his oral message, in person, to the Commander-in-Chief.[52] But by then, Rhodes was not expected to be able to hold out against the Germans.

The occupation of the rest of the Dodecanese Islands depended on Jellicoe and the SBS.

Chapter Six

The Last Seadogs

Churchill wanted a Dodecanese Campaign to gain control of the Aegean and Jellicoe seized the moment of his departure from Rhodes to help launch it. He had been planning raids on the Dodecanese Islands for some time but in the light of the Italian armistice and the fall of Rhodes he needed to reconsider the strategy.

Jellicoe discussed his plans with those closest to him before putting them to MEHQ. As the campaign progressed, the planning of individual raids became more impromptu. Preparation often took place informally with a small group on the deck of a caique a matter of hours beforehand, while in the background stores were being assembled, equipment checked and the latest intelligence information gathered.

There was, however, nothing spur-of-the-moment about the overall aim. Despite the failure to acquire Rhodes, with its important airfields, the Prime Minister's ultimate wish – the Aegean once taken – was to get Turkey and its forty divisions on the Allies' side. This would open a Russian supply route through the Dardanelles, as he had hoped in his 1915 Gallipoli Campaign.[1] But if control of the Aegean did not work, they would tie down the enemy through ceaseless attacks.

On the morning of 11 September, with the indefatigable Sergeant Kesterton and Fanetza, and flying the Italian flag, Jellicoe sailed into Castelrosso, the main port on the island of Castelorizzo. Their rather majestic entrance was marred only by

81

Colonel Fanetza falling into the harbour as he went ashore. He emerged with his previously immaculate uniform streaked with oil and flotsam while Jellicoe and Kesterton strove to keep straight faces. This severe dent to his dignity cost Fanetza any serious role in the ensuing proceedings.[2]

The island of Castelorizzo lies at the south-east end of the Dodecanese, very close to the Turkish coast. Castelrosso was beautiful in the morning sunlight, with a scenic waterfront and little white-painted houses set off against grey, volcanic hills. On arrival, Jellicoe learned that Turnbull, a stockily built man in a beret pulled down over heavy, dark eyebrows with the inevitable field glasses round his neck, had already been and gone. He had flown into Castelorizzo by seaplane from Cyprus and after summing up the situation there, had continued on westward to Simi, an island about fifteen miles north-west of Rhodes.

David Sutherland with Walter Milner-Barry and about twenty men had reached Castelorizzo by sea. After deciding to risk landing directly at Castelrosso, they received an enthusiastic welcome from the local people, who saw the SBS as liberators.[3] The islanders were desperately impoverished but had retained a spirit of great fortitude.[4]

Restored by a large whisky and soda, Jellicoe went straight into a meeting with Sutherland and Milner-Barry. After some deliberation, it was decided that despite the failure of the Italians on Rhodes to join the Allies, it was still vital to press on and persuade the comparatively small Italian garrison on the island of Kos, which had an airfield, and the more substantial Italian headquarters and naval base on the island of Leros, that they should do so. It would be another race against time to get there before the Germans.[5]

Still early on the same day, 11 September, Jellicoe set off again due north with Fanetza for Kos. However, shortly after putting to sea, Campioni himself sent a signal ordering them to return to port. Jellicoe decided to ignore this instruction, persuading the Italian captain, Commandante Del Viso, that Campioni would not have sent it if he had known that Turnbull had reached Simi. Exhausted from several days of only snatched naps, Jellicoe then fell asleep in the sun, rocked in the bosom of the Aegean. His written report records his indignation with ensuing events:

> I woke up to find that the land, which when I had dozed off had been to starboard, was now to port and to realize that we had about-turned. I remonstrated violently with Colonel Fanetza, and the fact that he had given the order purposely while I was asleep and that I had been unable to restrain a smile which he had seen during his earlier and involuntary immersion in Castelrosso Harbour, did little to improve our tempers.[6]

They were almost back at Castelrosso and it was too late in the day to turn round again for Kos. Jellicoe learned that Rhodes was expected to surrender to the Germans within hours and Turnbull had received orders to deploy more widely across the surrounding islands. The promise of further troop reinforcements was followed by the arrival next day of a motley selection of boats, including some large caiques and a few small trawlers – hardly the armada needed to achieve Churchill's lofty aims.[7]

MEHQ having blessed their hastily readjusted plans, Jellicoe then set off again for Kos, this time with Sutherland and ten men of 'S' Detachment in an ML. Early the next morning, on 13 September, in warm sunshine, they approached the rather barren south coast of Kos. They made their way round the island to the harbour itself on the north coast. It was beautiful, with the usual rows of small white houses, surrounded by vineyards. As they sailed in, the inhabitants could not hide their joy and welcomed the new arrivals with rapture. There was, however, a heavy Italian military presence. Fortunately, uncertainty about their reception was brief. After some hesitation, followed by the realization that they were to be treated as an ally, not a defeated foe, the Italians received the two British officers very well and the garrison came straight across to the Allies. The SBS immediately deployed around the airfield at Antimachia. The Italian garrison commander provided a feast of tagliatelle verde and Chianti, while the local barbers offered free haircuts and shaves. So far, so good.[8]

In the early afternoon, Jellicoe set off yet again in an Italian MTB for Leros. His purpose was to contact the Italian Governor, another admiral called Mascherpa, with the aim of persuading him to change sides and allow Allied forces onto the island. As they made their way, the weather worsened. Jellicoe and the helmsman spoke French together and the latter kept shaking his head and repeating, '*C'est grave. Oui, c'est grave ...*'.[9] Then he changed to, '*C'est pire. ...*',[10] to which Jellicoe replied very firmly, '*Il faut continuer, quandmême*',[11] until finally they reached Leros.

At Leros, Jellicoe lost no time in making for the Governor's palace and Admiral Mascherpa. The Italian had laid on a great feast, complete with a Banquo's ghost in the form of Fanetza skulking beside him. Still using French, Jellicoe quickly convinced Mascherpa and the Italians to join the Allies. He then swiftly extracted key information about the island defences and suitable dropping areas.[12]

This time, the requested back-up was immediately forthcoming. That afternoon a Dakota and a flight of South African Spitfires landed on Antimachia airfield, followed late that night by a company of 11 Parachute Battalion near Marmeti in the north of the island.[13] Over the next few days, 234 [Infantry] Brigade from Malta arrived, piece by piece, with other elements of the SBS, LRDG and the Greek Sacred Squadron, while a parachute battalion was dropped onto Kos.[14] As if all this were too much for the powers that be to sanction, MEHQ also appointed General Anderson to Kos, to command the increasingly mixed force, and gave it the title of Force 292. By 15 September, 'thanks to Jellicoe and the SBS, the British now had a foothold in the Dodecanese'.[15]

Having achieved his Leros objective of making sure that the Italians came over to the Allies and setting up a headquarters on Leros, Jellicoe set off again to visit as many other islands as possible. He flew by seaplane to Stampalia to secure the large Italian garrison there. The seaplane carried on to another destination but was shot down next day on its way back to pick him up, so he returned by boat.

Meanwhile, Jellicoe was not the only one to mix business with pleasure. In line with the agreed strategy, Sutherland, with twenty-five SBS, went to Samos, the second largest island in the

Dodecanese. After being wined and dined by the commander of a 1,500-strong Blackshirt battalion, and being relieved by a battalion of the Royal West Kent Regiment, Sutherland and his men set off for Kalymnos, due south of Leros. The island was famous for its sponges and the owner of the sponge business, Madame Vouvalis, known as The Sponge Queen. This doughty lady immediately laid on a celebratory dinner and sent the SBS men into her garden with spades to dig up the fine wines she had hidden from the Germans.[16]

By then, the SBS were not the only force active in the Dodecanese. The Greek Sacred Squadron was also operating jointly with the rather less sacred SBS in carrying out raids on the enemy-occupied Dodecanese Islands and elsewhere in the Aegean. The honour of taking the island of Knossos was reserved to them, under Tsigantes. He also had the honour of taking Samos, making there, untrained, his first and only parachute jump. He then occupied it successfully with a large contingent of his squadron. Tsigantes had overall command of the Greek forces in the Dodecanese Islands but the high quality of the Sacred Squadron was not really tested in the campaign.[17]

The Germans, however, had no intention of giving up the Dodecanese. Over the next two months, both sides continued to see the islands as a strategic counterbalance that might influence Turkey to come in on the Allies' side. The Germans mounted sustained and very heavy bombing raids, during which the Royal Navy suffered serious, sustained casualties. While these attacks continued, Jellicoe went back by Royal Navy destroyer to Alexandria to report personally to Jumbo Wilson in Cairo. On the destroyer, which was commanded by his cousin on his mother's side, Jellicoe met Alan Phipps, the son of the British Ambassador in Germany, whom he had seen in Berlin before the war.[18]

The quickest way for Jellicoe to return was by a night parachute drop onto Kos. Parachuting was never his favourite occupation and on that occasion the knowledge that the enemy had mined most of the landing areas was particularly disconcerting. But he landed safely and made immediately for Leros. By 5 October, after a depressingly short fight, Kos had fallen; Simi was invaded a few days later.[19]

Jellicoe then based himself on Leros, where 'his jeep was a familiar sight all over the island and he seemed to bear a charmed life'.[20] He visited other islands with David Sutherland to direct operations and boost morale. On 11 November, intercepted German intelligence revealed that a German invasion was expected that night. Leros was in the middle of the strategically important chain of Dodecanese Islands hugging the south-west coast of Turkey. There was no point in maintaining Special Forces strengths on the island so Jellicoe ordered Sutherland and part of his squadron, to join Lassen and the remainder on Samos.

A hard-fought battle raged on Leros for four or five days, in which both sides sustained heavy casualties and the very fine CO of the LRDG, Lieutenant Colonel Jake Easonsmith, was killed.[21] The Germans landed troops, commando-style, by sea and mounted a number of daring parachute operations, at one point landing German paratroopers almost directly on top of Jellicoe. He was in the north of the island, which managed to hold on longest.[22]

On the afternoon of 16 November, Brigadier Tilney (who had taken over from General Anderson) asked Jellicoe to report to 234 Brigade HQ, high up on a hill in the central part of the island. Tilney thought he could mount a winning offensive and wanted Jellicoe to help plan, and no doubt lead, it though Jellicoe was unaware of this at the time. The HQ was in a fortress that Jellicoe had previously visited with Mascherpa. After waiting until dark so that he could get through the German lines, Jellicoe set off with one man. As he reported in, after a climb of 1,200 feet, a German full colonel appeared at the entrance to the headquarters. Tilney then appeared and said rather sheepishly, 'I'm terribly sorry George. When I sent for you, I didn't know we'd be captured. But your friend Alan Phipps is missing. Do you think you can find him?'[23] The Germans had sprung a surprise rearguard attack through the Italian positions. Jellicoe had seen sleeping British soldiers on his way up the mountain and had been unaware that the German attack had begun.[24]

Speaking German, Jellicoe persuaded the German Colonel to let him look for the missing man in turn for giving his word that he would return. He was impressed by the Germans' fighting effectiveness and by their agreement to let him look for his friend.[25] It was a sad business searching for Phipps. British and German soldiers lay dying on the mountainside and Jellicoe injected many with morphine to relieve their misery. He did not, however, find Phipps.[26] Having given his word, he reported back to the German Colonel. The Germans marched Jellicoe down to their temporary headquarters on the east coast. But he was determined not to become a POW. On arrival at the German HQ, he overheard the German officers discussing how to end the continuing British resistance and said quickly to them in German, 'Look. I'm your prisoner. You can do what you like but I can assure you that my chaps are going to continue to fight on unless I tell them to stop.' Since the Germans didn't want any more fighting, they agreed to let Jellicoe go and find his men. They omitted, however, to ask for his word that he would return. They seemed confident that he would, as Jellicoe heard the Commanding Officer explaining to his men, 'He cannot get off the island anyway as there are no boats'.[27]

Jellicoe marched rapidly northwards and found some LRDG and SBS about two miles from a little harbour in Pandeli Bay on the north-west coast of the island. With about twenty men, he commandeered a boat just as it was getting dark. They sailed north to Lipsos, a small island north of Leros which had not been occupied by the Germans. After lying up next day, they sailed at night due east to the Turkish mainland. Jellicoe then sent some SBS back to Leros to pick up the men who had not surrendered, with the result that no member of the Raiding Forces went into captivity. Three thousand other British troops and 5,000 Italians were taken prisoner.[28] The Germans had taken five days to batter the small island of Leros into submission, with horrifying losses on both sides.[29] Jellicoe then went by boat to Samos and then to Kusadasi in Turkey.

On 24 November, after driving the short distance by road to Izmir, he took the train to the British Embassy in Ankara. The Ambassador had already received a message from Cairo and greeted Jellicoe with, 'They want you back in Cairo – urgently'.

He went by train to Adana in southern Turkey and caught an early flight next morning to Cairo. A waiting car drove him straight out towards the pyramids to the Casey Villa,[30] a large house near the Mena House Hotel.[31] He was to see the Prime Minister.

Churchill was sleeping but Jellicoe was told to report straight away. He went up to see the great man who was indeed in bed having his customary post-prandial nap. He seemed preoccupied with the failure of the Teheran Conference but wanted to know from someone who had been on the spot in the Aegean how things were and what had gone wrong.[32] Remembering how the Prime Minister had dozed off when listening to his account of the Crete raid, Jellicoe delivered a crisp summary of events.

Churchill listened very attentively. He made no comment but appeared desperately disappointed. The two men talked for about forty minutes and Jellicoe must have made the situation clear because Churchill said that it all meant that there were great prizes to be won if the British could have a successful Aegean operation. However, he thought all now depended on dealing with German air superiority if they continued to control the vital airfields on Rhodes. He said he had always felt that there was a real chance of the Turks coming in on the Allied side.[33] Perhaps too, he still hoped for an opportunity to lay the ghost of Gallipoli. Unfortunately, he had pressed the campaign without carrying his American friends with him.

The next day, Churchill described his meeting with Jellicoe in a letter to his wife, Clementine, in which he told her the whole story, concluding:

> I could see he was very much impressed with the German behaviour both in the severity of battle and afterwards. On the other hand, they treated the Italians like dirt and certainly shot several of the officers, how many we do not know. Strange combination of military vice and virtue![34]

A few nights later, Churchill invited Jellicoe, his cousin Bernard Burrows, a counsellor in the embassy, and a number of young officers to a dinner at the embassy in Cairo. Churchill engaged Jellicoe, Fitzroy Maclean and Chris ('Monty') Woodhouse[35] in discussion about the Balkans. Woodhouse was playing a similar role to that of Fitzroy MacLean in Yugoslavia, liaising with the Greek resistance forces and political leaders. Towards the end of the evening, the conversation gradually fell quiet. Everyone was listening to Churchill and Smuts discussing whether or not France was finished. Churchill ended the discourse by saying, 'I hesitate to dismiss a great nation because of the temporary state of its technical apparatus'.[36]

In Cairo, news of the fall of Leros had led to concern for Jellicoe's safety. This was swiftly dispelled on 24 November when he appeared in the office of Hermione, Countess of Ranfurly.[37] Her diary records that he and an Italian with him were wearing Turkish civilian clothes.[38] He was also spotted in the bar of Shepheard's Hotel, rather curiously dressed, as he pushed past an acquaintance muttering that he needed a drink.[39]

Jellicoe went back to Athlit to plan more raids on the now German-occupied islands. It was important that the Greek people there could see Allied activity on their behalf. One December evening in Beirut, Jellicoe met his future wife, Patricia (Patsy) O'Kane.[40] Patsy was tall, slim, blonde and beautiful and widely acknowledged as 'the toast of Beirut'.[41] She must also have been clever because she worked for the British Press Attaché in Beirut and Damascus, Bill Allen,[42] writing enemy misinformation in French and English. That evening, Jellicoe went over to chat to someone at a table where Patsy was sitting with friends. They were introduced and it transpired that he had read a letter that she had written to Peter Stirling in Cairo. There was a spark between them and Jellicoe then had one more reason to go to Beirut.[43]

Patsy had been brought up in Shanghai where she became a lifelong friend of another expatriate daughter, Margot Fonteyn. Patsy's father had been the chief engineer of the electricity company in Shanghai, which like many utilities was mainly internationally controlled after the First World War. She was artistically talented and had trained at the Slade and then under Sutherland at the Chelsea Art School. After returning to Shanghai, she was working for the British Consul General when Japan entered the war and was evacuated under diplomatic privilege to Durban. After disembarking at Laurenço Marques as part of an exchange of Allied and Japanese prisoners she never forgot the heavenly smell of fresh orange juice and coffee. She then joined the war effort in the Middle East and got herself to Beirut, via Cairo where she met the Stirling brothers.[44]

As their relationship developed, Jellicoe and Patsy never had enough time to see each other because of their separate, and in his case highly secret and dangerous, duties. Patsy had earlier been engaged to marry Leigh Fermor's Second in Command, W. Stanley Moss. Since Leigh Fermor's chance meeting with Jellicoe off Crete, he had continued to operate as an SOE agent.[45]

The SBS regrouped and spent the remainder of the winter mountain warfare training and planning future raids. They were frequently in Beirut liaising and training with the Royal Navy and the Greek Maritime Squadron. Henceforth, the objective of the SBS was to terrorize the German occupiers, forcing them to garrison the islands with increasingly large numbers of men. Operations became more diffuse and more difficult for the enemy to counter. The SBS sank enemy supply ships and destroyed enemy ammunition and POL dumps. Their increasingly successful raids, combined with the lack of easy transmission of Nazi propaganda to perpetuate the Aryan myth, wrecked German morale. The three squadrons commanded by Sutherland, Patterson and Lapraik were constantly deployed throughout the Aegean,[46] often operating with the Greek Sacred Squadron in the Dodecanese, the Cyclades and later the more northerly Sporades.

They took their leisure when they could. One evening in December, Jellicoe had a long chat about the future with David Lloyd Owen, commander of the LRDG in the Balkans, and David Sutherland. The evening then developed into 'a most alcoholic and amusing party'.[47]

From early spring until autumn 1944, Jellicoe and Tsigantes directed East Aegean joint raiding operations – in the form of a long series of continuous raids – often from hideouts on the Turkish coast. The Greek Sacred Squadron concentrated on the northern islands, leaving those in the south to the SBS. Tsigantes was an audacious leader but looked like a prosperous restaurateur.[48] Yet he was also highly sophisticated and charming, spoke four languages and was totally fearless in action.[49] This constant belligerence was highly successful in pinning down

German forces that were desperately needed elsewhere in the Greek islands, while the Turks seemed quite content to turn a blind eye to these activities.[50]

Anders Lassen, under the command of Ian Lapraik, played an outstanding part in the raids. In January, in an attack on Calchi, the Dane was disappointed to find only six Germans, whom he captured. He was in the middle of blowing open a German Pay Office safe when he was surprised by a German supply boat.[51] He and his men immediately switched their attention to attacking it and took the boat as a captured prize, complete with another set of prisoners, back to base.[52]

Other raids followed.[53] In February, Lassen attacked Simi, partly to avenge the death of the Abbot of Panormiti Monastery, who had been killed by Italian Fascist soldiers for working clandestinely for the British. He destroyed an artillery post, killing three Italians in the process.[54]

Amid all these warlike activities, Jellicoe found time to marry Patsy. He was having an exceptionally dangerous war and each time he chanced himself in action, though he gave it no thought, he risked the succession of his title. Patsy was talented and intelligent but Lady Jellicoe thought the match unsuitable. No doubt she still had the Princesses Elizabeth and Margaret in mind. Never one to give up easily, she approached Churchill to see if he could stop the planned nuptials.

'*How* old is George?' Churchill enquired.

'Twenty-five,' she said.

'Then he's old enough to make up his own mind,' came the rather final response.[55]

Jellicoe and Patsy were married in Beirut and after a brief honeymoon in Cyprus, Patsy continued with her job while Jellicoe went back to raiding.

Lassen was still at it and still keen on safe cracking. In April, he and his party raided Santorini in the Cyclades. With his sergeant, Nicholson, Lassen made straight for the main Bank of Athens in the town. With deadly efficiency, they worked the rooms of Germans above the bank, kicking open each door, heaving in a grenade and shutting it again before taking cover, either side, against the wall. They then raked each room with Bren-gun fire, killing more than fifty Germans. The SBS had never attacked Santorini before and the enemy were totally unprepared.[56]

While the Germans were picking up the pieces and reinforcing the garrison there, Lassen attacked Paros. Although he could not destroy a landing strip that was under construction, he divided his party of thirteen into four groups and under cover of darkness wreaked simultaneous havoc on equipment and stores dumps, killing some Germans in the process.[57] The volatile Dane, recruited by Jellicoe, was proving his worth as an exceptionally courageous and effective leader.

The most important thing about these raids was that they were unremitting. The mass of small operations kept the German eye firmly on that part of the world. Raids were widely dispersed and since the Germans could not anticipate where the SBS would strike, they had to deploy a disproportionate number of men. This tying up of men and resources continued to be the main SBS strategic aim, together with signalling the Allied presence to the Greeks.[58] The operations had virtually on-the-spot planning and something of the spirit of the Elizabethan seadogs seems to have come alive in the eastern Mediterranean and Aegean. The SBS raiders, like 'legitimised pirates' as John Verney called them,[59] in an assortment of commandeered and battered-looking caiques, schooners and fishing boats sailed out from secret bays to sink and capture enemy ships, land raiding parties on idyllic but German-occupied islands and give the enemy a bloody nose when he was least expecting it.[60]

Jellicoe's mother ship, often his HQ when planning Aegean raids, was an unlikely-looking caique called the *Tewfik*. Usually moored at Port Deremen in Turkey, she rolled and yawed even in the gentlest of swells and had rather unpredictable engines.[61] Though the *Tewfik* was hardly a proper 'flagship', Jellicoe's father would have been very proud of his son.

In midsummer 1944, the SBS became the Special Boat *Service Regiment*, with five squadrons, and moved its headquarters to the mountains in the Italian province of Bari. The Raiding Forces set up camp to the south of them. Both were operating with the LRDG and there was a very close bond between them. This new group of units, together with 2 Marine Commando, made up

Land Forces Adriatic. Increasingly, the job of raiding the Aegean Islands fell quite rightly to the Greek Sacred Squadron and by September the SBS had ceased to operate there.

In July 1944, the SBS again raided Crete, the object of their attack being petrol dumps, rather than airfields. They aimed to force the Germans to venture an oil tanker out into the Mediterranean and into a submarine ambush. Ian Patterson duly arrived on the island after the usual 'hush, hush' preparations to be met by a whole crowd of enthusiastic Cretan helpers. Another party, led by Lieutenant Dick Hardman arrived later in July and together they blew up 165,000 gallons of fuel, as well as a bridge near Kouphi and a truck. Two SBS men, Captain John Lodwick and Bombardier Nixon, were captured but later escaped from a POW train taking them to Germany. After some terrifying adventures, they finally reappeared and presented themselves to Jellicoe, who said, 'Ah, you're back. Damned slow about it weren't you?'[62]

On 24 July, Jellicoe breakfasted in Bari with David Lloyd Owen. Lloyd Owen did not want the LRDG to come under command of Turnbull and HQ Raiding Forces. At a meeting chaired by Brigadier Davy's Chief of Staff, Colonel MacNamara, he told Turnbull bluntly that he was not wanted. Things then got 'rather heated'. But the result was from Lloyd Owen's point of view, very satisfactory since the SBS was to be a completely self-run affair.[63] The next day, after lunching with Fitzroy Maclean, Dan Ranfurly and David Lloyd Owen at the Allied Officers Club, Jellicoe met Davy, MacNamara and Lloyd Owen in the evening to discuss operational roles. It was decided that the 'LRDG would primarily recce and the SBS primarily beat up'.[64]

In terms of the ambitious aim to take and hold the Dodecanese Islands in the face of German air-power supremacy, the campaign had been a failure. But on another level, and seen in the context of raids on the other island groups, the Raiding Forces as a whole had inflicted incalculable losses on the enemy. From August 1943 until the end of the war they carried out 381 raids across seventy islands of the Aegean, including many small and remote localities. Their reign of terror, with a maximum of 400 men at any one time, struck fear into the hearts of German forces 100 times their own size. They destroyed enemy resources and morale, played havoc with German planning and stiffened the resolve of the Greek population.[65] This was classic singeing of the King of Spain's beard.

The SBS Regiment then had a new mission – to liberate Athens and prevent civil war in Greece – in which Jellicoe was to take a dashing and highly dangerous lead.

Chapter Seven

Liberating Athens on
a Bicycle

As part of the Land Forces Adriatic (LFA), the SBS Regiment was to mount raids into Italy and Yugoslavia. Since it was important that Marshal Tito approved, Jellicoe flew to see Fitzroy Maclean. He was with Tito on the Croatian island of Vis, off the Dalmatian coast in the Adriatic Sea. Over lunch, Tito with his high cheekbones, piercing gaze and *en brosse* haircut was taciturn but, Jellicoe thought, impressive. They sat outside, overlooking a view of the rich agricultural landscape of the island. Tito spoke in Serbo-Croat and even though MacLean with his flair for languages had picked it up well, they had to use interpreters.[1] With few words, Tito let it be known that he was content with the SBS's plans.[2]

No sooner said than done. Lassen opened the batting by blowing up a railway bridge at Karasocici, on the Yugoslav side of the border with Albania. Typically a man of few words, and even fewer when they had to be written down, Lassen's report recorded baldly that they landed, reached the bridge, blew it up and came back. Unsatisfied with this rather perfunctory account, Jellicoe called for more only to learn that Lassen's group of twelve men had been surrounded at a partisan HQ by about 400 troops – an unpleasant mixture of German troops and Yugoslav *Ustachi* Fascists. To quote Lassen, 'fighting began'. He succeeded in withdrawing successfully, losing only three men as prisoners, but

95

noting 'Nearly all enemy troops are *Ustachi* who are highly trained and skilled in anti-Partisan and anti-SBS work. They are very good'.[3]

Despite Tito's high-level approval, the tides of war were changing. The Germans were seen as losing and Tito's Communist partisans, who were supposed to be supporting the SBS, were already at best lukewarm towards those they perceived to be the forces of western capitalism.[4]

Although Jellicoe's task was to cover Italy and Yugoslavia, he was to have one last, but highly significant, personal contact with wartime Greece. In mid September, Brigadier Davy, Commander of Land Forces Adriatic (LFA) at Bari, told Jellicoe that a German withdrawal had begun in the south-west Peloponnese – the large tongue of Greece that lies south of a line from Araxos on the west coast to Corinth in the east. The Germans were moving northwards.

The political situation was complex. The Communist Greek partisans, ELAS, were watching for their chance to seize power in Greece. They seemed to be adopting an approach to the Allies similar to that of the Communists in Yugoslavia. There was therefore cause for concern that discord between ELAS and the political parties opposing them, and between ELAS and the vestiges of Greek local government, would lead to confrontation, possibly even civil war. It was also believed that the German withdrawal would accelerate, precipitating just such a crisis. Another Jellicoe special operation was on the cards.[5]

It was tragic that after four years of German occupation and having suffered the privations of war, Greeks were killing each other even as the Germans were departing. But Britain's objectives were not entirely altruistic. Churchill had no intention of seeing Hitler's occupation of Greece replaced by a Communist one. Eyeing Jellicoe speculatively, Davy concluded that there was therefore a good deal to be said for getting a neutral British force on the spot as soon as possible to help prevent internal hostilities. He then asked Jellicoe to take a small force to the north-west Peloponnese and occupy the airfield at Araxos.[6]

So came into being 'Bucketforce', which Jellicoe thought a ghastly name. Nevertheless, he was excited at the prospect of assisting the German departure from a country in which he had been operating for so long. He had a deep admiration and affection for Greece and the Greeks. Ordinary people, such as the peasants, skippers of the ships used to carry out SBS raids, their wives and families were already risking their lives to serve their country and help the Allies. Jellicoe was worried about what would happen if civil disorder could not be averted. Apart from having a British force available to accelerate the German withdrawal, there needed to be an Allied, probably British, presence there as soon as possible in order to keep the peace.[7] There was in Greece at the time a desperate need for a legitimate Greek government supported by a military presence to establish authority and stability and assure Greece's political recovery.[8]

Plans were hastily implemented, with the result that Bucketforce was a curious mixture of military and other elements provided by HQ LFA and HQ Balkan Air Force (BAF) in the form of 'L' Squadron of the SBS under Ian Patterson; two companies of the Highland Light Infantry; 2908 Squadron of the RAF Regiment; an LRDG Patrol; a half-troop from 40 (Royal Marine) Commando; and various assorted maintenance and support elements, comprising a force of about 450 in total.[9] The preparation time was similar to that for Operation RODEL onto Rhodes, that is, it was almost non-existent.

Patterson had been Second in Command of the parachute battalion dropped with 234 [Infantry] Brigade on Kos the year before and had then joined the SBS. He was very bright, versatile, energetic and sensible. During his short time with Special Forces, he had proved himself and Jellicoe was thankful to have had officers of his calibre, including Sutherland, Lapraik, MacLean, Lassen, Verney, Milner-Barry and others.[10] But Jellicoe had made it his business to acquire good men so it was not all down to luck.

The operation on Araxos, called TOWANBUCKET, was fairly straightforward. Patterson with a small advance party from his squadron parachuted onto Araxos on 23 September and occupied the airfield. As soon as it was captured, Jellicoe flew in by Dakota escorted by eight Spitfires. He then went down to meet the rest of their small force coming in by sea further down the west coast at

Katakolon. They moved north-east to join Patterson who was by then just outside Patras. Things then became more complicated.

Jellicoe's job, as the saying went, was to 'exploit' eastwards with Bucketforce and, if possible, capture Patras, the main city of the Peloponnese.[11] This was essential to the main operation which was to liberate Greece: Operation MANNA. Patras was a gateway to the rest of the country. Gradually it became clear that Jellicoe was to spearhead the operation.

He and his men took some days to advance on Patras, where they lay up west of the city. A powerful German battalion under General Magnus was threatening to blow up the port. The Greek Second Security Battalion there, the Evzones, was not necessarily pro-German but had been helping the Germans to defend the eastern side of the city. The battalion was, however, distinctly anti-ELAS, many of its young men having been obliged to make the unpalatable choice of joining either the Communists or the Government's Battalions.[12] It was a chilling sight, as British forces advanced towards Patras, to see ELAS trying to kill their compatriots instead of fighting the Germans.[13]

On 3 October, while he waited for the right moment to act, Jellicoe made contact with Hans Evenstoll, a Swedish representative of the Red Cross from Athens, who acted as a go-between with both the Germans and ELAS. Evenstoll noticed that 'although Colonel Jellicoe was very young, he was wearing a Military Cross[14] and his men clearly worshipped him'.[15]

Jellicoe told Evenstoll that bad weather had hindered his operations. 'I do not have,' he said, 'more than a hundred men with me. But don't tell the Germans. Ask the German General if he is related to Willy Magnus. He was one of my best friends when I was studying in Berlin.' Evenstoll duly related to Magnus the encounter with Jellicoe. 'The son of the great Jellicoe?' said Magnus in surprise. It transpired that Willy was his nephew but much as Magnus would have liked to meet Jellicoe, he said that under the circumstances he could not.[16]

Jellicoe immediately sent an ultimatum to Magnus to surrender. This was followed by a night of hard talking, with Evenstoll playing a key role in the secret communications which took place close to the German front line on the western outskirts of Patras.

Everything depended on this crucial negotiation, since it would be impossible to capture Patras without persuading the Germans to withdraw. At the same time, the ELAS guerrillas needed to be contained. They were committing horrendous atrocities elsewhere in Greece and were poised to move into the city and begin a reign of slaughter and destruction as soon as the Germans left.[17]

The outcome of the talks was that Magnus and his forces withdrew rapidly.[18] After some typically protracted Greek-style negotiations with Colonel Courkalakos, the commander of the Security Battalions supporting the Greek Government, Jellicoe and Patterson were suddenly surprised to find that around 1,400 Evzones began to slip across early in the night to surrender to them as POWs. This meant that ELAS could not touch them. Jellicoe then sent them back under guard to Araxos.[19]

In all of this, Patterson had shown extraordinary diplomatic skill and sensitivity in handling negotiations, not least while Jellicoe was still bringing up the force from Katakalon. He analysed each situation carefully and applied his effort where it counted most. Now also he showed his great courage and military skill. He quickly filled the gap left by the Greeks in the eastern defences, sending SBS and RAF men into the centre of the town. Here they clashed with the Germans in street fighting but sustaining no losses. As the Germans' hold loosened, Jellicoe sent more SBS and RAF detachments into the city with orders to force their way through to the harbour. The Germans finally abandoned their positions and took to the sea in less than half an hour, leaving key port installations mined and booby-trapped, all of which devices the SBS found and defused in the nick of time.[20]

Jellicoe's presence had not only accelerated the liberation of Patras from the Germans. With his tiny force he also fulfilled what is surely the obligation of any military invader to maintain law and order and protect civilians. Panayiotis Kanellopoulos, George Papandreou's representative of the Greek Government in exile, was expected from Cairo soon but order had to be established first. Jellicoe imposed a strict street curfew to prevent wholesale destruction by ELAS. Together with the Evzones and a number of citizens from Kanellopoulos's birthplace, between 1,500 and 2,000 people were saved.[21] To assess the magnitude of the calamity that might have ensued, one had only to compare Patras with what had happened in Kalamata. There, the ELAS guerrilla leader Aris Veloukhiotis, had carried out an appalling massacre of innocent people.[22] Aris, who went by a number of aliases, of which Aris was one meaning 'God of War', was known to butcher and torture Greek anti-Communists with his own hands.[23] He self-avowedly wanted to 'punish the traitors' who had joined the Greek Security Battalions and was only prevented by an order of the government, enforced by Jellicoe.

There was no rest. On 4 October, Jellicoe received fresh orders franked Top Secret. These were to keep order in Patras, move on and take Rion if possible, recce towards Corinth, send a detachment from 40 Commando to recce north of the Gulf of Corinth and support the RAF with transport and labour to establish a forward aerodrome.[24] This was a tall order. Even the first item on the list was a fulltime job, coupled with keeping ELAS under control.

Davy then flew in and sent an Immediate Top Secret SITREP to HQ BAF the following day, 5 October, reporting,

> ELAS forces moving into town ... Victory parade tomorrow in which British taking small part.... Jellicoe keeping direct control of Police but ELAS command dislikes this.... Unless Commission from Greek Government arrives quickly, Greek Government may be the loser and Greek Commissioner find it hard to establish his authority. Local inhabitants nervous of ELAS ... Kanellopoulos expected this evening....[25]

The next day, Patras was quiet. Kanellopoulos accepted that ELAS, in the person of Aris, was the only organized power in the Peloponnese. It was clear that Kanellopoulos faced a much more complicated task in Patras than in other Greek cities. Aris was a dominating figure. Kanellopoulos asked for British troops to remain in the city for a few more days.[26]

Outwardly, Jellicoe ensured that relations with ELAS were cordial. On 7 October 1944, Panayiotis Kanellopoulos walked to the Cathedral Church of Patras to celebrate the city's liberation. Behind him, as recorded by Kanellopoulos 'walked the young.... Colonel Lord Jellicoe of the British Commando Force, son of the glorious Admiral of the First World War'.[27] Beside Jellicoe, having been persuaded by him to take part, walked Aris. Part of Jellicoe's strategy was to keep ELAS happy while curtailing their power. He was clearly effective in doing the latter because later that day, 7 October, he received a reproachful signal from HQ BAF:

> [General] Sarafis [the ELAS General] is complaining that you are not, repeat not, treating local ELAS in Patras as ally which can be trusted. Basis of Caserta Agreement[28] is that ELAS is to be treated with complete trust and confidence. Amongst other complaints, Sarafis reports (1) that you refuse to allow ELAS share of guarding Security Battalions; (2) that ELAS identity cards must be countersigned by British officers; (3) curfew has been imposed 1900 hrs to dawn; (4) that friendly demonstrations by locals are forbidden ... vital importance that fullest trust be shown to ELAS and dignity of Sarafis upheld ... suggest you redress above grievances unless there are the strongest local reasons unknown here against this course....[29]

Jellicoe was indeed doing all of the above and for very good reason. ELAS were up to no good. They were concentrating on Patras and had even imported crowds for demonstrations. About 80 per cent of people in the city were anti-ELAS but since the Communists had all the available arms, nobody dared openly to lead any other political party. ELAS aimed to dominate Patras and only fear of British intervention prevented their elimination of the police, wholesale 'arrests' and widespread killing.

Jellicoe then discovered that ELAS were taking anti-ELAS Greeks north across the Gulf of Corinth to a part of Greece under their control. He put a stop to this practice immediately and tightened the curfew. A signalled reply from Davy to General Scobie, the British General commanding the Allied forces that were to liberate Greece, confirmed,

> Jellicoe already deals with local ELAS command and is most tactful.... As regards confidence, it is difficult to show [it] to ELAS when we do not arm them from security battalions

or clothe them and we *do* give them orders not to go out of the Peloponnese to attack the Germans. Agree with you that Jellicoe indeed in difficult position.[30]

In any case, Davy now wanted Jellicoe to press on again for Corinth. He sent a Most Secret cipher message from the newly established RAF Araxos specifying several urgent requirements including reinforcements 'to relieve Jellicoe of political and base duty'. The message went on:

> Jellicoe magnificent but no staff to cope with Aris and company ... consider politically essential we maintain contact Germans all the time and hunt them out of Greece. In view of situation, feel I must stay here with Jellicoe, as these two days are crisis of Anglo-Greek future ... Locals still nervous. Genuine popular affection for British ... 1200 hrs parade showed popularity of Kanellopoulos, who was well clapped to and from church. British troops got a little rather nervous clapping but genuine pleasure on faces. ELAS troops got less clapping and scared faces.... Total ELAS about 1,200 regulars, 1,600 reserves.[31]

By now, Jellicoe commanded the coastal belt about ten miles wide from Katakolon to Corinth. All armed ELAS were under his command and those ELAS forces he did not require were moved elsewhere. He began an investigation into arrests carried out by the Secret Police against his orders and demanded a list of those arrested.[32] After a lunch on 9 October with Jellicoe and Aris, Davy reported,

> Aris ... made excellent speech ... of which general theme [was the] more we help him fight Germans, which is [the] only object [the] more we cement Anglo Greek friendship. Want arms and will fight barefoot. This of course poetical. Need boots and clothes.[33]

On 9 October, at twenty-six, Jellicoe was promoted to local acting colonel.[34] He was immediately dubbed 'Military Governor of the North West Peloponnese'. This title was a good deal less grand than it sounded. Despite Jellicoe's success in limiting ELAS's freedoms, Aris actually wielded considerable power in the area. It was therefore with some relief that Jellicoe handed over responsibility for the city to Panayiotis Kanellopoulos, as Greek Commissioner for the Peloponnese, and the British Military Mission's able commander, Colonel Chris ('Monty') Woodhouse. Woodhouse was liaising with the Greek resistance forces and political leaders.[35]

Jellicoe, now an acting brigadier,[36] pressed on eastwards. The Germans were leaving Athens but their mines on the airfield threatened to prevent the main Allied invading force, led by General Scobie, from landing on time. It was vital there should be no power vacuum in the capital. Reaching Corinth on 9 October, Jellicoe was too late to prevent the enemy from doing a demolition job on the Corinth Canal. Davy confirmed to HQ BAF, 'Striking force SBS and guns RAF Regiment assembled Corinth to chase Germans out of Athens and prevent demolition....'.[37]

At 1800 on 11 October, Jellicoe sent a SITREP:

B Patrol, L-SBS reached Megara E 0349. Germans left 1800 Oct 8 now 6 miles east town ... Intentions: 3 patrols L moving forward to cut Thuvai Piraeus road ... Intelligence: Road eastward from Corinth bad.... All quiet Corinth. 5 PoW. 1 Australian deserter today....[38]

Because of the need to prevent ELAS from seizing power in Athens, HQ BAF signalled Jellicoe half an hour later to ask him whether 4 British Independent Parachute Brigade should parachute onto the plain of Megara, east of Corinth:

Plan to drop one coy (company) parachutists 1300 hours 12 October ... on Megara. On 13 ... Oct build up of one parachute brigade begins. Confirm airfield and vicinity is clear of mines. Send all information enemy own troops and state of airfield.[39]

They crossed the canal north of Corinth. The weather deteriorated rapidly and Jellicoe was faced with the difficult decision of whether to signal that the drop should go ahead. After some

103

deliberation, he did so and 4 Parachute Brigade dropped in a 25-knot wind. Where they could, Jellicoe's men drove their jeeps across the parachutes' riggings to prevent the men from being dragged across the rough ground. But the combination of mines, enemy fire, accidents and bad weather meant that casualties were heavy. Then came a very difficult personal decision for Jellicoe.[40]

Near Megara, as he watched from his jeep, he saw a young man about 400 yards away being dragged into a minefield. Jellicoe knew that he could drive his jeep across the parachute's cords but he did not know exactly where the boundary of the minefield lay. He was truly caught between his desire to save the parachutist and the knowledge that it was crucial that he lead the advance into Athens. He did not go to the soldier's rescue and remained troubled about it ever afterwards.[41] But the decision to go ahead with the drop was right. The reinforcements were very badly needed and without them the outcome would almost certainly have been civil war and a bloodbath.[42]

Jellicoe pressed on again towards Athens. The Greek Government and ELAS had agreed that the latter would remain outside the city until a legitimate government was in place. In the interim period, authority was vested in General Spiliotopoulos, the General commanding the Greek forces, who had recently been appointed Military Commander of Attica. But he had few military forces at his disposal while ELAS still had troops in Athens. The situation was tense. Would ELAS break the agreement and take control as the Germans left the city? Jellicoe's way was blocked by the enemy flank that was protecting the withdrawal of the main German force. He would have to go by sea instead.

Because of the extreme urgency, Jellicoe and Patterson commandeered a caique in the evening. Together with Shan Sedgwick, the *New York Times* correspondent, and a few others, they skirted the shores of Salamis, just west of the city. After disembarking at Scaramanga, they lay up observing as the last of the Germans were pulling out of Athens. Jellicoe and Patterson then spied two bicycles and deciding that their need was greater than that of the owners, mounted their unlikely transport and set off to cycle the last remaining twelve miles into Athens.[43]

Arriving in the capital just as the last Germans were leaving, the two SBS cyclists headed for Constitution Square and the Hotel Grande Bretagne, next door to the former German HQ. There they were met by Lieutenant Colonel Frank Macaskie, an SOE agent known as the Scarlet Pimpernel of Greece because of his ability to slip through the fingers of the Germans during the Greek occupation.[44] Macaskie had recently returned to Athens to help facilitate Jellicoe's entry and was being sheltered by Archbishop Damaskinos. At the meeting with Damaskinos, Jellicoe learned that the rearguard German commander in Athens had released prisoners at the last moment, without which they would have faced an uncertain end. He had also refused German orders to blow up the Marathon Dam.[45]

Jellicoe then reported the same evening to the Greek authorities and General Spiliotopoulos, who was staying at the house of a Greek called Markejinis. Jellicoe, the insignia of his rank covered with dust, duly presented himself, saluted and said, 'Brigadier Lord Jellicoe sir', before reporting that he had just arrived from the Peloponnese and had come to ask for the General's orders.[46]

Using the only language common to both of them, Jellicoe spoke in French, introducing himself as 'Brigadier Jellicoe'. Spiliotopoulos appeared suitably unimpressed and it was only later that Jellicoe realized that 'brigadier' is one of those 'false friends'[47] between French and English that look the same but mean something completely different. 'Brigadier' in French means 'corporal' in English.[48]

Having described the situation in the Peloponnese and Kanellopoulos's difficulty in restraining the unimaginable atrocities of Aris, Jellicoe then left with General Spiliotopoulos for the Old Palace to meet the directing staff of the ELAS Second Division. From there they went straight to the large Tameion building, next door to the Hotel Grande Bretagne. It was now early on the morning of Thursday, 12 October 1944. By command of General Spiliotopoulos, the people of Athens began to gather in the square, all the Greek officers in full military uniform. When Jellicoe appeared on the balcony of the adjacent Hotel Grande Bretagne, frenzy seized the crowd.[49] 'Yellico! Yellico!' they chanted amid thunderous applause.

105

Jellicoe's presence in the city had indeed had a remarkable impact. He was already known for his activities in Patras and this carried conviction with the departing Germans, the citizens of Athens and ELAS alike. When the Greeks saw him with Macaskie, they saw salvation. His arrival had prevented, at least for that crucial moment, the outbreak of civil war in Greece. In ancient Greek tradition, they offered the two men wreaths of fresh laurel.[50]

Among the crowd, was a beautiful young Greek Red Cross nurse called Mary Cawadias. She had been born in Greece but educated in London, where her father was a doctor, and had returned to Greece when the war broke out. She had worked as a nurse until the Germans had incarcerated her and her mother. Both had been under sentence of death for helping Allied prisoners of war to escape from occupied Greece. She had been released thirty-six hours before Jellicoe's arrival in the city.[51]

As Mary Cawadias looked up, she saw two other officers behind Jellicoe on the balcony. With them was a Greek beauty, Sophia, who had also been in the prison camp but had been the mistress of a German senior officer and had spied on Mary and the other women prisoners. One of the officers was young, tall and blond. It was Anders Lassen.[52] Whilst Jellicoe had been on the west side of the Peloponnese, Lassen had with great skill and courage and a small band of men made his way via Kythera round the south-east coast of the Peloponnese and arrived in Athens at about the same time.

The timing could not have been better. Athens had been hanging by a thread so Jellicoe's dash to the city had been decisive. Whoever controlled the capital, with about a quarter of the Greek population, controlled Greece. To the Greeks, Jellicoe was symbolic of British power. The troops dropped at Megara had been delayed so he was perceived as a forerunner, the tangible proof that the British were not far away. It was wonderfully stabilizing and ELAS were held at bay. They had gambled on respecting the agreement but still being able to win the day. They had hesitated and lost. Thus Jellicoe passed into Greek history as a war hero, more than he has in Britain.[53]

Later that day, the celebrations continued and Mary Cawadias invited Jellicoe to her mother's flat. He went with three or four of his SBS men. There was no food but they brought their rations of spam and water biscuits. There was however plenty to drink. During the evening, Mary Cawadias asked Jellicoe what his next move was. He told her that he was to go to Thebes the next day. They quickly agreed that she should accompany him to interpret for him, not least because it would be important when guerrillas were making speeches.[54]

The next morning, Friday 13 October, they set off north towards Thebes, from which the Germans had just departed, noting with some concern that all the ELAS traffic was going south towards Athens. Mary Cawadias was struck by the quite extraordinary hold that Jellicoe had over his men. She was offered pride of place in the front of the vehicle, while Jellicoe rode in the back. It soon became apparent that the front seat was in fact not a good place to be as the well-meaning Greeks showered the approaching jeep with ripe grapes. She got pelted while Jellicoe remained serenely in the back. The Germans having left Thebes, Jellicoe made a speech, which Mary Cawadias interpreted.[55]

Returning to Athens that evening, they found that 4 Parachute Brigade had marched into Athens during the day and were billeted in the building next to the Hotel Grande Bretagne, their presence finally reinforcing the new HQ of the Greek Government.

On Saturday 14 October at 10.30 a celebration began in the metropolitan Cathedral to the enthusiastic applause of the crowd. At the end of the service, Archbishop Damaskinos showered those present with rose petals and laurel leaves. Themistoclis Sofoulis, a leading Greek politician and head of the Liberal Party, later Prime Minister of Greece, offered these in turn to Jellicoe and Macaskie.[56] It was all very moving.

The next day, it was back to the war. Jellicoe had orders to take a battalion group up to Kozani and the Yugoslav frontier to show the flag and chase the departing Germans out of Greece. On 17 October, with 4 Para, a battery of light guns, most of Bucketforce and also Patterson, Woodhouse and Milner-Barry, Jellicoe drove north towards the Greek border with Yugoslavia.

After passing through Larissa, Grevena and Elassona, they had a difficult encounter at Kozani south of the frontier. In this action, Jellicoe took on more than he had bargained for. As he made a forward flanking movement to cut off the rear part of the German force, he intercepted their column further forward than intended, thereby cutting off quite a large part of the German battalion. They fought back vigorously and effectively, inflicting a number of casualties.

After hastily disengaging themselves, Jellicoe and his forces pushed north to Florina just south of the Greek/Yugoslav frontier. There they joined forces with B Squadron, LRDG, who had parachuted in earlier in October to harass the Germans, and then pursued the enemy up to the border. Here Jellicoe stopped; he was under orders to go no further. Milner-Barry went on into Albania to recce while Jellicoe headed for Salonika.[57]

There Anders Lassen, with only a small force of M Squadron SBS and a few LRDG, had inflicted considerable damage on the Germans and prevented the demolition of the harbour. Lassen had gone up the east coast of Greece in caiques, trying to win the cooperation of ELAS but to no avail. He reached Salonika just in time to save it from them as the Germans left. Having only about thirty-five men, six officers and a few jeeps, Lassen commandeered the only other vehicles available, a number of fire brigade engines. With these, they chased the rearguard German force and took control of the city, becoming known in the process as 'Pompeforce'.[58] Rather as Jellicoe had done in Patras and Athens, Lassen saved Salonika from destruction and was feted as the saviour of the city. The hero who had had such a marvellous career fighting in the Aegean for the last year had also become the hero of Salonika.[59]

But far from being jubilant, the Dane seemed rather depressed. The most attractive former mistress of the Germans had transferred her affections to Lassen. But she had been making comparisons. Lassen's predecessor had apparently performed far better than he. He felt he was letting down the entire British Empire.[60]

After a week in Salonika, Jellicoe returned to Athens where Sutherland joined him. Jellicoe's standing with the Greek people was assured. On 28 October, the fourth anniversary of the invasion of Greece by the Italians, the Greeks gave him a tremendous reception when he appeared in Athens. They continued to clap and shout 'Jeellicoe!' whenever they saw him.[61]

At the beginning of December, Jellicoe had come to the end of his involvement in wartime Greece. The Greek Sacred Squadron was also disbanding for the first time in 2,300 years. They were going home in victory, carrying the torch of freedom. Many took it back to their units throughout the Greek army, carrying the culture of the Greek Sacred Squadron with them.[62]

From Colditz, via various clandestine means, Stirling had indicated that he wanted Jellicoe to be his Staff Officer in China. The SAS founder expected to have command of a special contingent to operate against the Communists there.[63] The Prime Minister was keen on the idea and Stirling wanted Jellicoe to take a major staff role. But it was not until the beginning of December that he made the difficult decision to accept the offer. He hated the idea of leaving Special Forces but did not want to pass up Stirling's invitation. Jellicoe then relinquished his SBS command to Sutherland, who was the obvious choice.

Jellicoe's return to Patsy in December was celebrated by the arrival of their daughter Alexa, who was born in Alexandria. He reverted to his substantive rank of major and dutifully brushed up on his staff work in preparation for a course at the Army Staff College in Haifa. The deskwork was immensely boring after all his active service.[64] But Stirling's special unit in China was not to be. It was called off because of the nuclear attacks on Japan.

Jellicoe never saw Patterson again, who had so much ability and potential. He was killed when his aircraft crashed on landing in Italy as he returned from Greece. The young Anders Lassen, still only twenty-four, was killed winning the Special Forces' only VC at Commachio, Italy in the last three weeks before the end of the war. He had been an inspired leader, a master of the skills of his fighting profession and his men would have done anything he asked of them. He had also been extraordinarily good and kind to the poorer Greeks, caique commanders and their families.[65] Such outstandingly able but complex men often find it difficult to adjust to normal life in peacetime.[66] But Jellicoe, Lassen's CO for

109

the last two years of his heroic SBS life, has no doubt that Lassen as he knew him would have made an outstanding contribution to post-war Denmark.[67]

The war had also taken its toll on the friends of Jellicoe's Cambridge days. Just after the collapse of France, Pease joined the Cambridge Air Squadron and was picked to join a fighter squadron. He was shot down in the fiercest day of fighting during the Battle of Britain. Jacobson joined the Tower Hamlets Rifle Brigade. He was killed in the first Rommel offensive near Derna in North Africa. Mark Howard, the Coldstreamer, had been killed in Normandy. It was like losing three brothers.

On 8 August 1945, Jellicoe lunched with the newly reunited Dan and Hermione Ranfurly at the Savoy Grill in London. They had all just seen the *Midday Standard* headline 'OBLITERATION' and learned of the dropping of the atom bomb on Hiroshima. They discussed this awful development as they ate and its possible significance in changing forever the world of conventional warfare. Walter Monkton, who joined them, said that it was the biggest event since Christ came and that it was so enormous that there was unlikely to be anything that would not be changed by it.[68]

A new post-War order was dawning. For Jellicoe, the challenges and dangers of the Foreign Service, the Cold War and political high office lay ahead.

Part Two

A Different War

(January 1945 – December 2004)

Chapter Eight

Washington and the Cambridge Spies

Jellicoe's army days were over. On his last night in Cairo, he and Burrows dined at a club near the Mena House Hotel and were invited over to King Farouk's table.[1] Farouk was twenty-five, two years younger than Jellicoe, and already spoiling for a fight with the newly forming state of Israel. His wife was very beautiful.

Jellicoe wanted to join the Foreign Office but with fifteen months to kill before demobilization he went back to London to arrange his next move. The Jellicoes arrived on VJ Day. Lady Jellicoe senior had to be at home to welcome them instead of attending the great celebration in St Paul's Cathedral.

'You've ruined my day,' she said.[2][3]

Shortly afterwards, Jellicoe lunched at White's Club with Stirling – who appeared none the worse for wear for his stay in Colditz – Fitzroy Maclean, Randolph Churchill and Johnny Cooper.[4] It was a signing off at the end of a phase in Jellicoe's life.

That autumn, he failed the Foreign Office graduate selection board but resolved to try again the following year. Meanwhile, instead he accepted a job as second in command of the UN Refugee Relief Agency (UNRRA) at Klagenfurt in Austria looking after Europe's displaced persons, of whom there were millions created by the war. After a short course in London and familiarization with the UNRRA machinery, he went to Austria before Christmas. Delayed in Vienna by a bout of flu, it was the turn of the year when he reached Klagenfurt.

111

As head of operations, Jellicoe was responsible for UNRRA's five camps in southern Austria, located near its headquarters at Villach, and around 25,000 displaced persons. There were Russians (who sometimes pretended to be Poles or Ukrainians because they thought they might do better that way), Poles, Ukrainians and about 1,500 Jews. Many succeeded in reaching the UK, South Africa and above all the US, while the Jews wanted to get to Palestine. For the Jews especially, the UNRRA camps were more like transit centres than permanent refugee camps.[5]

From time to time, a senior official from the Soviet Embassy would try to persuade the Russians to return home. The Soviets regarded Russian refugees who had fled during the war as traitors. Many who had fought alongside the Germans were being sent back to Russia and disposed of. The refugees in turn hated the Soviets. Jellicoe was always very worried that the refugees might attack the Soviet officials when they came to visit the camp. He would walk round with them, feeling very anxious. At times he even worried about his *own* safety. But his presence did seem to have the effect of preventing serious trouble.[6]

The British Embassy in Vienna was also a problem. Senior officials there twice sent for Jellicoe and remonstrated with him for allowing the Jews to use the UNRRA camps as a transit to Palestine. But he remained firm. 'My job', he pointed out, 'is to do the best I can for these people. It's your job to run prisons.' The UNRRA authorities supported him totally. Despite these difficulties, Jellicoe had more fun than if he had stayed with the Army.[7] There was very good skiing in Austria. He soon recovered his competitive edge and began racing in major competitions.

In April 1946, the Jellicoes took a house at 20 Chapel Street, SW1, conveniently near the Foreign and Commonwealth Office. In late autumn, Jellicoe tried again for the Foreign Office and was accepted into the German Political Department as a Third Secretary. For the first time in his life he had an ordinary day job and, except for the occasional trip abroad, went home each night to his family. They were happy days; he relished at last starting out on his chosen career and settled in well. He shared an office with two other young diplomats: Reginald Hibbert, later British ambassador to France and Director of the Ditchley Park

112

Foundation and Norman Reddaway, who became ambassador to Poland. Post-war power cuts in the days before central heating meant that the office was dreadfully cold. Being so junior the three were not entitled to a fire. Not caring what anyone thought, Jellicoe wore his quilted dressing gown with large lapels.[8]

That winter, he skied in St Moritz and took part in the Cresta Run. The British Winter Olympic team captain was talent spotting and in one week Jellicoe received two invitations to train for the 1948 Winter Olympic Games in St Moritz – one for the ski team and one for the Cresta Run. Thankfully, from his point of view, his new job in London gave him a good excuse for not accepting either of these challenging opportunities.[9]

The Cold War had begun. Jellicoe worked initially on Austrian affairs but gradually took on coverage of German affairs and foreign policy more generally. In February 1947, he made his first visit to Moscow as a very junior member of a delegation to a Council of Foreign Ministers of Russia, France, Britain and Germany, led by Britain's Foreign Secretary, Ernest Bevin.

The night before they left London, Jellicoe spent the evening with a fellow delegate, the American journalist Cy Sulzberger of *The New York Times*.[10] Jellicoe had known Sulzberger in the Middle East; he was filing stories from Ankara when Jellicoe dashed through after his escape from Leros.[11] The two men had a good night out, only just making it next morning to catch the train from Victoria Station.

The delegation crossed the Channel by boat to France, where Bevin signed an accord with the French before the two delegations caught the train to Moscow. The women with the French delegation were much better looking than those with the British party. Sulzberger got the best one and Jellicoe had to make do with the second best.[12]

After visiting Berlin and Hitler's bunker, they arrived in Warsaw. Jellicoe was sobered by the sight of the ghetto where the Jews had held out at the end of the war. The British and Americans had dropped in supplies for them and when the Russians were almost at the gates, the Jews had risen against the Germans. But the Russians then halted their advance and the Jews had been slaughtered. The Germans blew up the city leaving

113

it a blazing ruin. The delegation continued on by train to Moscow, through a bleak landscape of ruins, rubble and dearth of trees, which had all been used for fuel.

Relations with the Russians were difficult. They were exacting about formalities and frequently failed to show up for meetings. But Russia in winter was captivating as thick blankets of snow covered the Kremlin and Red Square. Tickets were available for any member of the delegation who wanted to attend the Bolshoi Ballet and Jellicoe quickly took up the offer. He watched Ulanova, who had become the Bolshoi's prima ballerina after leaving the Kirov a few years before. Not for the last time, he regretted that he had never learned to speak Russian.

The first formal meeting in Moscow began with a diminished British team. A third of the party due to fly from Berlin had been delayed by bad weather. As a Third Secretary, Jellicoe suddenly found himself representing Britain in a committee discussing the future frontiers of Germany and Poland. His opposite number, the senior Soviet, was a Russian Field Marshal. But Jellicoe had been studying maps and reading up about frontiers. When he was well into the meeting, Bevin sent him a note: 'I apologise for landing you with this at such short notice. Please let me know if you need help.' Jellicoe sent a hastily scribbled reply, 'Thank you for your kind offer. I'm fine. But do let me know if *you* need any help.' Bevin was amused. Another head of delegation might have reacted more stuffily and even sacked the precocious Third Secretary.[13]

In March 1948, just before his thirtieth birthday, Jellicoe was posted to the British Embassy in Washington, still as a Third Secretary, where his main responsibility was the Balkans. The job meant close contacts with MI6.

In post-war Washington, British prestige was high. The NATO Treaty negotiations were at an advanced stage and the Anglo-American special relationship made for a strong affiliation. Even as a junior member of the Embassy, Jellicoe could see almost anyone he wanted at the State Department. Promotion to Second and then First Secretary swiftly followed.

For the part of his job relating to Greece, he already had excellent contacts and background. Yugoslavia was more difficult.

114

Tito was opting for independence from both the West – he was after all a Communist – and from the Soviet Bloc.[14]

Jellicoe's boss and Head of Chancery was Donald Maclean. Like the other Cambridge spies, Kim Philby and Guy Burgess, Maclean was an idealist. After being attracted by Burgess, he had become a Communist while at Trinity College in 1933. He and they saw Communism as the only answer to Fascism. At the same time, they believed in the dream of workers and peasants building a socially equal world of common ownership and freedom from the capitalist mode of production.

Maclean had lived a double life from an early age. His father, Sir Donald Maclean, had been a Liberal politician and a minister in the Presbyterian Church. But his son had made a commitment to Communism while at Gresham's School, Holt where, 'to encourage purity and limit adolescent experimentation, each boy's trouser pockets were sewn up'.[15] Young Maclean's first experience of prolonged deception had therefore been to keep his father thinking that he still believed in Christianity and eschewed left wing politics.

During his interviews for the Foreign Office, Maclean admitted that he had Communist views he had not entirely shaken off. But this had not stopped him from entering that establishment in 1935, the first of the Cambridge spies to be admitted to the club of those who know the nation's most sensitive secrets.[16] The weight of the old school tie and Cambridge University seems to have overcome any doubts about Maclean's loyalty to his employer and country.

Maclean was already an experienced diplomat of considerable ability. He understood diplomatic behaviour and had excellent connections in Washington and the States. He was tall, charming and the best looking of the spies but slightly more intense than Philby.[17] Jellicoe liked him. He was a highly effective policy administrator and adviser. They got on well and played tennis twice a week, weather permitting, on the Embassy courts. Colleagues in the Foreign Service never imagined that Maclean or Philby could be spies.[18] Patsy Jellicoe found Maclean extraordinarily nice. Philby appeared warm, almost cosy. One would never ever have suspected that he was capable of defecting. It was

115

only later that Patsy realized that rather than being cosy, he was cold, with a dual personality. He never said very much or shared anything of what he was thinking.[19]

Jellicoe became firm friends with a First Secretary in Washington, Nicholas (Nicko) Henderson. He had gone into the Diplomatic Service after Oxford and served in the Minister of State's Office in Cairo in 1942 and 1943. After being Assistant Private Secretary to the Foreign Secretary, he went to Washington in 1947.

In September 1948, Tim Marten, fellow juvenile raider of the peach house at St Lawrence, and Wykamist, who had also joined the Foreign Office, arrived to work on the NATO negotiations. As one of the First Secretaries, he was responsible for atomic energy, a very high profile and politically sensitive policy area.[20] His boss, Roger Stevens,[21] head of the Economic Relations Department, invited the newly arrived Marten and his wife Avis to lunch to meet the Macleans and hear about Washington. Melinda Maclean was very proud of her new (real mink) coat. Maclean had two salaries to go with his two jobs.

Marten found Jellicoe a good colleague. He was agreeable, persuasive and yet persuadable, displayed a sort of inborn judgement and was an excellent negotiator.[22] They and Henderson became close friends. Jellicoe sometimes wondered which of the three of them would get to the top of the Foreign Office. He always thought it would be Marten, then Henderson, followed by himself.[23]

On 4 April 1949, Jellicoe's thirty-first birthday, he witnessed the signing of the North Atlantic Treaty in Washington. It was an impressive ceremony with Ernest Bevin, still the Foreign Secretary, signing for Britain. But the day was significant for another reason. Jellicoe had for some years (of increasing girth) made a habit of weighing himself on his birthday. That awesome day, he noted that he was beginning to lose the battle of the bulge.[24]

Signing was followed by intense preparations and briefing for the 4th Session of the UN General Assembly in New York. The growing disillusion with the UN needed to be curtailed; other delegations were reported to be 'tired of holding the ring at

East-West slanging matches, which the USSR were using as a sounding board for their propaganda'.[25]

The international mood was sombre. Bearing down on a prostrate, demoralized and virtually unarmed Europe was the Russia of Stalin, fresh from the rape of Czechoslovakia. There was twofold fear. The first was that the immeasurably superior Soviet armies would simply make a military promenade to the Channel. The second was that the Communists might come to power at the polls or by putsch in Italy. The French and Italian Communist parties were militant and confident. So NATO was intended to be the shield under which Europe would recover her prosperity, her nerve and her self-confidence.[26] There was no difficulty in selling the concept of NATO in the United States or in Western Europe – Europe was the front line against the Soviet Union. The difficulty faced by the American administration lay rather in selling NATO to less well-informed American public opinion.[27]

Getting Europe back on its feet economically had long been a US priority aimed at reducing demands on the US for financial assistance and providing a democratic counterpoint to the Panglossian claims of the Russians. The Americans therefore promoted European economic integration. France and Germany subsumed this policy into their own objective: to bind Europe so closely together economically that another European war would be physically impossible, if not unthinkable.

Integration began with the OEEC (Organization for European Economic Cooperation), set up in Paris to administer US Marshall Aid funds for rebuilding Europe. Unlike the later use of an occupation authority in Iraq, the Americans got it right psychologically. They said the OEEC could decide how to hand out the money, provided all its members agreed. Cooperation was rewarded with money: non-cooperation with penury. Cooperation happened. The OEEC eventually transformed itself into the OECD and still exists as a rich country economic policy club.

Separately, the Europeans pursued their own interests. Coal and steel were the backbones of twentieth century warfare, while oil was considered the blood of victory, though at that time none was produced in Western Europe. So the 1952 Treaty of

Paris set up the ECSC (European Coal and Steel Community), the forerunner of the EEC and the EU. By 1956, the Treaty of Rome was in negotiation. Both treaties were explicitly federalist in objective: economic integration would, it was thought, force and also underpin the goal of political integration. So it has proved.

To Jellicoe in Washington, all this seemed a good idea. Britain tended to see the lessons of two World Wars as being that the Europeans caused trouble and you could only rely on the Americans to help. For Britain, NATO meant the Americans had bound themselves to do so again, against the Russians. This analysis remains at the heart of British official thinking to this day. But Jellicoe thought this Atlanticist argument wrong for two reasons. First, the Americans would only help if it suited them. They were opposing the Russians in Europe because that was where American interests lay. Second, he saw that the French and Germans were right: stopping European wars would remove a huge economic, social and political drain. And it would remove the need for the American guarantee. Geographically, Britain could not really leave Europe. So, he concluded, Britain should join before it was too late.

Jellicoe advocated this policy for the rest of his political career. Unlike many of his political contemporaries (and almost all of the British establishment) he did not make the mistake of assuming that European integration would not happen, or that it would be slow, or fail, or that the Americans would oppose it. In fact, the reverse turned out to be true.

Kim Philby arrived in Washington in October 1949, fresh from Turkey, where he had been Secret Intelligence Service (SIS) station head and a Soviet spy. Philby had betrayed to the Russians and sent to their deaths countless British agents he had dispatched into Russia, as well as their contacts and families inside the USSR.[28]

As the SIS representative in Washington, Philby liaised closely with the CIA and was therefore ideally placed to pass secret and highly sensitive information about US as well as UK special operations to his KGB controller in New York.[29] Marten's atomic communications were Top Secret; they did not go through ordinary Foreign Office ciphers but instead through

Kim Philby's super secure MI6 ciphers – and therefore straight to the Russians.[30]

Philby had had a splendid example of how to live the double life from his father, whom he idolized. Sir John Philby had been a senior civil servant and Arabist who wrote for *The Times* but also converted to Islam, took a second Muslim wife and occasionally wore Arab clothes. To complete the model, Philby senior had also sold secret information about British policy on the Middle East[31] to Ibn Saud.[32]

Philby's Civil Service selection board had gone so far as to turn him down at his first attempt to join the Foreign Office on the grounds that 'his sense of political injustice might well unfit him for administrative work'.[33] But the final selection board overturned this sound piece of judgment and let him in.

Philby was *the* pre-eminent Cambridge spy. He did enormous damage to the West, due to his encyclopaedic knowledge of British Intelligence operations. Jellicoe worked closely with him and liked him enormously. Highly intelligent, efficient and quick in his judgments, Philby was sound, sensible and industrious while remaining pleasant and good-humoured. Attractive rather than classically good-looking, Philby was seen as a possible future head of MI6. He was easy to work with – the more so because he was doing two jobs.

For about a year Jellicoe was deeply involved in an attempt on the part of Britain and the US to undermine the Enver Hoxha regime in Albania. The main objective was to infiltrate agents into Albania to obtain intelligence on the state of the regime and assess how easy it would be to undermine it. The No. 2 in the CIA and the No. 2 in the Policy and Planning staff at the US State Department worked very closely with Jellicoe on this initiative. As the fourth man in this enterprise, Philby was in a position to sell US and British secrets to his masters in the KGB. Jellicoe was always puzzled by the fact that all their agents seemed to disappear. They were recruited from all over the world but put into the field mainly from Malta. The last thing he ever suspected was that Philby was a double agent.[34]

After the signing of the NATO Treaty, Jellicoe and Philby went to New York to brief Bevin on Albania. Everything said in the meeting went almost certainly straight to the Russians.[35] In October that year, Philby told the MGB/KI (the precursor of the KGB) about the impending first SIS seaborne landings into Albania and the West's plans to infiltrate agents across the borders and parachute them in the following year.[36]

Guy Burgess had come to Washington with Philby but had a very minor role as a Second Secretary. The son of a Royal Navy Commander and a wealthy mother, with whom he had a close relationship, he had gone after Eton up to Cambridge and Trinity. There he had met the fourth Cambridge spy, Anthony Blunt, as well as Philby and Maclean. Burgess had been academically brilliant, talented and self-confident, with complete contempt for what he saw as bourgeois morals, and a passion for his own particular brand of champagne Communism.

Fifteen years later in Washington, he still had his boyish looks, chubby build and crinkly brown hair. He was flamboyantly homosexual, which was then illegal, and an alcoholic. He must have become a liability to the Russians, as well as to his own government, but the Soviets probably kept him on because of the close bond between him, Philby and Maclean. The Cambridge spies worshipped Communism and a faith that was shared was more likely to endure. Burgess was also Philby's courier to New York.[37]

Burgess lived with Philby and his second wife Aileen, his first marriage to an Austrian member of Comintern having ended in divorce. Burgess's presence made life difficult for Aileen and the children. Philby did not sleep around but, like the other Cambridge spies, he was very ideological and close to Burgess.

Burgess had the office next door to Jellicoe's but was seldom there. Jellicoe did not take to him.[38] Scrofulous, with filthy hair and nails and a perpetual adornment of dandruff on his collar,[39] he was dealing, in a somewhat desultory fashion, with the Middle East. He would come into his office at about 11 o'clock. At lunchtime, he went to a typical American diner with a compartment to himself. There he would sit with a gallon stone jar of red wine and a plateful of spaghetti. At about 3 o'clock, he would return to the office, his waistcoat spattered with Bolognese sauce.[40]

Sometimes, usually with ill-judged timing, Burgess went onto the attack. When Lord Cairns, RN, who was a listener in GCHQ, came to Washington to talk to his opposite number in the US equivalent of GCHQ (the National Security Agency), the Philbys invited Cairns to dinner, along with the Martens. Cairns had had drinks with the Martens beforehand, as had Burgess, whom Avis disliked intensely. The four of them were on their way to the Philbys by car when Burgess started questioning Cairns in the most searching and unpleasant manner. It was all about GCHQ stuff, what Cairns did, which departments he dealt with and so on. Cairns was clearly very annoyed.[41]

Finally, something happened to put the skids under Burgess. His mother came out to visit him and somehow managed to arrive at a point half way down the east coast. Burgess had a splendid white Lincoln Continental with a twelve-cylinder engine and an immensely long bonnet. The only thing wrong with the car was that Burgess was driving it.

He set forth to fetch his mama but had hardly crossed the Potomac Bridge when he was stopped for speeding. The Interstate Highway Police grilled him but were unable to do anything since he had diplomatic immunity. However, they warned their colleagues further down the road to look out for him. Burgess carried on and ten or fifteen miles down the road broke the speed limit again. This time the police took him in but could not hold him. At large again, Burgess spotted a fair-haired boy thumbing a lift. Being addicted to such, Burgess gave him a lift. After a while the boy said, 'Gee. It's a swell car,' at which Burgess invited the boy to have a go at driving it. The boy accepted. He broke all the speed limits and when the police stopped the car again there was nothing to prevent his being jailed. Burgess really was a very dissolute character.

The news buzzed around Virginia. The State Governor, Governor Battle sent an immediate, detailed protest report to the Deputy Secretary of State, Dean Acheson, who passed it to the British ambassador, Oliver Franks. He and Derek Hoyer-Millar, the Minister,[42] agreed that at last they could get rid of him.[43]

In September 1948, Maclean was posted to the British Embassy in Cairo. His American colleagues, including the CIA, gave him a

121

slap up farewell lunch and on his last night in Washington, he and Jellicoe dined down on the Washington waterfront in one of the many delightful fish restaurants. It was summer; the wives and children were away in Maine so their meal was unhurried. Jellicoe was slightly surprised when Maclean began to criticize certain aspects of US policy, making clear that it was his personal opinion. Jellicoe thought no more of it – until it he learned late the following year that deciphered Russian signals meant that the finger of suspicion of espionage was pointing at Maclean.

In Cairo he went off the rails because of his drunkenness and was sent back to London. After some months recovering, he was put in charge of the American desk in the North American Department at the Foreign Office. The search then narrowed down to four people, of which three were eliminated, leaving only him. Maclean and Burgess then defected to the Soviet Union and Philby immediately came under suspicion.[44]

Jellicoe and Marten were surprised that nobody came from London to ask them about their former colleagues. They assumed that London had instead talked to Philby, in which case the Russians would have known all about it and the answers he gave to London would have been fabricated.[45] Maclean had clearly been in a position to do immense damage to Britain through his spying activities – though not on the scale of Philby.

Burgess did his share too. According to Alan Bennett, 'No one has ever shown that Burgess did much harm, except to make fools of people in high places'.[46] Unfortunately, the evidence proves otherwise. After the collapse of Communism and the USSR, the KGB made their files on the Cambridge spies available to Random House publishers, showing how many secret documents the spies gave to the Russians. Burgess sent them over 4,000. Moreover, he worked closely with ministers and was in a position to give the Kremlin US and British military intelligence on the Korean War. No doubt the Russians passed some of it on to the Koreans. Had there been a Third World War, the damage would have been even more devastating.

Why the Cambridge spies betrayed their country is a conundrum. Communism satisfied them intellectually and they certainly believed that there would be a world revolution.[47] They would have given Britain Communism run from Moscow with themselves in top jobs in London. Perhaps Bennett came closest to the truth in his characterization of Burgess. 'I can say I love London. I can say I love England. I can't say I love my country because I don't know what that means.'[48]

In early summer 1951, Philby too was recalled from Washington. But not before he had attended a high level British/American intelligence meeting there to coordinate joint SIS and CIA special operations in the Balkans. He later boasted in his memoirs that he had given his controller 'precise information about three groups of six agents being parachuted into the Ukraine. I do not know what happened to the parties concerned,' he went on, 'but I can make an informed guess.'[49] They were almost certainly tortured and killed.

While in Washington, the Jellicoes had another daughter, Zara, and two sons; Patrick, to whom Marten became godfather, and Nicholas. Jellicoe's elder daughter, Alexa, and Marten's daughter Jenny went to the little class run by the ambassador's wife. The new ambassador, Oliver Franks, allowed no formal lessons.[50] At the time, the UK Government restricted the amount of money that could be taken out of the UK and consequently the Jellicoes never had enough. Patsy increased their revenues by painting portraits and pictures of people's houses.[51]

Old Lady Jellicoe came out to visit, crossing by sea to somewhere in Louisiana. The Jellicoes then drove down to pick her up. This journey of some 1,000 miles took about two days. On the second day driving up to Washington, she said, 'George, what a big country it is. I had never realised. What a pity we let it go.'[52]

At a welcoming party for her, Evelyn Waugh upset large numbers of Americans. He had just given a derisory lecture about the US while gathering information for his book, *The Loved One*. Lady Jellicoe senior also tended to make comparisons between America and Britain and her interactions with the Americans needed careful handling.[53]

Jellicoe made many close American friends, travelled widely and was in considerable demand as a speaker. The Jellicoes lived in three different beautiful houses, including one in Georgetown. Social life was international and cultures mingled. The Russians always offered brandy before lunch. One Soviet asked Patsy whether if Jellicoe defected to the Soviet Union as Maclean had done, she would follow him. 'Certainly not!' she replied.

In September 1951, Jellicoe was appointed Head of Chancery in Brussels, his first job with a European dimension. In May 1950, the UK had declined to join France, Belgium, the Netherlands, Luxembourg, Italy and the Federal Republic of Germany in negotiations on the European Coal and Steel Community (ECSC). The subsequent signing of the Treaty of Paris by the six had made the ECSC a reality but Britain was outside it. Jellicoe was deeply disappointed. His new job was therefore significant, not only in raising his interest in European issues and the UK's response (or lack of it) but also because it enabled him to forge new and wider personal European contacts than had been possible in Washington. Some of those had already moved on. Nicko Henderson had been posted from Washington to the Embassy in Athens carrying a letter from Jellicoe to Mary Cawadias saying that the bearer was a good friend of his. 'Look after Nicko, Mary darling', Jellicoe had said. She did – and married him.

Patsy could not come to Brussels for some months because of the children. So Jellicoe took a temporary flat in the centre of Brussels near the Frère Orban. Here he met Ronnie Grierson,[54] who had the flat below and had already embarked on an extraordinarily successful business career. Grierson had the biggest address book Jellicoe had ever seen.[55] He had been born Griessmann, in Bavaria in the 1920s and educated in Germany, France and England. While at Oxford University in July 1940, sharing a tent with Roy Jenkins on a summer forestry camp, there came an ominous knock at the tent flap. Following the Battle of France, Grierson, like other German nationals, was being interned.[56]

Under Article 18b of the Defence of the Realm Act he was whisked away to a barbed wire camp in Shropshire. After four months, when the threat of invasion was seen to have receded, he was examined by MI5 and allowed to join the Army. Only one Army unit accepted aliens and within one hour he was in it, as a private in the Auxiliary Military Pioneer Corps. From this most unpromising situation he had emerged, through sheer ingenuity, personality and probably the most rapid series of promotions in British military history, to become the only German to end up as an officer in the SAS and later the only German colonel in the Black Watch.[57]

When Patsy arrived, the Jellicoes took a beautiful house by the lakes and made many new friends, including Louis Camu, the eminent Belgian banker and economist who had organized the wartime Flanders Resistance before being betrayed and handed over to the Gestapo.[58] Not long afterwards, the Embassy was told to expect a new Defence Attaché. Jellicoe was the first to greet the new arrival, Group Captain Peter Townsend, whose love affair with Princess Margaret had been making the headlines. Old friends reappeared too; Julian Dobrski had seen an article about Jellicoe in a Brussels newspaper. The former SOE Agent had become an international businessman and was in charge of the European operations of AT&T, the major US telephone company. When the company transferred to Geneva, he had moved to a house[59] in the hills at Crans-sur-Sierre in a valley running up into Italy. The families became firm friends and Dobrski helped old Lady Jellicoe to buy a flat there. Eventually, with characteristic forthrightness, Lady Jellicoe said to Nikki, Countess Dobrska, 'I might as well give up this flat because I can always come and stay with you'. One day Jellicoe learned that Dobrski had died suddenly on the train from Sierre to Geneva.[60]

Jellicoe liked and admired his new ambassador, Sir Christopher Warner, who had a fearsome reputation for meticulous drafting. It was well merited. During his two years in Brussels, the most familiar sight for Jellicoe was that of his drafts, pearls of wisdom and precision as he thought them to be, made mincemeat of by the ambassador and returned full of scribbles, hieroglyphs and red-ink balloons.

But Sir Christopher had another, equally well merited, reputation for kindness and humour and became a great friend. He was also an impressive professional. It had become fashionable to think that ambassadors counted for little and there was something in that. Ambassadors could not act with the superb and audacious independence of Stratford Canning. But seeing Sir Christopher in action taught Jellicoe a thousand ways in which an ambassador's influence can change the image of the country he represents in the mind of the country to which he is accredited.[61] Working for Warner made up a little for the fact that the work was not intellectually stimulating; indeed, Jellicoe sometimes felt that his role obliged him to be ineffectual. This new culture took some getting used to. It was an interesting but also disheartening time.[62]

Jellicoe's concern about Britain's attitude to Europe increased. Paul-Henri Spaak, the Belgian Catholic Christian politician who became known as 'Mr Europe', was encouraging the UK to play a more positive role. Jellicoe could see the French busy advancing their policy interests. He and Warner made frequent representations to the Foreign Office in London. But their efforts bore no fruit. It was really very depressing that the British in Brussels could not be more *communautaire*.

Brussels was definitely a place for burning the candle at both ends and skiing was one of the best ways to do it. In 1951, under the aegis of the Army Ski Association at St Moritz, Jellicoe and Stephen Hastings, who was by now a military attaché in Helsinki, met up again skiing. Jellicoe had a friend who ran a pub between Davos and Klosters. There was a fine run nearby and as the pub was at the bottom, they would finish up there and have supper. One evening, they swept down and in the middle of the ensuing party Jellicoe got up and announced that he had mumps. They reeled out of the pub, where he stood on top of a car shouting, 'I'm mumped! I'm mumped!'

'Get off you bloody fool!' Hastings shouted. The following week when he got back to Finland he found that he was mumped too.[63]

In spring, 1953, Jellicoe and Marten skied the Haute Route from Chamonix to Zermatt and on to Saas Fée. Each day, they started out at 3 or 4 am with a guide, climbing with skis and sticks until they reached one of the ski huts. They would then climb to one of the high points, fix their skis and ski down to the next hut. This took five or six days. After flying back exhausted from Zurich to Brussels, they went that night to a ball given by the Lambert Banking family and danced until 6 am.[64] And so Jellicoe spent an interesting, if not entirely productive, two years in Brussels.[65]

In September 1953, he returned to the Foreign Office in London as No. 2 in the Northern Department in charge of the Soviet Desk; an important policy dossier to hold at a crucial time in East-West relations. It was a time of immense change in Russia, with the succession to Stalin a key issue. The Soviets had delivered an ultimatum on Berlin and a summit was due to take place with Khrushchev, Eisenhower and Macmillan.

Jellicoe was about to enter the world of James Bond.

Chapter Nine

Cold War Warrior

Early October 1953. The Iron Curtain was down. The first Russian satellite was in production; Soviet guided weapons were imminent or had started.[1] The West was working in line with the policy of long-term containment of the Soviet Union originally outlined in George F. Kennan's 1946 'Long Telegram'. From within the US Embassy in Moscow, Kennan, an ordinary American official, had understood that if the West could live with Communism long enough, the Soviet regime would eventually implode. In the meantime, he advocated a strategy of curtailment of Soviet bloc expansion and avoidance of any overt *casus belli*.

Jellicoe's job was political relations with the Soviet Union and Soviet policy – including military strategy and disinformation. His section monitored, sifted and analysed information from Posts, MI5 and MI6 agents. Joseph Stalin had died at 9.50 pm on 5 March, though the news was not broadcast until 4.00 am the next morning. But the West took no satisfaction from Stalin's demise. He had shown cautious commonsense and avoided armed conflict. Whoever became President of the Soviet Council of Ministers, the real power was likely to be wielded by a small committee including Beria, Bulganin and Kaganovich. There would be no one person to whom the West could turn in time of crisis.[2] By July, Beria had been dismissed.

Jellicoe's Foreign Office boss chaired the Joint Intelligence Committee (JIC), the high-level committee operating under a Charter from the Cabinet Defence Committee, where Jellicoe sometimes deputized for him. Otherwise, he attended the meetings, as did 'C', the Chief of the Secret Intelligence Service, otherwise known as 'M' in the James Bond stories. (The original 'M' in real life was Mansfield Cumming but in the Bond parallel universe Ian Fleming chose to use the first initial.) Other regular attendees were the Directors of Intelligence of the three armed services, the Head of MI6, the Director of the Joint Intelligence Bureau (JIB), the Director of Scientific Intelligence and the Director of GCHQ Cheltenham, where Jellicoe was occasionally briefed.[3]

The JIC and other intelligence organizations were so secret that half of Whitehall and Posts abroad did not understand what they did. A Top Secret publication: *A Child's Guide to Certain Intelligence Organizations* aimed to rectify this ignorance. Originally, the four overt organizations were the JIC itself, the Joint Intelligent Staff, the JIB, administered by the MOD and directed by the Chiefs of Staff through the JIC and the Security Service (MI5). The covert organizations consisted of the Secret Intelligence Service (SIS) (according to the *Child's Guide* the 'British Secret Service proper'), the SOE, 'C's Organization', MI6, GCHQ and two other parts whose name and role are still secret.[4]

The SIS had two main functions. The first was to 'obtain, evaluate, collate and communicate to Departments of HMG such intelligence as cannot be obtained by overt means'. The second function is also still withheld under the Public Records Act. In April 1956, Roger Hollis – according to Peter Wright a major spy – replaced Sir Richard White as Director General of MI5.[5]

Jellicoe knew no Russian, had spent only a couple of months in Moscow and found the Marxist-Leninist scriptures incomprehensible. Unfortunately, he also had insufficient Soviet jargon to hide his ignorance. He was not alone in that. Gerry Hennan, the former US ambassador to Moscow, a world expert on the contemporary Soviet scene, said there were no experts on the Soviet Union – only people with varying degrees of ignorance. Jellicoe kept asking himself, 'What processes are at work in the Soviet Union today? Has the regime emerged weaker or stronger from the transfer of dictatorial power?'

At the end of the first year of the post-Stalin regime, he concluded that the USSR had weathered the crises of Stalin's death and the elimination of Beria with an astonishing economy in manpower. The seven remaining members of the Praesidium of the Central Committee (the Politburo) with Malenkov presumed *primus inter pares* seemed to operate as collective leadership in the style of a western Cabinet. But, like all totalitarian states, the regime was presenting a smooth, monolithic face to the world. Senior soldiers had replaced several civilian officials. The USSR faced huge economic problems and its internal propaganda urged the peasants to improve their productivity. Otherwise, the focus was on rapid expansion of heavy industry to close the gap between the US's economic potential and that of the Soviet bloc. It seemed to Jellicoe that the Soviets had no hope of bringing this off quickly. The situation was dangerous because Stalin's personal control over the war machine had been replaced by seven sets of fingers on the buttons.

In 1956, Ulanova, whom Jellicoe had last seen dance in Moscow in 1947, came to London with the Bolshoi Ballet. Covent Garden asked if the Foreign Office would sponsor the visit and having agreed, Jellicoe watched her performance from the Royal Box. She danced as if oblivious of the audience, totally absorbed in her role. When she joined them afterwards, Jellicoe again regretted not having learned Russian.

After two years of spies, listeners and dealing with the Soviets, the Foreign Office offered Jellicoe the post of Deputy Secretary General to the Baghdad Pact, an international mutual security organization.[6] Harold Macmillan invited him for a weekend in the country to discuss it. However, the major event in Jellicoe's life was not professional but emotional. In early 1955, arriving one evening at a party at the house of his friends Morys and Sarah Aberdare,[7] he looked across the room and saw a stunningly beautiful girl. On learning her name – Philippa Bridge, neé Dunne – Jellicoe realized that he had heard of her through a shared acquaintance, Giulio Pascucci, then a Second Secretary at the Italian Embassy.[8]

Philippa was tall, with dark hair and eyes. She had a wonderful, greyhound bone structure, was very courageous on horseback and men adored her.[9] At twenty-four, she was already divorced and certainly not thinking about marriage.[10] Her father, Philip Dunne, was the 8 Guards Commando Captain from whom in 1941 when gambling on HMS *Glenroy* on the way out to the Middle East, Jellicoe had won back the large sum of money. After being introduced, Jellicoe said, rather formally, 'I'm very pleased to meet you since I know you're a great friend of an Italian friend of mine'. She responded and those were the only words exchanged at the time. Jellicoe's marriage to Patsy had been stalling and he fell hopelessly in love.

Philippa shared a flat at 58 Rutland Gate, Knightsbridge with her brother Thomas. She had heard of Jellicoe, with his war hero reputation and completely devil-may-care attitude to life. He was a swashbuckling and fearless figure, always joking and very attractive to women. He did not care what anyone thought and by now had a name for being rather reckless as far as women were concerned. He was also a great tease. 'You know, I don't find you at all attractive Sue,' he would say to Philippa's old school friend, Susan Baring. 'I must be about the only man in London who doesn't. Aren't I lucky?'[11]

Jellicoe flew to Baghdad for the first meeting of the Baghdad Pact Council on 21 and 22 November 1955 at Qasr-al-Zehoor, a royal palace two miles outside Baghdad lent by King Faisal II. The following spring, with a backlog of leave and short of a car in Baghdad, he decided to drive there, accompanied by Philippa for the trip, and fit in some skiing on the way. Not liking the sound of these plans, Philippa's mother, Peggy Dunne, summoned Jellicoe shortly before the impending departure. They had met in 1940 when she visited Dunne while he was training with 8 Guards Commando on the Isle of Arran.

Peggy had inherited a share of the Johnny Walker whisky fortune at the age of twenty-one, was very much a woman of the world and not one to mince her words. She knew that Philippa was keen to accompany Jellicoe on his skiing holiday but she thought it a great mistake since Jellicoe was still married. He was courteous and careful. He had enormous respect for Peggy but he held firm.[12] She then prevailed upon her ex-husband to intervene. Dunne dutifully left his racehorses and drove up from

131

Newmarket to see his potentially errant daughter.[13] They had a very pleasant evening together. Then, just as he was leaving and standing in the doorway he said, 'I suppose it's asking too much to ask you not to go?' 'Yes Daddy,' she replied resolutely, 'It *is* definitely asking too much.'[14] So much for a father's firm hand. But Philippa was clearly Jellicoe's equal in the relationships stakes. Just before their departure she holidayed with her brother Thomas Dunne in Nice, where she consulted him about the merits of two marriage proposals, neither of which was from Jellicoe. Dunne returned to London to find a note from his sister, 'Gone to Baghdad with George Jellicoe'.

Philippa learned to ski at Courchevel and took to it immediately. After skiing in Italy, they drove to Naples and took a boat via Sicily to Beirut where Jellicoe introduced Philippa to the famous Hotel Saint Georges. She then went to Rome, while Jellicoe drove on through Jordan to Baghdad.

In 1956, Iraq was politically stable. Britain's 1919 mandate over the country had quickly resulted in a rebellion in which 400 British soldiers died. The solution was a monarchy. Britain put a Hashemite prince on the throne as Feisal I. He was a son of the Sheriff of Mecca – head of the Hashemite clan related to the Prophet Mohammed – who played a leading part with T. E. Lawrence in the Arab revolt against the Turks. They still rule Jordan.

By 1956, the Hashemite monarchy was failing to win public support, particularly from the younger generation. The Prime Minister, Nuri as Said, a former Army general, statesman and political leader, maintained close links with Britain and worked for Arab unity. In 1930, he had negotiated a treaty with Britain, which remained in force for twenty-five years after Iraq's entry to the League of Nations in 1932. From then on, the treaty gave Iraq control over its internal affairs and defence but British influence remained strong through its retention of two major air bases at Habbaniya and Shu'aiba. Nuri had been Prime Minister fourteen times since 1930 and had always pursued two policies: a pro-British attitude and support for the dynasty.

Rising young army officers supported neither of these principles and their antipathy had led to open conflict at the beginning of the

Second World War. Nuri and the King had fled into exile. Britain had defeated the rebel Government of Rashid Ali Al-Gailani and Nuri had returned as Prime Minister under British sponsorship until 1944. He maintained political order in Iraq while continuing to advocate the union of several Arab nations and ensured that Iraq became a charter member of the Arab League in 1945. It was a difficult balancing act – sticking close to Britain while preaching pan-Arabism was the proverbial each way bet. Eventually it would come unstuck; the policies were simply inconsistent.

Through tough, effective use of police and the press, Nuri repressed critics of the Hashemite Crown. He seemed to see the Baghdad Pact as a solution to the troublesome problem of the expiry of the Anglo-Iraqi Treaty. Since the pact brought in other Arab states, Britain's treaty with Iraq was less noticeable while the other states had a more audible voice.

However, the key non-participating state in the region, Egypt, made plain its opposition, seeing the pact as a military accord that threatened Arab unity and independence. (Under the Anglo-Iraqi Treaty, Britain's Royal Air Force was enjoying the use of the bases at Habbaniya and Shu'aiba.) Gamal Abdul Nasser, the Egyptian President, was saddled with a bilateral – and from his perspective lop-sided – treaty of his own with Britain. But he had resisted British attempts to turn it into a multilateral one. The British saw Nasser as rather pro-Soviet and hoped for his political demise.[15]

Britain had long been aware that social revolution in Iraq was possible. In 1950, the then Counsellor at the British Embassy, Humphrey Trevelyan, had greeted a newly arrived Third Secretary with the words, 'I am going to bequeath an agreeable duty, which is that on Fridays instead of coming to the office you will go out foxhunting with the Crown Prince's pack, because there you will meet the young officers, doctors and lawyers who sooner or later are going to carry out a revolution in this country.'[16]

Baghdad was not a particularly beautiful city. Jellicoe lived in one of the lovely old Turkish houses on the west bank of the Tigris, belonging to an old friend, Jock Jardine, the British Council representative in Baghdad, who was away on a long leave. After Jardine returned, Jellicoe moved into the newly vacant neighbouring house of Agatha Christie.[17]

The pact was founded in 1955, sponsored by Britain and the US to counter the threat of Soviet expansion into the vital Middle East oil producing countries. It consisted of Iraq, Turkey, Iran, Pakistan and the UK. Britain had wanted the US to be a member but had failed to persuade Washington. However, a senior US official represented the Americans on the military committee.[18]

Baghdad was one of the last vestiges of the British Raj. Jellicoe had close contact with his Foreign Office colleagues in the British Embassy, a parchment-coloured Ottoman building at the end of a long drive, beautifully situated by the river. The large, adjacent, colonial ambassador's residence had a ballroom and billiard room. To the right of the portico stood an old brass cannon, known as the Baghdad Cannon, inscribed with 'The Gates of Constantinople', which the Iraqi caretaker used to polish.[19] Relations with the ambassador, Sir Michael Wright, whom Jellicoe had known since his Cairo days, and particularly with his wife Esther, were difficult; both could be rather conservative.

British-Iraqi relations had been founded on a trading relationship as long ago as 1635 when the East India Company had first opened an office in Basra. But the links between the two countries went deeper than the merely commercial. Many of the Iraqis in administrative posts concerned with foreign affairs or in medical or educational appointments had been educated in Europe or the US. Jellicoe found it easy to do business with them and relations at the bureaucratic level were warm. Before long, the gregarious Jellicoe made many Iraqi friends.[20]

The Secretary General of the Pact was a congenial Iraqi called Oiaow Khalidi. But the main task of making it work fell to Jellicoe. All the member countries seconded a Deputy Secretary General, with varying degrees of involvement. Jellicoe was well qualified to oversee the activities of the Liaison and Counter-Subversion Committee, the Economic Committee, the Military Committee, the Economic Experts Committee and the Council itself. Much of the work turned, as it often does, on money. He was determined to put the Pact on a proper financial footing but

1. Like father, like son. A confident look from the one-year-old George Jellicoe with his father, Admiral Viscount Jellicoe of Scapa, 1919.

2. Cowes week, St Lawrence, Isle of Wight, 1935. *Front: left to right,* Lady Myrtle Balfour (George's sister); Countess Jellicoe; HM Queen Mary. *Standing, 2nd from left,* Viscount Brocas (George); *3rd from right,* Earl Jellicoe; *4th from right,* Prince Frederick of Prussia ('Fritzi').

3. In Court dress as a page at the Coronation of HM King George VI; the young Earl Jellicoe, aged nineteen *(highlighted)*, 12 May 1937.

The Long Bar, Shepheard's Hotel, Cairo, where David Stirling invited Jellicoe to be Second-in-Command of the SAS.

Paddy Mayne, when CO 1 SAS Regiment, 1944. He and Jellicoe led columns to the right and left of David Stirling during the daring 'gangster style' SAS desert raid on Sidi Haneish.

6. David Stirling, who founded the SAS and made Jellicoe his Second-in-Command, North Africa, 1941.

7. David Sutherland, the courageous, natty dresser known as 'Dinky', 1942.

8. Anders Lassen, 1944, to date still the SAS's only VC, who was under Jellicoe's command in the SBS. Lassen also won three MCs.

9. SAS jeeps. Their introduction in early 1943 marked a turning point in SAS operations.

Colonel Tsigantes, Commander of the Greek Sacred Squadron, 1942, who was buried just over Jellicoe's garden wall in the local churchyard – a bit of England that will be forever Greece.

11. The SOE Agent 'Major Dolbey', alias Count Julian Dobrski, in 1942. With Jellicoe he parachuted onto Rhodes to persuade the Italian Admiral Campioni to change sides.

The trawler HMS *Porcupine*, commanded by the SOE skipper John Campbell, which picked Jellicoe up after the raid on Crete in June 1942.

13. Fitzroy MacLean with Marshal Tito. Jellicoe had a meeting with them on the Island o
Vis during the summer of 1944.

14. Greek liberation day, 13 October 1944. *From left to right*, Jellicoe, Archbishop Damaskinos, Frank Macaskie, Shan Sedgwick.

15. Jellicoe and Patsy on their wedding day, Beirut, 23 March 1944.

16. The only Brit in sight. Outside the Cathedral in Athens at the service of thanksgiving the day after Jellicoe liberated it on a bicycle, 1944. *Front row: 2nd from right*, Jellicoe; *3rd from right*, General P. Spiliotopoulos, representative of the Greek Government; *4th from right*, the Mayor of Athens. Aristides Skliros; *5th from right*, Brigadier P. Katsotas, former Commander of the Greek Brigade that fought at El

17. Skiing at Courchevel, 1955. In one week in 1948 Jellicoe received invitations to train for both the British Olympic Ski and Cresta Run teams.

18. In Baghdad, 1955, as Diplomat and Deputy Secretary General of the Baghdad Pact.

19. Jellicoe in love. Almost the first meeting at The Prospect of Whitby, 1955. *Left to right:* Geoffrey Keating (one of Field Marshal Montgomery's wartime photographers); Philippa; Cecilia Weikerstein (later McKeown); Jellicoe; Cecilia Weikerstein's father.

20. In flying gear as Navy Minister, *left*, about to fly out to the Fleet, east of Malaysia, with former Cabinet Minister Anthony Head, 1963.

21. Jellicoe's mother, the formidable Lady Jellicoe, 1964. Her brooch is of HMS *Iron Duke*, Admiral Jellicoe's Flag Ship at the Battle of Jutland.

22. Lord (Edward) Shackleton, a worthy opponent in the House of Lords but also a friend and another significant influence in Jellicoe's life

23. A shadow Cabinet meeting in one of the House of Commons Committee rooms, Jellicoe between Edward Heath and Quintin Hogg with Margaret Thatcher, 1968-1970.

24. The last speech as Cabinet Minister and Leader of the House of Lords at Greenwich, 1973, when Jellicoe knew that news of his resignation and scandal was about to break. Jellicoe (*right*) with his cousin, Sir Charles Madden (*left*).

5. Cartoon from the 1972 Concorde sales tour. Jellicoe (*left*) who assumed responsibility from Michael Heseltine, with George Edwards (*second from left*) and Brian Trubshaw, (*second from right*) the famous test pilot, who died in 2001.

6. As Chairman of Tate & Lyle with the Prime Minister, Margaret Thatcher, at the launch of one of the company's own ships at the Richards Shipyards at Lowestoft in 1982.

27. As Chairman of the British Overseas Trade Board amusing HRH The Princess
    Anne at Tesco's Annual Dinner in 1984.

28. As Chairman of the Medical Research Council with Diana, Princess of Wales and
    Sir James Gowans, Chief Executive, at the opening of the MRC's Cognitive
    Development Unit in London, 1983.

29. As Chairman of the British Overseas Trade Board, visiting Taha Yassin Ramadhan, Saddam Hussein's powerful Deputy Prime Minister, Baghdad, 1985. After the 2003 Iraq war, Ramadhan became the 'Ten of Diamonds' in the Coalition Forces' pack of cards (*see back jacket*). He was captured at Mosul on 19 August 2003.

30. Jellicoe with Sir Patrick Leigh Fermor at the 60th anniversary celebration of the liberation of the Greek Islands, Athens, 2005.

36. The 'Three Musketeers' fifty years after the war walking in Spain – Sir Stephen Hastings *(left)* and Sir Carol Mather *(right)*. Jellicoe is unencumbered because the others are carrying his kit!

could not purloin resources, SAS-style. As chair of the Budget Committee, he dispatched a secret minute to the Foreign Office, pointing out that the UK must keep the post of Deputy Security Adviser.[21]

Shortly after his arrival, Jellicoe flew to Teheran to attend a meeting of the Pact in 'the capacious building of the Ministry for Foreign Affairs, a creation of his late Majesty Reza Shah'. There was minimal ceremony with only one formal dinner party by the Shah and another by the Iranian Prime Minister.[22]

The meeting resulted in 'useful' reports from the committees. The Liaison and Counter-Subversion Committee proposed to 'coordinate, initiate and control action in the propaganda and public relations field and counter Communist propaganda and subversive activity'. They aimed to combat hostility to the Pact in uncommitted states and operate a publicity campaign in its favour. Arrangements were finalized for the establishment of an Atomic Energy Centre in Baghdad, a proposal which had electrified the first Council meeting in November 1955. Some countries, Iran and Iraq among them, preferred to recruit their own technicians from whatever country in the world could best supply their needs.[23] Interestingly (given later events in Iraq) the transfer of civil nuclear technology was seen as useful in spreading Western influence, largely because it was a cheap way of providing power for electrification, then synonymous with progress and development. Jellicoe achieved his main aim – a full-scale international budget and an approved establishment. One discordant note arose from an argument over the communiqué and references to neutralism and Kashmir. The final product was intended to satisfy Pakistan while avoiding Indian criticism.[24] Plus ça change.[25]

In Teheran, Jellicoe stayed with Tim Marten, by now Head of Chancery. While Jellicoe was there, he developed a very high fever. Marten sent for the Embassy doctor, who prescribed antibiotics. While Jellicoe was still sweating in bed, he sent for Avis Marten and gave her a letter for Philippa, swearing her to absolute secrecy – even Marten was not to know. But writing letters was not enough; after the meeting of the Pact, throwing caution to the winds, Jellicoe cabled Philippa to join him in

Teheran. They drove to Baghdad, visiting Isfahan and Persepolis on the way, before Philippa caught a flight back to England.[26]

In July, Baghdad sweltered in the midsummer heat. Most of the embassy staff were away and Philippa returned to Baghdad. Jellicoe had plentiful excuses for visiting the other members of the Pact – Turkey, Pakistan and above all Iran – to which he always drove by different routes to take in the scenery and archaeological sites. They travelled extensively in beautiful northern Kurdistan. After being entertained by grand elders in a little teahouse, riding alone through a mountain village, they met a group of men armed with Kalashnikov rifles. Their leader was rather taken with Jellicoe's cavalry twill trousers, eyeing them with such longing and making so many pointed complimentary remarks, that he began to fear for their lives, let alone for the trousers. They made a tactical withdrawal, half expecting to hear a rifle report as they moved off. Within Iraq, Jellicoe made journeys north to Kirkuk and Mosul and south to Basra.[27]

That autumn, the Suez Crisis saw the beginning of the end of the British Empire in the Middle East. On 26 July, in a clear challenge to Britain's status as a world power, Nasser decided to nationalize the Suez canal. His action threatened British oil supplies from the Middle East and other economic interests in the region. Since the canal was under the joint ownership of Britain and France, the Prime Ministers of the two countries, Sir Anthony Eden and Monsieur Guy Mollet, together with Israel, after some dithering with the United Nations over a Security Council Resolution, attempted to invade Egypt. By late autumn, the US had forced both Britain and France into a politically humiliating withdrawal.

Like many Britons at the time, Jellicoe was appalled by British policy on the Suez issue and came close to resigning over it. Baghdad had been relatively peaceful but Britain's extremely unpopular action as far as the Arab world was concerned, seriously impaired Iraq's relations with Britain. It made Nuri's position impossible and wrecked everything the Pact was trying to achieve.[28]

The Cambridge spies still had an impact on Jellicoe's life. While he was in Baghdad, Philby arrived as *The Observer* correspondent for the Middle East. The Foreign Office immediately instructed Jellicoe not to associate with him. Given that the two men had been such good friends, Jellicoe found acceding to this request both difficult and embarrassing.[29]

He made several trips back to the UK for meetings and Philippa went out three times for short visits. On the third occasion, Jellicoe went to Baghdad Airport to meet her off a BOAC flight at two o'clock in the morning. Out came the usual tired and crumpled businessmen, followed by Philippa. She was nervous about flying and usually had a few drinks to fortify herself. On this occasion, she had had one too many. Staggering down the gangway, she fell into Jellicoe's arms saying, 'Marry me George! I'm really terribly rich.' He took her at her word. But it was to be ten years before he was free to do so.[30]

In March 1957, Jellicoe's Foreign Office superiors suggested a long leave from September, probably hoping that this would resolve the increasingly apparent problem of Philippa.[31]

In October, he and Philippa left Baghdad and drove back to England through southern Turkey, Greece, and southern Italy to Sicily, where Jellicoe had to fly back to England to his brother-in-law's funeral. After rejoining Philippa, they visited a friend in Tunisia before driving to Rome for a party near the Coliseum. There, Jellicoe met Edda Ciano again, Mussolini's daughter with whom he had danced to the tune of the Italian national anthem when staying in Potsdam before the war. By 1945, her father had had her husband shot and Mussolini himself had been assassinated.[32]

In February 1958, back in London, the Permanent Secretary at the Foreign Office, Sir Derek Hoyer-Millar, asked to see the repatriated diplomat. The senior mandarin was forthright. 'George,' he said. 'You have a choice of ceasing your relationship with this lady or changing your job.' It was one of the easiest decisions Jellicoe ever had to make. He refused to give up his relationship with Philippa and resigned from the Foreign Office.[33] Many thought Jellicoe would have gone to the top as a diplomat.[34] Hoyer–Millar agreed. 'I had hoped that some other way out of the difficulty might have been found,' he wrote in response to Jellicoe's resignation letter. 'You were one of our most promising young men and it is a great pity from the Service's point of view that we shall not have the benefit of your services in future as I'm sure you would have gone far ...'[35]

Jellicoe accepted a job from his first cousin, the then Sir Nicholas Cayzer, who ran the family shipping firm, British and Commonwealth. They owned the Clan Line, with some seventy cargo vessels and the Union Castle Line of passenger ships. Jellicoe expected to become responsible for the South African office but somebody else got the job. He made some interesting trips to South Africa, staying in the best hotel in Cape Town, which belonged to the company.[36]

Like many people visiting South Africa at that time, he was very worried by what he saw of apartheid and the trouble that was being stored up for the future. He was keen to help, particularly as no British Ministers were going there, and spoke out whenever he could. Ever afterwards he retained a fondness for South Africa. Since the firm's head office was at St Mary Axe in the City and another was in Southampton, Philippa began to look at houses within easy reach of both.[37]

In July, social unrest finally boiled over in Baghdad.[38] A dissident army officer called Abdul Karim Qassem led a military coup and overthrew the monarchy. On 14 July, revolutionary forces captured the capital and proclaimed a Republic and a provisional Constitution declaring that 'Arabs and Kurds are considered partners in this homeland'. King Feisal, Crown Prince Abdul Illah and the rest of the Royal Family were murdered and their bodies dragged through Rashid Street in Baghdad. Feisal was a first cousin of King Hussein of Jordan, with whom he had had a good relationship. Everyone had always thought that it would be Hussein who would not survive. Nuri tried to escape dressed as a woman but was caught, killed and dragged through the streets. The Jellicoes had met him in Claridges Hotel only a few weeks before.[39] Amid all the chaos, a twenty-one year-old Iraqi called Saddam Hussein committed his first murder for the Ba'ath Party, killing a Communist political opponent called Saadoun al-Tikriti. The following year, with other Ba'athists, he made an unsuccessful attempt to kill Qassem.[40]

Then came one of the strange turns of fate which had sometimes attended his father: the House of Lords launched a debate
on the revolution in Iraq. No longer in the Foreign Office, Jellicoe
could say what he thought. He felt impelled to make his maiden
speech and wrote it in Brooks's Club. Philippa was in the gallery
on 28 July 1958, as he rose at 2 pm to make his first recorded
utterance from the cross-benches.[41]

His diffidence in addressing their lordships was increased by
the fact that he was speaking after the lunch break. He craved
their indulgence, saying that he would restrict himself to Iraq and
the Baghdad Pact. Despite the recent repellent scenes of violent
revolution, he was at pains to point out that there was another
side to the picture – the courtesy, kindness and hospitality of the
Iraqi people. They displayed no inferiority complex towards the
West, and this could only help in establishing sound relationships
with the new Iraq. He expressed his deep shock at the deaths of
the Royal family and 'that great, and greatly human, statesman,
Nuri Pasha', whose regime could not be written off as feudally
corrupt, though it had been unresponsive to public opinion with
at least 75 per cent of political opinion against it.

Jellicoe then made three suggestions as to how Britain could
normalize its relations with the new Iraqi Government, whose
statements should be taken as sincere, unless and until they proved
otherwise. First, the Baghdad Pact powers' meeting then taking
place at Lancaster House should clearly denounce the circulating
reports of a planned intervention into Iraqi internal affairs.[42]
Second, he urged that the Baghdad Pact powers should at their
meeting announce their recognition of the new Iraqi Government
because it met the two normally applied criteria of controlling
the country and being willing to discharge its international
obligations. Third, there was the human aspect: even though Iraq
had been independent for a long time, the Iraqis themselves had
not always felt so. 'They have somehow suspected,' Jellicoe said,
'that the British were in some way still running the country.' For
example, the Nuri regime had been implementing a large schools
programme. 'These schools,' said Jellicoe, 'were built for the
purposes your Lordships might expect – to educate Iraqis in. But
the Iraqis did not believe that; they thought – it was a very

139

widespread belief which one could not eradicate – that these schools were camouflaged barracks intended for the British Army when they reoccupied Iraq. These are', he said, 'the sorts of ingrowing toenails in the Iraqi consciousness which I feel we must try to eradicate.'

On the Pact itself, Jellicoe urged flexibility and understanding if Iraq decided to leave it, and support for the other member countries who would be more exposed and who had stood by Britain during the Suez crisis. In conclusion, he found it hard to understand why the Americans were members of every Pact committee but jibbed at membership itself, particularly as joint British US regional policy deplored this sort of anomaly.[43]

The Marquis of Salisbury was first on his feet to congratulate Jellicoe on his speech. 'The noble Earl', he said, 'bears a famous and honoured name and I am sure your Lordships would agree with me ... how worthy he is to bear it.' Viscount Astor congratulated Jellicoe on a 'surprisingly constructive' maiden speech. 'I say "surprisingly",' he added, referring to Jellicoe's nefarious wartime SAS and SBS career, 'because when I knew him in the Middle East, his activities were entirely *de*structive. He was engaged in blowing up all sorts of things ...'. [44]

Jellicoe's maiden speech prompted considerable press comment. Subsequent correspondence led to more active involvement in the Lords, after which he moved to the Tory benches. At the same time, after about eighteen months working for British and Commonwealth, Jellicoe had come to the conclusion that there was room for four first cousins in the business but not five.[45]

A career in politics beckoned.

Chapter Ten

Whitehall Warrior

Harold Macmillan's first government was in office; Edward
Heath was Chief Whip. Jellicoe began a meteoric rise in politics.
In October, he spoke again in the Lords to move 'an humble
address' to the Queen from the Conservative benches:

> The last time I addressed your Lordships, was from the
> platonic sanctity of the Crossbenches. I then had the aesthetic
> pleasure of seeing your Lordships in profile. I now have the
> equal pleasure of seeing some of you full face. I do not know
> why I find myself in this particular hotspot ... I can only
> surmise that the noble Earl [the Leader of the House] was
> fishing for a large Tory trout, cast over the Crossbenches
> for an ex-Ambassador and hooked an ex-First Secretary by
> mistake.[1]

In March 1959, he followed Lord St Oswald, in a debate on
Britain's Five-Year Defence Plan.[2] The following spring, in a
debate on the shipping industry, he declared his business connection: a good deal of salt water flowed in his veins from both
sides of his family. He outlined ways in which government could
help the industry to help itself. It was time for a really effective
partnership between vigorous private and progressive public
enterprise, both inspired with a dash of what he called 'the Jackie
Fisher spirit'.[3]

141

His private life however was unresolved. Old Lady Jellicoe took to Philippa while Peggy Dunne was more redoubtable. Though she admired Jellicoe, as President of the Stratford Division of the Conservative Party and Constituency Party Chairman for Jack Profumo,[4] the charming and amusing Secretary of State for War, Peggy knew that politics and divorce did not sit well together. But eventually even she succumbed and Jellicoe and Philippa began house hunting in earnest.[5]

One Friday when Jellicoe was dining at Brooks's, the waiter came to tell him he was wanted on the telephone. Peggy had seen a house in *Country Life*. He had seen one too – a beautiful 1741 Georgian manor house near Marlborough, with twenty acres and a swimming pool. It could not be viewed that weekend because the owners were away. The next day, he and Philippa were due to have lunch with Peggy at Radway in Warwickshire and decided to go via the property. They stopped just up the hill at a little church. Walking through the churchyard to the edge of the property, they looked down through the late morning mists to the sweep of lawns and beautiful manor house. In less than a minute, they turned to each other. 'That's it,' they said in unison. After ten minutes inside the house, they knew they wanted it. Tony and Barbara Hunt looked after the gardens and house respectively. Tony had been born in one of the village's thirteen houses and had never worked anywhere else.[6]

Jellicoe still made time for leisure, often dangerous. On a walking and skiing holiday in the Atlas Mountains with Carol Mather and Robin Fedden[7] they climbed the highest peak of the Jebel, the 4,265 metres Jebel Toubkal. After skiing ahead of their guide in thick mist, they stopped and waited. He appeared and they all went back to their primitive ski hut. The next morning, they discovered that their ski tracks stopped right at the edge of a precipice; Jellicoe laughed.[8]

The following February, he had one last contact with the Cambridge spies. After a trip to the Middle East for a major oil company, visiting sheikdoms in the Persian Gulf, Bahrain, the Trucial States and Qatar, he stayed on the way back with Humphrey Trevelyan, ambassador in Baghdad. To their delight, a telegram from London brought news that Edward Heath had

142

announced in the House of Commons that Kim Philby, who was *Observer* correspondent in Beirut, was cleared. Jellicoe and Trevelyan immediately sent Philby a congratulatory telegram and suggested that he and Jellicoe meet up when his flight home stopped for five hours in Beirut. As the plane landed, Philby was waiting on the tarmac. They passed some very pleasant hours at the Hotel Saint Georges before Jellicoe caught his flight to London. In 1963, Philby defected to the Soviets. Jellicoe was appalled and saw to it that Philby never made contact with him again.[9]

The July 1960 reshuffle of the second Macmillan government cleared the decks for action on Europe. The Kennedy Round of the GATT[10] was about to begin. The original EEC Six would be engaging as a single entity for the first time and the UK was on its mettle. The European Free Trade Area, EFTA, had been established (a sort of UK-led opposition to the Common Market) and so the general atmosphere did not augur well for opening negotiations on British entry to the EEC. But by 1961, Macmillan had appointed Heath to lead the British negotiations, supported among others by Sir Eric Roll.[11]

The Communist challenge was urgent and the West's response seemed ineffective. In January 1961, Jellicoe chaired part of a two-day British Atlantic Committee Round Table Conference in Parliament on 'The Battle for the Minds of Men'.[12] Viscount Hailsham PC, QC, presided; speakers included Paul-Henri Spaak, Secretary General of NATO, Lord Pakenham and Professor Hugo Seton-Watson[13]. This sort of involvement, together with his activities in the Lords, got Jellicoe noticed.

In February 1961, the Prime Minister wrote to Jellicoe inviting him to become a Lord-in-Waiting and a Conservative Whip. He was also to support Lord Mills, the No. 2 government spokesman in the Lords on defence and aviation.[14] 'I hope,' Macmillan continued rather less formally, 'you will find Government as exhilarating an experience as the organizations you served during the war!'[15] Following the usual announcement in the *London Gazette*, the Lord Chamberlain's office confirmed that Jellicoe would take up post from 8 February. The job appeared to consist of representing the Queen at funerals and memorial services –

often at very short notice – and meeting VIPs arriving in the country.[16]

Letters of congratulation arrived from ministers, foreign ambassadors, chairmen of organizations, friends old and new and from people Jellicoe hardly knew at all. Many mentioned the possibility of further promotion, though one said, 'I hope you won't languish as a Whip for seven years as I did!'[17]

Profumo wrote enthusiastically, 'A thousand congratulations. I'd wished for this earlier ... all your friends and admirers will applaud loudly...'.[18]

Tim Marten was delighted but added, alluding to Jellicoe's marital situation, 'Only wish all your matters progressed so well'.

Jellicoe described his new job as 'rather varied. At one moment I am a combined bottle-washer and lady-in-waiting. At the next, I find myself a sort of pseudo Defence Minister ... I handle all Housing and Local Government matters in the Lords and am No. 2 Government Spokesman on Defence and Aviation matters. I really don't know which I know least about!'[19] In a speech to the Anglo-Belgian Union, he described his new appointment as something of an anachronism. In the age of Blue Streak[20] and Baroness Somerskill,[21] not only had the Union's President, Lord Swinton, produced 'that almost extinct political animal, that dinosaur of politics, an hereditary peer. He has gone one better and produced a Lord-in-Waiting to boot'. Jellicoe had pictured himself in knee breeches and powdered peruke, opening carriage doors for the Shah or, better still, his wife. To his dismay, things had turned out rather differently. He was expected to know something about obscure subjects like rating law and Polaris submarines. Reluctantly, he had come to the conclusion that the only old-fashioned thing about the job was the pay, which had clearly been fixed some time before the South Sea Bubble burst.[22]

Barely five months later, in July 1961, Jellicoe was promoted to Joint Parliamentary Secretary at the Ministry of Housing and Local Government. Profumo wrote on the headed notepaper of the Secretary of State for War, commenting on a recent performance in the House, 'Full marks ... thank you *so* much. The debate can have done nothing but help us.'[23] A letter from Susan Baring suggests just how hard Jellicoe had worked for the promotion:

> So thrilled ... relished the newspaper comment, viz: that never before had there been anyone in the Lords sufficiently versed in housing problems to be able to deal with the subject and how *you* could. I thought of our lost weekend when you were swotting up those formidable Ratings Acts (or whatever they were) ... you had never worked so hard since Cambridge finals ... Heaven knows, you've deserved it and now it looks to me like a clean run up to – oh, anything you like ... Your mother was very sweet when I lunched with her, said not a word ... but whispered to me as I left, 'Get the evening paper – there's good news about George!'[24]

'It is becoming monstrous writing to you every six months like this,' wrote Evelyn Waugh,[25] while another correspondent was more self-interested, asking if Jellicoe was now too busy to shoot and whether he still wanted to continue with his half-gun.[26]

Housing, or the lack of it, and the slums were a huge political problem. Jellicoe was responsible for National Parks and environmental matters, including building restrictions in London.[27] Very tall buildings were being approved without any proper planning. He vetoed some potentially catastrophic constructions scheduled for Pall Mall and Harley Street. He continued to speak on Defence and Aviation matters.[28]

As the only Minister for Housing and Local Government in the Lords, Jellicoe also spoke for other Government Departments when the need arose, seeing through some important EEC/EFTA legislation. He learned to spot when he had not been properly briefed. Within his own area, he took on some major and controversial tasks, for example, one concerning water resources in the north-west.[29]

Manchester Corporation had deposited a Bill in Parliament seeking to abstract water from Ullswater and construct a reservoir in Bannisdale Valley. Twenty-six petitions laid against that part of the Bill during a Lords' debate the previous November had ensured that it failed. But the Manchester area risked serious water shortages by 1965 if nothing was done and the Ministry decided to accept a Manchester Corporation suggestion for further consultations.

The aim was to examine the points of contention and provide a basis of agreed fact. Jellicoe chaired a regional conference of varied, and fairly vociferous, interested parties. The job involved mountains of correspondence, Parliamentary questions, tenacious and sometimes hostile regional media and frequent travel to the Lake District.

At the first conference meeting in March 1962, the views of the participants were entrenched. After getting his head round survey reports and technical data, Jellicoe found common ground and brought people together.[30]

He moved on to his second appointment in eighteen months. In July 1962, he succeeded Lord Renton, a leading lawyer of his day, as Minister of State at the Home Office under Henry Brooke, the Home Secretary. With promotion came a more high-profile job and discrete portfolio.[31] Everyone in the Ministry from Keith Joseph and Evelyn Sharp[32] downwards was delighted. 'There is no one in the Lords whom I would half as soon have had to be our new Parliamentary Secretary as yourself', Brooke concluded.[33]

But Macmillan put the seal on it, 'This is a remarkable tribute from a man who knows how to pick men. Few people can have made such substantial progress in such a short time – will be fascinated to see how you team up with Rab...'.[34] A message from the Hendersons read simply, 'Capability of new climber exceeding all expectations'.[35] One of the most touching letters came from his former embassy driver in Brussels.[36]

Much of the correspondence also regretted his departure from his previous job. Profumo wrote, 'How sad we have only had a "that was George that was" relationship in politics![37] We shall miss your great interest and help here. However, *warmest* congratulations on getting a key responsibility of your own. *No reply* please – and that's an ACI!'[38]

Jellicoe invited Renton to lunch at Brooks's to get his views on his new responsibilities. The two men had met before, in the last year of the war when Renton was president of the British Courts of Tripolitania and presiding over a court in the ballroom of Marshal Faldo's palace.[39]

Monty Woodhouse was Parliamentary Under Secretary of State in the Home Office. Carol Mather was working in the Conservative Research Department and was Secretary to a weekly policy group on Home Office affairs, chaired by Brooke, of which Jellicoe was a member. The group produced a pamphlet 'Crime Knows no Boundaries', which recommended the amalgamation of some of the many police forces in the country. Politically, Jellicoe was seen as middle of the road.[40]

Brooke was good to work for but like other junior Home Office ministers Jellicoe did not much enjoy his job. The Home Secretary, a Minister of State and two Parliamentary Under Secretaries of State handled all the work. (Nowadays, the Cabinet Office struggles to rein the Home Office back to *seven* ministers.) But the Home Secretary made all the running and junior ministers had little active role in policy making. The Home Office was the worst of all the departments for this. Jellicoe was deeply interested in the prisons; the more he discovered about them, the more concerned he became. On visiting them, he was horrified by the overcrowding. To his great frustration he was unable to do much about it. Instead, he became a member of the Home Office Committee on Penal Reform.[41]

In midsummer 1963, the Profumo Affair became the sex scandal of the decade. It was a politician's nightmare, involving call girls, sex parties, KGB spies, secret FBI investigations, lies told in Parliament and the suicide of an eminent London osteopath. It led to the downfall of a Cabinet minister and ultimately the resignation of the British Prime Minister. These awful consequences imprinted themselves on British political culture for the rest of the century.

Profumo had a relationship with a call girl, Christine Keeler, who lived, platonically she said, with Stephen Ward, a fashionable London doctor, at his Wimpole Mews flat, together with another call girl, Mandy Rice-Davies. However, Ward's main vice appears to have been social climbing. He threw sex parties involving two-way mirrors, sado-masochism and orgies for high-ranking and influential members of the establishment, including

147

Roger Hollis, head of MI5. It was said that an unknown man, rumoured to be a Cabinet minister, used to serve Ward's guests naked, except for a mask, and eat his own meal from a dog bowl.

Keeler met Profumo at a party at Cliveden, the Berkshire country home one of Ward's patients, Lord Astor, in 1961. When the story broke in late 1962, Profumo denied any affair and went to stay with Peggy Dunne at Radway to escape the media. In March 1963 he lied to the House of Commons, saying he and Keeler were just friends. Ten weeks later he admitted to MPs that he had misled the House to protect his family. That attempted subterfuge was his undoing and he resigned.

The class structure was still very much alive in 1963 and the public showed their contempt for the immorality and hypocrisy of the upper classes. Keeler had run away from home at sixteen while Profumo had been educated at Harrow and Oxford. Moreover, the girls themselves were not without wits. In response to a rather patronizing remark from a TV news interviewer that Lord Astor had denied having sex with her (after all, who was going to take her word against his?) Rice-Davies refused to be overawed and brought the house down with her deadpan one-liner, 'Well, he would say that wouldn't he?'

The affair became even more unsavoury when Ward was prosecuted for living off the immoral earnings of Keeler and Rice-Davies and committed suicide before the end of his trial. However, the scandal involved a major security risk. Keeler had also slept with Eugene Ivanov, a naval attaché at the Soviet Embassy, raising the question of whether British security had been compromised – and by its own Secretary of State for War. Keeler says she was used as a cover for an Anglo-Soviet spy ring.[42] Ward supposedly spied for the Soviet Union and asked her to get information from Profumo about nuclear warhead sites in West Germany. She then delivered it to Ivanov at the Soviet Embassy, who passed it on to Moscow. Fleet Street had a field day. 'Profumo quits over affair with girl', ran the headline in *The Daily Sketch*. 'Profumo quits – He lied to MPs over Christine to save his family' and 'Profumo quits – He tells Premier' appeared in *The Daily Mirror*. Even the more respectful *Daily Telegraph*

148

and *Financial Times* carried 'Resignation of Mr. Profumo' and 'Mr. Profumo Resigns'.[43]

Jellicoe was greatly saddened by Profumo's political demise and thought it a great loss to the country of an exceptionally able War Minister. He had been a great source of encouragement, friendship and practical help, even providing a helicopter to fly Jellicoe down to Salisbury Plain to visit troops on exercise there.[44]

In the aftermath of the Profumo Affair, Jellicoe was appointed in October 1963 to the post of First Lord of the Admiralty. The reconnection of the famous Jellicoe name with responsibility for the Royal Navy was greeted with an acclaim almost on a par with the famous signal to the Fleet, 'Winston's back'. Among another mountain of correspondence were letters from Fitzroy Maclean, Shan Hackett, Carol Mather ('thrilled to see that you'd become the ruler of the Queen's Navee') and Corelli Barnett ('I have sent you under separate cover a complimentary copy of my book *The Swordbearer*').

'They have really nailed you this time,' wrote another, 'and turned you into a sort of floating soldier.'[45] Many said how proud his father would have been. One letter from a man called Patrick Corcoran, who had served at the Battle of Jutland in the destroyer HMS *Narwhal*, touched Jellicoe deeply. 'We were the last in action in that engagement,' it said, 'and carried out a torpedo attack on six German battleships at about 2.30 pm on 1 June. I was also present when we lost the battleship HMS *Audacious* off the Donegal coast in 1914.' Years later, in 1935, Corcoran had seen a shooting party of men with double-barrelled shotguns near Tipperary, one of whose face was familiar to him. The next day he discovered that it was Admiral Jellicoe.[46]

Jellicoe was perfect for the job, having not only had wartime experience of the Royal Navy but also engaged in active operations with them. He occupied Churchill's old office in the Admiralty Building, at the end of the Cabinet Office. There he enjoyed one or two of its famous incumbent's better paintings and a good view over Horse Guards Parade. He could not believe his good fortune and threw himself into the work. He continued to broaden his political contacts, including within the Opposition,

Roy Jenkins being among the first of his Labour Party friends to 'swim in Jellicoe's freezing swimming pool'.[47]

The house halfway up Whitehall that went with the job was not available because the Prime Minister was occupying it while No. 10 was being renovated. During the week, Jellicoe lived with his mother in Eaton Square. On one occasion, a young flag lieutenant (known in Navy parlance as 'Flags') went to pick Jellicoe up for an appointment. He rang the bell and heard an interrogative shrill voice,

'Yes?'

'It's Flags Lady Jellicoe,' he shouted.

'Not today thank you!' she shrieked back.[48]

As First Lord of the Admiralty, Jellicoe had more autonomy and successfully saw through a major aircraft carrier programme, which was later partly unpicked by Denis Healey when Labour came to power. Had it not been for that programme, the country would have been much less well placed to send a taskforce to the South Atlantic during the Falklands crisis in 1982.

Jellicoe spent most of his time dealing with defence policy modernization issues and answering questions for Government in the Lords. He travelled extensively, visiting the Fleet in the Atlantic and the Far East and a number of naval stations en route. But he was never too busy to lend his support to important domestic naval projects, often combining this with diplomacy, for example, the Royal Canadian Navy submarine programme at Chatham.[49] Such support also required a studious approach to reports and technical detail so that he had an in-depth under-standing of the work.[50]

In April 1964, the Government decided to appoint one Secretary of State for Defence for the three armed services and replace the title of First Lord of the Admiralty with the more modern one of Minister of Defence for the Royal Navy.[51] So the last First Lord of the Admiralty was a real Lord. The abolition of the 200 year-old title caused some harrumphing in Parliament.[52] After thirteen years of Tory government, times were definitely changing.

In July 1964, the Tories were optimistic about a fourth term. They had secured a third even after the Profumo scandal. When the Government went to the country in October 1964, Jellicoe was galvanized into action speaking up and down the country on behalf of Heath and Tory candidates and writing innumerable letters of support. It was a time of huge optimism and belief that at last a new administration would crack the country's problems.[53]

It was not to be. The Tories lost the General Election. On 19 October, Jellicoe gave a farewell office party. The Navy were sad to see him go. The Naval member of the Canadian Joint Staff in London wrote on behalf of all in the Royal Canadian Navy 'with thanks for kindness and assistance on many occasions, for example, the negotiations surrounding the RCN submarine programme at Chatham where your interest in our problems ensured that discussions ran smoothly and the programme got off to a good start'.[54] Another conveyed gratitude for more personal benefits: 'Thank you for all the trouble you took over us at Devonport. We always enjoyed your visits and you certainly stimulated much activity, particularly in the married quarters line ...'.[55]

After a month working for Jellicoe's successor, the First Sea Lord wrote on crested notepaper with a jauntily slanted anchor, 'You kept us well up to the mark ... life in MOD is hectic ... The new Minister asks whether it is always like this and I tell him nearly always!'[56] The Controller of the Navy thanked Jellicoe for being '... such a dynamic and engaging boss. I have enjoyed working under your direction enormously, even when we've had a bit of a barney – in fact particularly then!'[57]

Tory MPs too wrote thanking him for his electioneering support. 'I was *very* lucky to win,' wrote one. 'And I shall be even luckier to hold it next time.'[58] Another thanked Jellicoe for his eve of poll support in Mill Hill and Edgware. 'As my majority was only 1,100,' he added, 'you can understand how particularly grateful I am.'[59] Yet another wrote with thanks for the eve of poll support in Portsmouth. 'The only thing that mars our pleasure,' he said, 'is the thought that it was your last appearance as Minister of Defence for the Navy.'[60]

His cousin, Sir Charles Madden, Commander-in-Chief of the Home Fleet, was particularly sorry, thanking Jellicoe for all his energetic work which the Navy had very much appreciated.[61] The Chairman of the Navy League wrote, '... how much the Navy are regretting your departure ... I know, of course, how well justified their regrets are ...'.[62]

Even Jellicoe's official driver wrote thanking his former boss for 'a wonderful farewell present. I feel it is something I did not deserve,' he said, 'for my bad driving in our short time together but then besides being a duty I found it a pleasure working for you.'[63]

And so Jellicoe became part of Her Majesty's loyal Opposition where he would play a leading role in attempting to reform the House of Lords.

Chapter Eleven

Opposition and House of Lords Reform

Even in opposition, Jellicoe prospered. A year after the election, he succeeded Lord Harlech[1] as Opposition Deputy Leader to Lord Carrington and became a member of the Shadow Cabinet. He remained on the front bench as Opposition spokesman on defence matters, the armed forces and some aspects of foreign affairs. As President of the National Federation of Housing Societies and an ex-Housing and Local Government Minister, he could also speak with authority on housing and homelessness. The issue was still high on the political agenda and an acute problem for the new Government.

Carrington was very much on the ball but always sensible and very human. He had served with distinction in the Grenadier Guards and won an MC. The respective opposites for the Government were Lord Longford and Lord Shackleton, the son of the great Antarctic explorer Sir Ernest Shackleton.[2]

Although Jellicoe was not a conviction politician he had a serious side, driven not by personal ambition but more by a sense of public service. In the House of Lords, Carrington found him able to master a brief quickly and turn his mind to a speech.[3] He was straightforward, not party political, but loyal.[4]

Shadow Cabinet meetings were usually held in one of the committee rooms at the House of Commons. Margaret Thatcher was always rather quiet. There was no inkling then of the extraordinary force that was to come from her later. Heath ensured proper debate, which appealed to the studious side of Jellicoe.[5] Though he *preferred* getting on with the job, he could also address policy issues. Heath relied on Jellicoe's judgment and his knowledge of the House of Lords.[6]

Jellicoe tackled the Government head on over what he called its 'mystery Defence Review', pressing for information about the status of the Falkland Islands and holding the administration to account on many other issues. He and Carrington said they would not oppose the Government 'just for the heck of it' but only when they believed its policies were not in the national interest. By November 1965, the Government's actions on defence were filling the Opposition with disquiet. When would the missing Review appear? Jellicoe maintained that the uncertainty was compounded by some very odd logic: on the one hand the Government was using the Review as a reason for not saying or doing anything. On the other hand they were blithely taking a whole series of basic defence decisions, for example, on aircraft procurement, which would affect defence and the Reserve forces right through the 1970s (and, it turned out, during the Falklands War).[7]

In December 1968, Jellicoe asked if confirmation of the status of the Falkland Islands had been received and if so whether the Government would now remove sovereignty from the agenda of the talks currently taking place. The Foreign Office Minister, Lord Chalfont, said the talks were *about* sovereignty and therefore the subject could hardly be removed. Jellicoe persisted, pressing to know what effect a transfer of sovereignty would have on the Falkland Island Dependencies, whether surrender over South Georgia would imply surrender over the other islands and whether the defence implications of such a transfer had been fully examined. Chalfont struggled to provide assurances.[8]

A year later found Jellicoe giving the Government a very hard time for agreeing, along with some other European countries, to suspend Greece's membership of the Council of Europe because of an alleged breach of the conditions. It was a sombre occasion, especially for him. 'Many of us remember,' he said, 'the days when Britain and the Commonwealth stood alone with Greece against the dictators. Greece is the country I know best, having spent many months in peacetime and in wartime on Greek soil and in Greek waters. It is particularly sad that Greece, to whom all Europe is indebted, should in any way be severed from the political community of Europe.' He elicited Government assurances that they would resist pressure for the expulsion of Greece from NATO.[9]

Being in opposition was not a fulltime job and Jellicoe revived his business interests. An introduction through Grierson in late 1964 led to a lunch in the City with Eric Roll[10], one of the most remarkable men Jellicoe was ever to meet, and Siegmund Warburg.[11] A non-executive directorship of S. G. Warburg followed,[12] Jellicoe's main role being to build on the company's existing involvement – particularly in Greece, Iran and Eastern Europe.[13] Jellicoe knew the difference between black and red figures and the importance of getting the noughts the right side of the decimal point. This was a pure bonus as far as Warburg was concerned; they could discuss with Jellicoe everything to do with the business.[14]

The world of Tory politics was unknown to Roll. So it was difficult for him to think of Jellicoe as anything other than a diplomatist, statesman and businessman. But they became close politically because Jellicoe was the kind of Tory he could live with (Roll sat on the Lords cross-benches) and they travelled extensively together. On a visit to the Beijing Museum in Hong Kong Jellicoe saw a portrait of his father; the locals were astounded to find his son in their midst. In Teheran, Jellicoe raised funds for Warburg and advised on structural changes to the company. In Greece, his high level contacts helped to open doors, particularly in the National Bank.[15]

Jellicoe's network of personal connections was by now global. In 1964, he had talks with Lee Kuan Yew, Prime Minister of Singapore and the following year wrote to congratulate him on his assumption of the premiership of the new State but regretting its separation from Malaysia. Lee replied, 'It took some fifteen years to build up a climate of opinion in Singapore to accept merger with Malaya ... after about a year of continual politicking by Malay extremists in the peninsula that even the Tunku[16] could

155

not control, I found myself in the silly position of agreeing in one weekend to unravel the ties that took one and a half decades to bring about.'[17]

In 1965, Jellicoe began a two-year stint as a delegate to the Council of Europe and the Western European Union, in which capacity he went to the US with an all-Party team, led by Duncan Sandys.[18] He had time for personal matters too, giving a silver tankard retirement gift to a member of staff whose thank you note said: 'I started as a Commander's messenger at sea in HMS *Courageous* at the age of seventeen and ended in the office of the Minister of the Navy himself, where I had the honour of serving Mr Mayhew and you.'[19]

One sad engagement was attending Churchill's funeral on 30 January 1965. After the service, a barge bearing the coffin of the great man slipped slowly under leaden skies up the Thames from St Paul's to Waterloo. Jellicoe thought of the lunch when Churchill had fallen asleep and the secret flight from Turkey to Egypt when they had talked in his bedroom.

A series of events then marked the end of an era in Jellicoe's private life. Philippa's father had to have an operation for lung cancer. Just before the surgery, they met him for a drink at Claridges. He was feeling quite well and half-wondered why he needed an operation. 'Shall I just run away?' he said. He never came round from the anaesthetic.[20] Jellicoe immediately stopped smoking his usual seventy cigarettes a day.

In 1966, he was at last able to regularize his private life. Patsy agreed to a divorce – just in time because at thirty-four Philippa had become pregnant. They were married in Marlborough Registry Office in April.[21] It had been ten long years since Jellicoe had first wanted to marry her. During that time, he had not lost his openness and sense of humour; he simply did not care about formality or what other people thought. But now he became happier and more relaxed, exuding warmth and giving free rein to the quirkiness of his character. It was his passport to success as Philippa too embraced the travel and representational aspects of his position.

Later that year, their first child, Johnny, was born, followed by Emma and Daisy in 1967 and 1970.[22] The children began to grow up in Wiltshire with those of Tony and Barbara Hunt, so closely that Emma and Daisy sometimes called Hunt 'Daddy' by mistake.[23] Friends were not far away. The Hendersons settled in nearby Combe, as did Michael Stewart, who had been in the Washington embassy.

In the same year, old Lady Jellicoe died in London. Jellicoe had offered her the opportunity to live in the cottage next to the church but she had characteristically replied, 'I think not. That might be rather *too* near the graveyard.'[24] Extracts from a poem written by Philippa say it all:

She was without pretence and without humbug;
She had colossal guts and an iron nerve.
She was completely self-assured;
She was very formidable;
She had a very simple, straightforward,
Direct approach to everything;
Very like a child.

She ticked off the doctors as she lay dying;
'You all said I was better –
How do you account for this?'

She was indomitable.
It was easy to make
The elementary mistake
Of thinking her immortal.

On 1 April 1966, Labour won a second General Election, improving its scant Commons majority from three to 100. But Conservatives still hugely outnumbered Labour in the Lords. The Tories therefore had the tricky task of balancing being an effective Opposition against the risk of the Labour Government abolishing hereditary peers and reforming the House of Lords.

Jellicoe had a first class, Wykehamist turn of mind and was a cautious operator. For someone so firm in his moral and executive judgements, let alone his military achievements, he was rather a consensus politician. He could be very amusing on his feet.[25] In the House of Lords, he was a more serious speaker, his élan not always showing up so well in official speeches.[26] He took on more

157

responsibilities, becoming a governor of the Centre for Environmental Studies and in 1968 chairman of the British Advisory Committee on Oil Pollution of the Sea. But by far the largest of these commitments was the part he played in the attempted House of Lords reform and related Inter-Party conference.

The background was a series of failed similar attempts to agree on reforms. An Act in 1911 had removed the Lords' power to reject Bills with a financial element ('money Bills') and in 1949 their ability to delay legislation had been reduced to a period of no more than one year from a First Reading in the Commons. Legislation introduced in the first four sessions of a five-year parliament could not, therefore, be passed without Lords' agreement. But hereditary peers still sat, spoke and voted in the House of Lords. They could delay the Government's legislative timetable and even cause a Bill in the last parliamentary session to be lost.[27]

Not surprisingly, the Government had promised in its Election Manifesto to remove this Lords' delaying power. In July 1966, it had even printed a House of Lords (Abolition of Delaying Powers) Bill. The abolitionist MP, Willie Hamilton, was described as being in full cry after their Lordships. 'The member for West Fife', ran a story in *The Guardian*, 'has put down a question ... to ask the Prime Minister whether he will initiate legislation to curb the delaying power of the Lords in respect of legislation.'[28]

Jellicoe *wanted* reform of the House of Lords. Being by accident a member of it, and an hereditary one at that, he wanted the Lords to work well and demonstrate the value he knew it added. But he also wanted a system in which the power of the Government majority was not overweening. His desire for reform was driven partly by the fact that the upper House was patently flawed and partly because the 'first past the post' Commons electoral system meant domination by the Party in power. So, in a sense, the Lords were being reformed to redress the deficiencies in the House of Commons. Even Bagehot in 1867 had said: 'If we had an ideal House of Commons, there would be no need for a House of Lords'. However, it probably suited some in the Commons to have a slightly eccentric Upper House which could not been seen as a candidate for usurping its role as the principal House of Parliament.

Lords' Reform began, fittingly for Jellicoe, with a meeting in a restaurant. By 1968, Richard Crossman, Lord President of the Council and Leader of the House of Commons, was leading an Inter-Party conference group on Lords' reform established in April 1967. Other members were the Tory MPs Iain Macleod and Reginald Maudling, Labour's Home Secretary, Roy Jenkins and Commons Chief Whip John Silkin. Carrington and Jellicoe represented the Tories in the Lords, while Labour fielded Lord Longford, the Labour Leader of the Lords and Lord Privy Seal, and his Deputy, Shackleton. Frank Byers attended as Leader of the Liberals in the Lords. The joint secretary to this heavyweight group was Michael Wheeler-Booth, a House of Lords clerk who had been seconded from being a Private Secretary to the Leader of the House and Government Chief Whip to be co-secretary of the Ministerial Cabinet subcommittee and of the Inter-Party conference.[29]

The Inter-Party conference was chaired first by Lord Gardiner, the Lord Chancellor and leading Government whip, then by Longford and then Shackleton when he succeeded Longford as Leader of the Lords. Most of the work was referred to a three-man working party of Jellicoe, Shackleton and Byers.[30] Despite the political divide, Jellicoe and Shackleton became increasingly close friends and he began to spend weekends at Tidcombe, where most of the real work was done, not least in give and take. Wheeler-Booth thought that Jellicoe excelled at this because he had a very liberal point of view.[31]

On 24 October 1967, Crossman arranged to brief the Tories about the mention of the Government's intention to reform the House of Lords that would be in the Queen's Speech. But Heath and Whitelaw knew that the Speech contained no reference to consultation. Carrington and Jellicoe had done some intelligence work and had informed their Commons colleagues of every detail because, as Crossman noted, 'Frank Longford can't resist talking to them out of office hours'. Consequently, Heath and Whitelaw refused to meet Crossman. He was obliged to go to Number 10 and tell the Prime Minister that the speech had to be amended to refer to all-Party consultation on reform, which it duly was.[32]

On 23 November, Longford gave a private and very amicable dinner for Carrington, Jellicoe, Shackleton and Crossman at the Café Royal. Longford persuaded Carrington and Jellicoe that he 'really wanted functional reform and ... an effective second chamber', and was convinced by the end of the evening that he could 'settle with Carrington and Jellicoe'.[33]

A few days later, the second meeting of the inter-Party group considered a working paper from Shackleton. The main problem they faced was that Heath, McLeod and Maudling were not really interested in Lords' reform. The second problem was that increasingly this became not the time for consensus politics. The Government faced many more pressing issues. The country needed repeated IMF loans and that summer, a Prices and Incomes Bill had been introduced. On 24 October, the French had vetoed Britain's entry to the Common Market. The Abortion Bill was another political hot potato. There was a six-month standstill of wage, salary and dividend increases followed by a price increases 'freeze'. A resulting fuel crisis had led to 'a kind of Suez atmosphere' – hardly the climate in which to win Tory Party agreement to proposals that would only be possible with full support via the usual channels on both sides.[34]

By early 1968, the group was making progress. After dinner at Carrington's house on 8 January, he, Jellicoe, Crossman, Longford and Maudling concluded that though many detailed points remained to be settled, they had an in-principle agreement. No hereditary peer would have a vote; existing hereditaries would either become life peers, and thereby acquire a vote or, alternatively, retain speaking rights only. Such speaking rights would not descend to their heirs. The Conservatives would waive their objections to the abolition of the inbuilt Conservative majority and Labour would concede the continuation of their longer delaying powers.[35] In fact, the Lords were very careful about exercising these powers.

By March, general agreement had been reached on a complicated two-tier scheme of reform. Voting and non-voting peers would include some hereditaries who could both vote and speak but who would eventually literally die out. Voting peers would be evenly distributed, apart from a small majority of ten for the Government, but the presence of thirty to forty cross-benchers would mean that the Government could occasionally be defeated. New peers would continue to be created. Delaying power was agreed as six months from disagreement with the Commons, which was effectively a year from Third Reading in the Commons.[36] (Wheeler-Booth had let Crossman know that the minimum the Tories would settle for was nine months from disagreement.)

Macleod thought that because popular support for the Government was waning (it had lost several by-elections) a White Paper and Bill on such a constitutional reform would only be possible if implemented in the next Parliament. But others thought to delay that long, especially if a Conservative government were elected, would mean the reform simply would not happen. On 26 March, Jellicoe, Maudling, Byers and Crossman met in a Lords Committee room (Carrington was ill and Macleod did not turn up). Given that the meeting was not quorate, they dealt instead with secondary issues such as the bishops, law lords and the problem of affirmative orders. 'When we deal with this kind of detail,' Crossman noted in his diary, 'Jellicoe clearly understands ... but Maudling is completely out of his depth ... amiable, conscientious and willing to go along with almost anything we propose'.[37] The only remaining real point of difference was the timing of the creation of the reformed House of Lords.[38]

But on 9 April, a crack appeared over whether peers with speaking rights but no voting rights should also be excluded from voting in committee. Jellicoe, Shackleton and Byers all urged that for an effective committee system, peers had to have such a right. But Labour saw agreement on this point as giving way on its central principle that the power of the hereditary peerage had to be eliminated completely.[39] On the whole, Tories in the Lords wanted implementation soon. But even if the Bill were passed in the next session, some Tories might insist it should not come into force until the next Parliament. And they might well ask why the Opposition was shoring up a Labour Government with no credit via a bipartisan agreement.[40]

By 7 May, the group had compromised on the idea of a White Paper with a paragraph from the Conservatives at the end about the disagreement over timing. Members of both Houses would have a free vote when the proposed legislation passed through Parliament. Crossman was left to draft the White Paper with the aim of getting it through Cabinet before the Whitsun recess and then through Shadow Cabinet.[41] But the group were unaware that in another part of the Whitehall forest a Cabinet Committee had already overseen the drafting of a short Government Bill to curb only the Lords' delaying powers. Then in June, the 1968 Southern Rhodesia (United Nations Sanctions) Order threw a large spanner into the works.

The resolution to support a UN resolution to impose sanctions in Rhodesia (following its unilateral declaration of independence) required affirmative resolution by both Houses. Tory peers seemed divided on the issue: many did not feel strongly about it while some even supported Ian Smith's stand. But if the Tory peers voted overwhelmingly against the Order, the two Houses would be in conflict. Jenkins then hinted in a speech in Birmingham that the all-Party talks on House of Lords reform might be jeopardized. The Lords Government frontbench then appeared to use his remarks to try and negotiate a trade off – the price of reform would be Lords support for the Sanctions Order. Jellicoe, despite his enthusiasm for modification, was having none of this. He told the Lord Chancellor that he 'had noted with interest, and some disdain, the minatory utterances of Ministers'. He said he would regret any abandonment of the talks but added, 'My Lords, we have our duty to do. The only right, the only honourable stance for us to take is to treat each issue as it comes before us on its merits.' His tone was, however, measured and reasonable. Carrington too spoke with statesman-like restraint.[42]

The Tory backbenchers were less tractable; once in a while they wanted to have their head. Some even wanted the inter-party talks to fail. Once the connection had been made between reform and the Order, those who did not want reform came into the House specifically to vote against the Order. On division, it was defeated by 193 to 184 votes. Of the Not-contents, 174 were Tory peers, signifying a moral victory for the Government. The Prime Minister, probably not realizing that it had been impossible to restrain the Tory peers, then announced the end of the inter-party conference and the introduction of a short Bill to reform the House of Lords. This smacked of vindictiveness and did nothing to further a climate of inter-party cooperation.

On 14 October, the Lord Chancellor, Shackleton and Crossman had a major discussion about revised tactics on Lords' reform and the timing of presenting the White Paper to the Tories. It was drafted as a Government White Paper, not an all-party one, and given to Carrington and Jellicoe over the weekend with a request that they ensure that Labour had faithfully carried out the plans laid down during the all-party conference. There was no mention of later inter-party cooperation via the usual channels. The Tories did as asked. They wanted the Bill to go ahead as a Government measure but they would let it be known that it was basically what had been agreed. In this way, both sides hoped to satisfy extremists in their parties who detested the all-party talks.[43] Members of the Shadow Cabinet made encouraging noises but, since they had not been asked, were silent about official support for the passage of the Bill.[44]

The substance of the White Paper, Cmnd 3799, published on 1 November, basically conformed to the May draft. It proposed reform not revolution. There was no agreement on a start date, the Government wanting to bring in the measures on Royal Assent while the Opposition preferred to wait until the next Parliament. Nevertheless, there was a compromise and Appendix II meant that a Bill could be introduced in either House and a public Bill could have a joint Committee stage of both Houses. But now, prominent Labour opposition in the Commons from MPs with standing, including Emmanuel Shinwell, Michael Foot, Tony Benn and Willie Hamilton, began to be voiced. From the extreme right, Enoch Powell and others also objected. In a House of Commons debate, a motion from Hamilton to reject the White Paper was defeated by 270 to 159. But many Labour MPs had voted against it and 100 had abstained.[45]

Before the debate in the Lords, Jellicoe wrote some 400 or 500 personal letters, pointing out that the Bill was very close to what the inter-party conference had agreed. The task of persuading his own side was not easy, some peers saying that it would be 'difficult to choose between being a dumb voter or an impotent spouter'.[46] The timing issue also remained important. The Conservatives wanted the legislation passed in the present session but to have *effect* in the next.

'We hold', said Jellicoe, leading for the Opposition in the debate on 19 November, 'that a grave constitutional change of this kind should not be brought into effect in the dying years of a discredited Government.'[47] But he pointed out that much had been accomplished. By the early summer, the inter-party conference had virtually finished its work. Then had come 'that fit of post-Rhodesian petulance. The talks were broken off and all bets from both sides were off . . .'.[48] The Conservatives could have taken the position that it was not they who had broken off the talks and ceased to coopcrate further but, Jellicoe argued, that would not have been a reasonable or honourable position to take. Too much was at stake. If the scheme was endorsed by the House, he said, the Party opposite would be agreeing something which they had never before formally agreed – namely that 'a viable Upper House has an essential part to play in our parliamentary structure. We now have a quite considerable constitutional prize within our grasp', he went on, 'the opportunity to build a really viable Upper House on the basis of a broad consensus of support from all Parties . . .'.[49]

The motion to approve was carried by 251 to 56, an over-whelming majority with one of the largest votes in the history of the House. The Government then introduced the Parliament (No. 2) Bill. Following a First Reading in the Commons on 19 December, the Prime Minister moved the Second Reading on 3 February 1969. A committee of the whole House then debated the draft Bill. It led to a public demand to publish peers' attendance figures for the first time since records began in the fifteenth century. The evidence was reassuring. About 250 peers were taking their seats daily, compared with between 100 and 150 ten years before. 'Therefore,' said an article in the *Daily Mail*, 'their attendance record is better some days than that of MPs.'[50]

On 3 March, Shackleton summoned Crossman to the Lords where he found him with Jellicoe (Carrington was in Australia). The Commons had spent six days in committee on the Bill without getting beyond the preamble and Jellicoe wanted to talk to

Crossman about a possible deal. After a friendly talk, Crossman said a deal wasn't on because there was simply nothing in it for Labour.

'You see George,' he said (completely overlooking the fact that Labour had not sought, and had not been promised, official support for the passage of their Bill) 'we shall only get it through if you face the fact that you and your people are absolutely failing to help. It's like running a Finance Bill without a voluntary [agreed] timetable. We only have our Whips there; yours aren't functioning at all and though it is making life virtually impossible we are jolly well going to slog ahead ... even if it means your people losing their Whitsun holiday.'[51] Jellicoe swiftly pointed out that this was not within his gift. The Lords had voted overwhelmingly in favour of the White Paper but the Commons was beyond his sphere of influence.[52] The Committee struggled on.

The following afternoon, Crossman told the Prime Minister that Callaghan, who had taken over from Jenkins as Home Secretary, wanted a Government guillotine[53] on the Bill, even if they were defeated on it. After the General Election (when Labour probably expected to be in opposition) Callaghan's own political prospects would be brighter if the Lords Reform Bill had been defeated. 'You've got to face it Harold,' said Crossman, 'he's playing for high stakes!' Callaghan then cancelled a meeting with Peart (the Labour Leader of the House of Commons and Lord President of the Council), John Silkin (Labour's Lords Chief Whip), Maudling, Whitelaw and Jellicoe. He talked instead to Maudling who said there was no question of Tory help in the Commons. Moreover, there would be a three-line whip against the guillotine. The Tory party had no further appetite for the Bill and least of all would they support a guillotine on a constitutional issue.[54]

In the attempted Second Reading in the Commons on 3 February 1969, it did not augur well when the Prime Minister, Harold Wilson, acknowledging that the Bill did not enjoy the full assent of all Honourable members, was greeted with shouts of 'Hear, hear!'. The Liberal Leader, Jeremy Thorpe commented that the Government's lukewarm backing for the Bill was effectively saying 'Tis a poor thing but mine own', while

Maudling supported it as long as the measure did not have effect soon – rather on the lines of 'Convert me, but not yet O Lord'. Michael Foot saw the Bill as the result of the Opposition – in which negotiation Jellicoe had played the leading role – having got the better of a bargain with the Government.

'I am an abolitionist', said Foot. 'We should kill this Bill now and prevent the country from being burdened in this modernising age by such an anachronistic and absurd institution as is being proposed, not surprisingly, by the collaboration between the two front benches.' The House divided and the Bill was defeated by 150 votes.[55] Although peers had wanted House of Lords reform because it would not eliminate their hereditary privileges altogether, many right-wing Tory MPs who thought it went too far, did not want it at all. On the other side, a large number of Labour left-wingers thought it did not go far enough. There was simply no way to bring these two extremes together.

By 12 April, after twelve days' sitting time since February, only the preamble and five clauses had been debated. Other urgent Government legislation, including Bills on Prices and Incomes, Merchant Shipping and Barbara Castle's Industrial Relations Bill, were seriously delayed. The tacitly agreed bipartisan measure had been dished in the Commons by a combination of attacks led by Michael Foot and Tony Benn from the left and Enoch Powell from the right.[56] Without cooperation between the Government's business managers and the Opposition whips via the usual channels, it was at the mercy of backbench hostility. On 17 April, despite political embarrassment and failure for the Government, the Prime Minister was forced to announce that the Bill was being dropped.

But that was not entirely the end of the affair. Two years later, a young Oxford graduate, Janet Morgan,[57] returned from a year at Harvard to do her PhD. While she was at Nuffield College, Shackleton gave a talk on the House of Lords. Afterwards, he mentioned to her that nobody bothered about the Lords and yet it was half of Parliament. He suggested that she tell Black Rod about her idea to write up the drama of the Inter-Party conference and the attempted reform of the House of Lords. When she began the work, Shackleton, Jellicoe and Wheeler-Booth 'adopted' her.

Jellicoe gave her the impression of never doing any work; in fact he did, but made no great bones about it.[58]

Jellicoe spent his remaining year in Opposition working with other Shadow Cabinet members on the strategy to win the General Election.

Unknown to Heath, just before the election, Jellicoe got into a spot of bother. Driving back to Onslow Square with a woman he had been asked to take to Annabel's restaurant and drop off again afterwards, he was running in a brand new car and stalled the engine. When he drove off again, he was overtaken within a hundred yards by a police car. He was wearing black tie and the officers asked if he had been drinking. He refused to take the breathalyser test, so they invited him to go to the police station. He took the test and was over the limit. The police drove him back to his flat at Onslow Square, whereupon he invited them in for a drink.[59] The impending court case was uncomfortably close to the election. Jellicoe immediately got in touch with Carrington, who had it postponed until afterwards. As Labour's days in office dwindled, Jellicoe devoted the full force of his energy to speaking up and down the country in support of Tory parliamentary candidates.

The Conservatives won and Jellicoe was back in Government.

Chapter Twelve

Sons of Heroes

June 1970. The Conservatives had won the General Election. Jellicoe did not know whether Carrington had told Heath about the drink driving matter. So it was a bit of a worry when No. 10 rang to say that the Prime Minister wanted to speak to Lord Jellicoe and he was in a Wiltshire pub called The Boot with the Hendersons.

Philippa took the call at Tidcombe and without batting an eyelid found some diplomatic way of saying where Jellicoe was. She then rang the pub to forewarn him. When the call came through as 'Mr Ten to speak to Lord Jellicoe', the hubbub of noisy post-Election celebration was clearly audible in the background. But the Hendersons could tell that all was going well by Jellicoe's repeated use of the phrase, 'There is nothing I would like more'.[1] Jellicoe was to be Leader of the House of Lords, Lord Privy Seal[2] and Head of the Civil Service Department (CSD). It was one of the briefest Governmental job acceptances in history as Jellicoe tried to terminate the conversation before his whereabouts were revealed.[3]

As Lord Privy Seal, Jellicoe referred to himself as 'a more or less human being who is both Leader of the House of Lords and Lord Privy Seal. I, of course', he would go on, 'look upon the Lords as a progressive and forward-looking body ... But you doubtless still regard it as the place where the former Duke of Devonshire dreamed that he was making a speech and woke up to find he was indeed doing so. But if Leader of the House of Lords is bad, Lord Privy Seal is worse. It may be likened to the Holy Roman Empire,

168

which was neither Holy, nor Roman, nor an Empire. The Lord Privy Seal may be a Lord, even under Labour dispensations, but he is not privy, nor a seal and he is always a target for ribald remarks.'[4]

Jellicoe had a Private Secretary (PS) for each major job: Leader of the House of Lords and Head of the CSD. The Lords PS also worked for the Chief Whip, a workload that would have finished most men. Jellicoe's first Lords PS, David Dewar, gave up after nine months: he couldn't cope with Jellicoe's relentless pattern of work (and play). Dewar had been used to lunchtime sandwiches with Eddie Shackleton to catch up on House business. Jellicoe would spend the morning in his main private office in the Old Admiralty Building, have a good lunch somewhere and arrive at the Lords at twenty minutes past two, so there was no time to be briefed. He worked into the evening before going to an official dinner.[5]

Dewar's replacement, Michael Davies, also took on the double PS role. It felt like more. Jellicoe rarely slept more than three hours a night. After a cold shower at 5 am, he did his boxes and discussed House business with Davies at quarter to nine before morning prayers. At weekends, he retreated to Tidcombe with more boxes. He liked them full so he could steep himself in key issues. It was part of his decision-making process.[6] Between March and October, he would have a 5 am swim before driving back to London.[7]

He attended all Cabinet meetings at which, apart from Heath, nobody was dominant though there was a coterie of friends. Socially, Jellicoe was not one of the 'Heathmen',[8] but together with Willie Whitelaw, Peter Carrington and Jim Prior they formed a group of 'old-style landed patricians who were ... more devoted to Heath personally and more in his confidence over the next few years than the others'.[9] Unusually, in Carrington and Jellicoe, Heath had two able Cabinet Ministers who were both hereditary peers, though they concealed their intellect under a relaxed manner.[10] Jellicoe got on people's wavelengths and got on with them while also being good fun.[11]

Although junior, Jellicoe was highly regarded for his wartime record and Foreign Office career. Post-war politics were often unified by a strong, crosscutting affinity among Second World War veterans. Jellicoe, Whitelaw and Carrington were all ex-Guards and often made common cause since they had no particular angle on many of the issues. When this happened, Heath relied on Jellicoe to put the emphasis in the right place.[12] He had an overview of the Whitehall chessboard. Sometimes he would move fast, without waiting for advice. Positions on an issue would be drawn up and then at the last minute Jellicoe would come in under the radar – SAS-style from out of nowhere. He was strategic, opting for all-night sittings in the Lords because he had the stamina for it and others didn't.[13] He had a strong, hard-drinking constitution, consuming quantities of his favourite champagne, and whisky, while his very dashing (but laid back) Government Chief Whip, Lord St Aldwyn, kept himself going on Bells.[14]

The CSD was still fairly new, Jellicoe's predecessor, Eddie Shackleton, having been its first ministerial head. Jellicoe was back in Churchill's old office in the Admiralty Building, over-looking Horse Guards Parade.[15] He had successively two able Under Secretaries of State in David Howell and Kenneth Baker, known rather disparagingly by officials as 'self-basting Ken', and an influential Permanent Secretary, William Armstrong.[16] His Private Secretary, Brian Gilmore, had served in the British embassy in Washington; Jellicoe liked his confident, jovial manner. His young researcher was Chris Patten.

Civil servants were intrigued. Jellicoe had been a civil servant too and his varied jobs across Government more than qualified him for his new post. Bill Kendall, General Secretary of the biggest Civil Service Union, the Civil and Public Servants Association (CPSA) invited Jellicoe to lunch. The ensuing article in their Whitehall in-house staff magazine about the 'new political boss of the Civil Service' described Jellicoe as 'lively, cheerful, ... friendly and unassuming, a good talker and very sure of himself'. Kendall played up the fact that the son of one famous father had taken over from the son of another.[17]

Not long after his arrival, Jellicoe spoke at a large gathering of staff welfare counsellors. They were predominantly female and predominantly not very young. So they could all see him, he climbed onto a chair on top of a table. For a moment he surveyed the throng of upturned faces. 'I know what you're all waiting to see,' he said. There was an uncertain pause. 'You're waiting to see the Lord Privy Seal fall arse over tit off this chair!' More silence. Then the whole room burst out laughing.[18]

1970 was the heyday of party politics but Heath was determined to face some big challenges with big policy arguments – on which he saw the CSD taking the lead. Jellicoe was to set up a new unit at the heart of Whitehall: the Central Policy Review Staff. The culmination of a series of reforms following a White Paper in autumn 1970, it aimed to advise Government on the changes. It brought in outsiders to work on policy analysis and review and was immediately nicknamed the 'Think Tank'.[19] The CPRS's first head was the Labour Peer Lord Rothschild, an ex-bomb disposal expert, pre-war scientist, and head of research at Shell. His appointment provided street credibility and independence. Of the other three main runners, the third, Professor Richard Ross, an academic economist, was 'turned down by Lord Jellicoe as too indecisive'.[20] It was all very US and MacNamara. Jellicoe henceforth became a great ally of the political staff in No. 10.[21]

One problem was that ministers had too much paper. The Foreign Secretary, Sir Alec Douglas-Home, asked Rothschild how it could be reduced. He had been having a good dinner with Jellicoe when, at about ten o'clock, he gave a frightful groan and said he had to go and do four red boxes before morning. Rothschild later exploded: 'Why the hell has he got four boxes of papers? Why hadn't they been properly digested in the office and condensed into four pages?'[22]

Jellicoe was generally nice to people but hard on those he did not like or who upset him. He was open about this and would tell Gilmore straight if he did not like someone. With officials, Jellicoe was courteous and appreciative. But if a civil servant served up a poor submission, he and Gilmore would look to see what could be made of it. More often than not, Jellicoe would say, 'Sorry. You'll have to go back to them.'[23]

The only thing that Gilmore and Jellicoe fell out about was the latter's tendency to accept all invitations and then decide late in the day which one he would attend. This suggested something slightly ruthless about Jellicoe and was more a trait from his mother than his father. The problem was exacerbated by the fact that his social life had doubled. With the job went invitations to 10 Downing Street, Chequers and Buckingham Palace. He was an appreciative boss and gave parties for his policy teams when the occasion called for it. The superannuation team had a splendid celebration when the Pensions Bill was safely through Parliament.[24]

Officials saw Jellicoe as a very good minister but he allowed others to think of him as laid back.[25] A civil servant cannot ask more than that the minister shares his or her mind with officials, expresses wishes clearly and does boxes promptly. If the minister is also clever, can master a brief quickly and speak well, that is a bonus.[26] Jellicoe would come into the office at 8.30 in the morning with his boxes all done and about eight handwritten personal notes to people. He would peer at officials' drafts with his head on one side, muttering to himself, 'Do I really want to say that . . . ?'[27] But on policy he was decisive. It was a joy to work with a minister who was prepared to make decisions.[28]

One of Jellicoe's major problems was public sector pensions. There was a lot to be done. Many civil servants' pensions had been frozen for a long time; the Foreign Office was particularly exercised about it. By 1970, John Herbecq[29] had been responsible for public sector superannuation for four years. The great joy of superannuation policy was that people were both afraid of it and bored by it. So he had been left more or less alone to get on with it. It was a political running sore for the Government of the day. High and rising levels of inflation continued to erode the value of pensions and the Opposition used this as a stick to beat the Government. Trades Unions too carped on about poor civil servants and what a disgrace it was that after all their years of hard work they didn't have enough to live on.[30]

Pensions were a mess. Previous work on them was pure ad-hocery. Successive Bills every three years or so were totally ineffective. They tried to help pensioners who had suffered most and those on smaller pensions, but offered no long-term remedy. Herbecq had worked up some proposals with Shackleton to create a link with the retail price index so there would be an automatic linked increase every two years. But the total mess of anomalies and inconsistencies first had to be sorted out to provide an equal starting position for all pensions. This would be very expensive because ad-hoc Acts of the past had fallen a long way short of restoring pensions' full value. Nevertheless, Shackleton and Treasury officials were all signed up to the new policy, which would bring every pension up to full compensation for inflation from the day the person retired but would not be retrospective. The link between pensions and RPI would thus be preserved, year-by-year. Fortunately, no public statement had been made before Labour lost the election, which left the way open for the Conservatives to pick up the policy.[31]

Shackleton had been good to work for, bright and a very astute politician. He never did get his mind entirely wrapped around superannuation but he was not alone in that. Douglas Houghton, the Opposition front bench spokesman, was probably the only man who did.

At Shackleton's post-election farewell drinks party in the House of Lords, he told Herbecq, 'I don't know who you'll get. It will either be Carrington or Jellicoe. I doubt it will be Carrington. He's got bigger fish to fry. If it's Jellicoe, I'll have a word with him because it would be a great pity if all the pensions work was lost.' Within twenty-four hours, Herbecq knew it was Jellicoe.[32] Shackleton *had* had a word.

'What's all this that Eddie's told me about pensions?' Jellicoe said. After being briefed he said, 'Well, we'd better get on with it.' He wanted to kill all ministerial correspondence on public sector pensions – fast – and declined more discussion. 'During the war', he said, 'If you wanted to escape you had to do it in the first ten minutes.'

They got on with it. The CSD was responsible for two million public sector occupational pensions and Herbecq never forgot it. Whenever somebody said there was 'a million to one chance' of someone being adversely affected, Herbecq would say, 'Don't tell me that. At those odds, we've *got two* of them.'

At a meeting with the Ministers of State of the ten interested Government departments, including the Financial Secretary, Patrick Jenkin, Herbecq being the only official present, Jellicoe presented the policy. The snag was that it had not been in the Conservatives' manifesto. Worse still, pensions *had* been included but only as an unworkable half-baked idea. The unease was palpable. Jellicoe reiterated that the manifesto alternative would only land them in trouble. Eventually, Jenkin said, 'We put a lot of work into this. How did we come to get it so wrong?'

At that moment, for the only time in his career, Herbecq knew what it was to have power. But Jellicoe still had to go and see the party chairman Toby Low, Lord Aldington. If he objected, the policy would be dead in the water. Jellicoe put Herbecq on the spot to explain it. Aldington was silent for what seemed an age. Then he looked at Jellicoe and said slowly, 'I *think* that's alright.' They were through to the next hurdle – to prepare a Bill and get it through Parliament.

To get Whitehall-wide agreement, the CSD needed Treasury approval. Contemporary public sector conventions helped. They focused on the demand Government expenditure made on available resources: if resources rose by 5 per cent, then expenditure could safely rise by the same amount without creating any extra inflationary demand. The continuing cost thereafter, using public sector conventions, was nil. Herbecq checked his line of argument with the Government Actuary, who pronounced it sound, and arranged to meet the official from the Treasury who would brief the Chancellor. The venue was the neutral ground of the Government Actuary's Department with one of his Under Secretaries to see fair play.

'When you're calculating next year's estimates', Herbecq began, 'you're assuming that pensions will make the same demand on resources. But to the extent that you are not increasing pensions they're a declining demand. So all you have to do', he said, driving home his point, 'in agreeing to this Bill, is to give up an un-covenanted saving you don't even know you have.' It took some time to get this rather 'Yes Ministerish' statement to register but finally he succeeded.[33] As they parted, the Treasury man seemed unsure whether what they had agreed was a good idea or not.

And so to the Bill. The First Parliamentary Counsel, Sir John Fiennes, decided to do a clean sweep and consolidate all previous provisions that were not to be repealed into the new Act. He also decided to do the work himself, though by halfway through the exercise he wished he had not done either of these things. He was a Rumpelstiltskin sort of a man who would become absolutely furious when things did not go his way.[34]

Fortunately, there was no real opposition. At Jellicoe's request, Herbecq went to brief Houghton.[35] He understood it all and Herbecq was impressed. Unusually, Herbecq then had to explain the policy to both sides of the House. The Act was passed and from that moment public sector pensions, once paid, stayed abreast of inflation – which was the major risk to savings in the generation that followed.[36] Moreover, the Civil Service final salary occupational pension scheme became the envy of the private sector.[37]

It had all been done in the nick of time. Not long after-wards, the Treasury got worried about public expenditure. Under Treasury's Leo Pliatsky, whose party piece was to spit peanuts all over the room, Government began to concern itself with 'cash costs' and 'cash limits'.[38] In such a climate, it would have been impossible to pull off the pensions stunt of the century.

Jellicoe also coordinated Civil Service matters affecting all departments. John Peyton, the Minister of Transport, was horrified at the idea of being coordinated by Jellicoe. Not because it was Jellicoe but because coordination usually just produced another layer of rubbish. But Jellicoe said little. The tricks of his Secret Intelligence Service days had stayed with him and no matter how long Peyton spent with him, he did not find out anything that Jellicoe did not want him to know.[39] Occasionally, Jellicoe had to knock heads together. When Margaret Thatcher was Education Minister, she came to see him because she was not getting on with her Permanent Secretary, William Pile. After talking to Heath, Jellicoe helped restore the relationship, which improved, at least for a while.

Jellicoe also saw coming to fruition work that he had pioneered since 1969 to promote the use of volunteers to help elderly, sick and lonely people in hospitals and the community. If youth at risk of becoming disaffected could be motivated to volunteer, two potential problems could be solved.[40] By midsummer 1971, he had a draft Green Paper and had persuaded Cabinet to spend up to £4 million more (a huge amount then) to support voluntary social service over the next four years. On 8 December 1971, Heath told the AGM of the National Council for Voluntary Service he believed very strongly that voluntary action could enrich the whole social and moral fabric of the nation. Jellicoe recommended that a Minister of State should coordinate matters that either concerned voluntary services generally or did not fall clearly to any one department. Too much had been falling down the Whitehall cracks. In February 1972, Jellicoe announced in the House of Lords that one of the Home Office Ministers would don this mantle.[41] By the time he left office the following year, this 'formative phase in the Government's relations with the voluntary movement was over. The ice had been broken in Whitehall'.[42]

Neither Jellicoe nor Eddie Shackleton, was a conviction politician. Hearing them together, it was often hard to tell which was Conservative and which was Labour. Moreover, they had become close friends. Both had lost their fathers while they were still very young; both had a famous name to live up to. But there the resemblance ended. Jellicoe grew up with his elderly father while Shackleton saw very little of his. Ernest Shackleton had left in the *Endurance* on his famous journey of exploration in the South Atlantic when his son was only three. In 1921, when Eddie was ten, his father died suddenly there. When Michael Wheeler-Booth mentioned to Jellicoe that he and Shackleton had both had famous fathers, Jellicoe responded 'Yes, but I really loved mine'.[43]

Shackleton more admired than loved his father.[44] Again unlike Jellicoe, Shackleton was always quite insecure financially until he became vice chairman of Rio Tinto Zinc in 1973. And Shackleton *talked* about women, whereas Jellicoe did not. Yet something about having had famous fathers gave them an affinity. In the Chamber they sometimes engaged in pitched battles. Roy Jenkins, then Deputy Leader of the Labour Party, compared them to the TV comedy duo 'Mutt and Jeff'.[45]

Outside the House, Jellicoe did his best to keep his predecessor informed of work he had initiated, sending Shackleton reports and papers and answering his queries on Government policy.[46] Shackleton asked why Government had chosen 1969, rather than 1971, as the baseline for the public service pensions updating exercise. Jellicoe replied, 'I attach an admirably clear note from a source you will no doubt recognise ... I hope you will find it as illuminating and useful as I did!' It was a page almost certainly drafted by Herbecq. Shackleton replied, 'I do appreciate the way you, and ... your office continue to service the ex-Minister'.[47]

Service with the SAS under David Stirling had made Jellicoe an inveterate bringer-on of people. As Leader, he influenced the choice of new Conservative peers and Lords-in-Waiting, among them Priscilla Tweedsmuir, who had been a minister in the Commons before 1964, Janet Young, who later became the first woman Leader of the House of Lords and Diana Elles who went on to the UK's European Parliament delegation. He also managed to increase Lords junior ministers' pay slightly above that of junior ministers in the Commons.[48]

He sometimes adopted as protégés hereditary peers who had what it takes.[49] A typical example was young Lord (Grey) Gowrie. Longhaired and trendy, a poet who wore carpet slippers instead of shoes and with a bomb plotter father-in-law, Gowrie hardly had the best credentials for a career in the Conservative party. He started turning up in the Lords in 1968. Carrington, Jellicoe and Shackleton encouraged him but Heath blocked progress. Undeterred, Jellicoe and Carrington mounted a strategy to make Gowrie a Conservative whip. He was unpaid and one of the real *Castrati* since he was not allowed to speak. In 1971, Jellicoe persuaded Heath to give Gowrie a job working for the Foreign Secretary, Sir Alec Douglas-Home as a Parliamentary Delegate to the UN. Finally, in 1972, Gowrie became a *paid* Lord-in-Waiting, undertaking representational duties for the Queen. But he was like the evil eye. No sooner had he welcomed someone than they went back to their country and got deposed, assassinated, or both.[50]

Jellicoe then put Gowrie into the Department of Employment where he could shine. Strongly qualified in the Arts and Literature, Gowrie even found himself winding up an economic debate. For the rest of his political career he had economic credentials. When Margaret Thatcher became Prime Minister, Gowrie went back to the Department of Employment as Minister of State before becoming Deputy to the Secretary of State for Northern Ireland and, as Chancellor of the Duchy of Lancaster, a Cabinet Minister.[51] Jellicoe had got round Heath.

Jellicoe was a workaholic and playaholic. He would ask Gowrie and his girlfriend Neiti out mid-week. Sometimes, they would talk nearly all night in his flat. At 7.30 one morning after Gowrie had staggered home, the Lord Privy Seal's office rang asking if Lord Gowrie could be there by eight o'clock! He went un-breakfasted and hardly shaved to the office, to find a bright-eyed and bushy-tailed Jellicoe waiting to attack the day's work. Sometimes Jellicoe would catch up on his sleep in the House and Gowrie had to kick him. Jellicoe's extramural socializing extended to his colleagues and their families; he laid on Trooping the Colour parties for children in his room with its splendid view across the Horse Guards Parade.[52]

Business in the House of Lords required expertise; political dog-fights, for example on Inland Revenue matters, were vigorously contested. Questions and answers were often handled by lawyers and had to be well prepared. Jellicoe had a natural bent for revenue problems and anything to do with the armed forces.[53] He also relished handling problems. The world economic situation and oil price hikes meant that Heath's Government had plenty of them. Rampant inflation and unemployment were accompanied by Union militancy, national strikes, the three-day week and the first mainland terrorism. Strikes, particularly annual docks strikes, had worsened under Labour whose failed attempt to pass legislation to deal with the problem following their White Paper, *In Place of Strife,* only made things more difficult for their successors. The class system was still alive and well in Britain. Disputes were emotionally loaded with personal and class resentments. The Trades Unions regarded legislation with deep suspicion, fearing it would curb their right to take industrial action or reduce the need for union protection. Employers did not want legislation either, fearing it would tackle what an internal Downing Street note on 'Proposals for Anti-Strike Legislation' called 'terrible British management'.[54]

In July 1970, following failed pay talks between the port employers and the dockworkers' unions, led by Jack Jones and Vic Feather, Jellicoe delivered a message from the Queen announcing a State of Emergency.[55] The following January, Tom Jackson, General Secretary of the Post Office Workers Union, led his 200,000 members into a seven week stoppage over a pay claim. The electricity supply workers, the firemen's unions and the BOAC pilots all seemed likely to extend their current industrial action. The Emergencies Committee (chaired by Jellicoe) reviewed its contingency plans.

Industrial relations was the most highly charged area of political life. Heath had grown up with unemployment and was convinced it was the worst possible scourge. In this unpromising political climate, the most high profile and controversial piece of Government legislation of the session – the Industrial Relations Bill – was prepared. On 24 March 1971, there was a postal strike.[56] The next day, looking rather like the antidote, the Bill came up from the Commons into the Lords for its first reading. The Opposition said the Bill had no senior minister in the Lords to answer questions on it and should be sent back to the Commons.[57] So Jellicoe had to be present for every division of the House.[58]

On Second Reading, the responsible minister, Lord Drumalbyn, said in the vital sphere of industrial relations there had been no permanent change for half a century. But this was not because all was well. There had been nearly 4,000 strikes in 1970. Ninety-five per cent were unofficial and most breached agreements. Trades Unions should be registered and liability for the harm done by strikes should be accepted by those responsible. Again, the Opposition was unhappy, noting 'This Bill is legalism run mad'.[59]

Shackleton moved to adjourn the debate because the Bill was already causing 'grave division within industry and the nation'. The Government should seek agreed solutions with both sides of industry and a workable code of industrial practice. Hailsham responded that the Bill did not only deal with unofficial strikes.[60]

After two days, Jellicoe attempted to unify; all agreed the need for legislation and soon. He reminded them of its benefits,

179

including positive and just management. The Bill was not mere 'Union bashing'. Nothing of the sort. Trades Unions could still call strikes that were judged fair. Members would be entitled to engage in union activities without fear of discrimination from their employers. There would be greater protection and safe-guards to workers from unfair dismissal and discrimination on grounds of Trades Union membership and longer notice of termination of employment. These new individual rights would be exercised through appeal to Industrial Tribunals.[61] Countless employees up and down the country would be protected from instant and arbitrary dismissal, while a new kind of conciliation officer would seek to resolve differences between employer and employee without the need for tribunal adjudication.[62]

Jellicoe reminded the Opposition that the Lords did not normally challenge Government Bills sent up from the elected Chamber.[63] Moreover, this Bill commanded wide popular sup-port – and from more Trades Unionists than the noble Lords opposite chose to admit. He asked their Lordships to reject the motion standing in Shackleton's name with a clear majority.[64]

Shackleton had been unwell, but was now restored thanks, he said, 'to powerful new pills – not *the* pill!' He seriously opposed the Bill. He knew of no Bill since the war that had caused such bitter controversy. The Government might believe it was in the interests of the nation and the working man. But Labour was always doubtful whenever the Tories said they were doing something for the working man. Inflation and the absence of an effective incomes policy were causing the strikes, not unfair dismissals.[65] Shackleton's motion failed on division, while a second division on the Second Reading was carried with 224 Contents and 15 Not-Contents.[66] So it went on, with the Opposition delaying progress to the best of their ability.

At the Committee stage, Shackleton attempted to goad Jellicoe.

'I do hope the noble Earl, the Leader of the House is satisfied with the very considerable progress we have made', (some thirty amendments had been dealt with) adding that at one o'clock in the morning they should perhaps all go home to bed. Jellicoe responded that they should make a little extra effort and tuck Clause 5 under their belt that evening while memories were fresh.

180

At 1.34 am, the House divided, the Government carrying the vote with Contents 109 to Not-Contents 27.[67]

In mid May, Shackleton complained that he had known one or two all-night sittings, when necessary, but now 'most of us are concerned as to whether we shall get breakfast tomorrow morning'. He begged the Government not to press ahead too hard. The Government had the majority and Labour did not want to resort to 'undesirable tactics'.[68] Ignoring this thinly veiled threat, Jellicoe said Labour's behaviour also had something to do with the Bill's lengthy passage, adding reprovingly, 'We have not maintained our usual standards of relevance in debate'.

As the debate continued, the Earl of Dudley adopted a teasing tone. 'I have read a number of accounts of the Battle of Jutland,' he said 'and it is clear that the noble Earl's father conducted himself with great *sang froid* ... by all accounts there is a great, grey battleship which appears out of the mist with all guns blazing and I think I am entitled to compare Amendment 194 to such an event ... The boy is on the burning deck and it is not reasonable to suggest that a worker should go forward and personalize his complaint in this respect.'

Jellicoe replied that the Government attached great importance to clear grievance procedures and employees' awareness of them. It was quite common for 'the ordinary employee not to have the foggiest idea what to do when he had a grievance'.[69] Moreover, he argued forcefully that it was unnecessary and undesirable for the new 'Industrial Relations court' to be 'tied into the trappings ... of the High Court. Judges ... will not robe and formal rules of appearance will not be applied'. It was to be 'a plain man's court'.[70]

By 20 July, the Lords had reached the end. No Bill has ever been debated at greater length. It passed and returned to the Commons, returning with amendments agreed on 5 August, and received the Royal Assent, along with twenty-two other Acts of Parliament later that day.[71] Though Labour later repealed the Industrial Relations Act in a single clause, protection against unfair dismissal was retained, as were industrial tribunals and conciliation officers.[72] Employment rights that had to be debated for days during the Bill's passage are now taken for granted.[73]

181

By mid 1972, Heath had clashed with the Trades Unions over his prices and incomes policy. Strike action clocked up an unprecedented 23 million working days lost.[74] Jellicoe took over the Cabinet committee on emergencies and contingency planning.[75] An hereditary peer dealing with strikes could have been anathema to the union side negotiators. But Jellicoe employed a disarming honesty. He was always in receive mode and learned a lot about how to handle his adversaries. During the dockers' strike, while collecting details about ships full of bad bananas, he was careful never to ask their leader, Tim O'Leary, a direct question because it always set him off.[76]

It was a busy time with Bills on education, inland revenue, local government reform and the European communities. But Jellicoe was determined to protect his family life. At weekends, he rode with them and they took family holidays in their Scottish croft at Rientraid, in a very beautiful part of north-west Sutherland. It was a place for an invigorating holiday rather than a self-indulgent sprawl. The weather was not always kind while in summer the occupants had busbies of midges around their heads.

Jellicoe was still picked for special jobs. While skiing in Zermatt in March 1972, Heath phoned. Concorde was about to undertake its first sales expedition to the Middle and Far East. Michael Heseltine, the British Aerospace Minister, would not be able to complete the tour and would Jellicoe take over?[77] Heseltine had managed to get the Shah photographed sitting in Concorde. With the Chairman of BAC, George Edwards, Jellicoe aimed to drum up some customers in Japan, the Philippines and Australia.[78]

It was still early days. Concorde was due to make its first flight – to Dallas – in September 1973. It was very luxurious, with only half a dozen passenger seats, the rest of the space being taken up by monitoring equipment. As usual, wives accompanied this remarkable sales delegation.[79]

Jellicoe joined Concorde in Singapore and arrived in Australia on 15 June. Aircraft of the Royal Australian Air Force came up to escort them down to Sydney Airport. On 19 June, Jellicoe spoke at the Sydney Journalists' Club, earning himself a headline in *The Sun* of 'My Lord, the super salesman'. After fourteen days and

20,000 miles, they had arrived in Sydney only half an hour late – due to Darwin fog. The Concorde pilot, Brian Trubshaw, was probably the subject of more newspaper cartoons than anyone at that time so he was used to enjoying a joke. At Tokyo airport a sick Concorde had been cured in about twenty minutes. Just before they taxied out, Jellicoe saw one of Trubshaw's merry men clutching a glass of water as he disappeared down the aisle. He asked what on earth he was up to. 'Oh', came the reply, 'he's putting water on the valve to test it for a possible leak', at which Sir John Pilcher,[80] a fellow Concorde traveller interjected, 'I can't think why Trubshaw doesn't use his spit.'

The newspaper article went on,

> There has probably never been a sales team quite like the aristocratic British contingent that is trying to sell the Anglo-French supersonic Concorde to Qantas ... The Earl is an astute salesman who has obviously done his homework on Concorde. He has the stamina to address a couple of Press conferences each day as well as make daily speeches ... cultivate politicians, DCA personnel and Qantas bosses. At fifty-four, the Earl looks a rugged character. He has a strong broad chin and speaks with a directness that appeals to Australians. One of his most effective points is that Britain does not need to be lectured on environmental matters. In recent years, its record on this has been good. In Australia, he has become known as 'Aeroplane Jellicoe'.[81]

On 24 January 1972 Jellicoe represented the Queen at the funeral of King Frederick IX of Denmark at Christiansborg Castle. His wartime connection with Anders Lassen VC was still remembered. On the same day in Brussels, Heath signed the Treaty of Accession, opening the way for British entry into the European Economic Community (EEC). At his side was Eric Roll.

Entry was *the* major political issue. In the Tory party, the original small minority in favour of joining had grown. In March 1970, when Labour were still in power, the Lords had debated a White Paper on Europe.[82] Government policy was that Britain wanted to join if the price was right.[83]

Jellicoe had declared himself straightaway. 'I believed', he said, 'in the early 1960s when our application was first made ... that it was the right path. Exclusion from the Community carries with it the risk that international negotiations affecting vital British economic interests will be ... decided over our heads.' He noted 'the gathering momentum behind the move towards closer monetary union ...'.[84] But he contested the proposed cost of the UK's contributions, recommending hard negotiations.[85]

After the 1970 General Election, the Tory Government had taken up the cudgel. In October, there was a free vote in a Lords' debate on a Government White Paper on EEC entry. Jellicoe took no chances, writing to large numbers of members on the Conservative and Cross-benches thanking them for their contributions to an earlier July debate and inviting them to speak again, the allocation of subjects for which he carefully stage-managed. So many members wanted to speak that the debate was extended from two days to three.[86]

On 26 October 1971, the Lord Chancellor, Lord Hailsham, moved that the House should approve the Government's decision to join the European Community. After a lengthy debate, during which the Chief Scientific Adviser, Lord Zuckerman, made his maiden speech, Jellicoe wound up for the Government. He said he had known Zuckerman 'for many years, ever since the time when, as an adviser to the Chief of Combined Operations he took a friendly interest in some experiments which a young Commando officer – myself – had been conducting into living off the land. I had tried to ... instil into my Unit, a taste for snails and grass – the sort of diet which some of the anti-Marketeers seem to suggest we are condemning ourselves to if we enter Europe'. His horse sense told him something very clearly: if Britain could not compete inside the EEC, it could not compete outside and the advantages of being inside seemed compelling. The World Wars had been in origin and essence civil wars and Britain should do all in its power to create conditions in which Europe could never again tear itself apart. The House Lordships divided, resulting in Contents 451 and Not-Contents, 58.[87] But it was to be nearly a year before the European Communities Bill came up from the Commons.

184

As ministerial head of the CSD, Jellicoe also had Cabinet responsibility for coordinating policy on Government's own research and development (R&D) and he chaired a Cabinet committee on science and technology.[88] One of his Assistant Secretaries, Ivor Lightman, had begun in the old Ministry of Works when Sir Edward Muir, a real 'Grandee' of the old Civil Service, was Permanent Secretary. Lightman was always tearing about. 'Ah, Lightman,' Muir would say, seeing him flying down the corridor. 'Dashing around as usual. There's one thing you should know. The more work you do the more harm you'll do.'[89] Another favourite comment was, 'Ah, Lightman. Unremitting toil.'

Lightman was happily running a branch on science policy and consultancy management when he was pitchforked into Jellicoe's area. Lightman found Jellicoe's working methods very informal – mostly featuring a large bottle of whisky in the Lords. Rothschild had published a report on science and technology which enshrined a new 'customer contractor principle' – anyone carrying out publicly funded R&D *had* to have a customer. Henceforth, only the scientific Research Councils would be funded to do pure research. The heavens of the research establishment promptly fell in. They regarded the whole thesis of the customer contractor principle with deep mistrust. Rothschild had been chairman of the Agricultural Research Council, which made his treachery all the more heinous.[90]

The relatively young Margaret Thatcher was responsible for funding pure scientific research in the Science Research Councils while departmental ministers were responsible for applied research in their own fields. Jellicoe was coordinating the Government's response to Rothschild's report and had overseen a Government Green Paper.[91] He asked Lightman to analyse shoals of responses from the science and technology community and advise on policy.[92]

Jellicoe then held meetings with each of the Research Councils. They would sound off while Jellicoe listened and Lightman strove to look impassive. Then Jellicoe and Thatcher would decide what line to take, since R&D expenditure was getting out of hand. Although she appeared very competent, Thatcher did

185

not particularly impress Jellicoe; he was still unaware of her enormous potential. The work completed, a Lords' debate on the Green Paper was timetabled for 28 and 29 February.

On 27 February, Lightman attended a meeting about science funding with Thatcher. He thought how nice she was to her civil servants – quite careful and more circumspect than she was later. But he did not have long to admire the young Thatcher in action because Gilmore called him out of the meeting.

'The LPS has to make the opening and winding up speeches on Government research funding tomorrow and Thursday,' he said. 'Can you write them?' A colleague was off sick so Lightman had to step in. He sat down to draft. He had plenty of atmosphere because there was no electric lighting. The miners had struck on 9 January over a full pay settlement of an extra £5 to £9 per week while the National Coal Board were only prepared to pay £1 to £3. So Lightman had to work by candlelight. He stared desperately at an otherwise blank piece of paper bearing only the words 'My Lords'. What to say next? Jellicoe supported Rothschild's approach but he needed to show that he was listening to the views of those reluctant to accept change. Lightman had a copy of Chairman Mao Zedong's *Little Red Book* and quoted it in Jellicoe's speech:

> If we have shortcomings, we are not afraid to have them pointed out and criticized, because we serve the people. Anyone, no matter who, may point out our shortcomings. If he is right, we will correct them. If what he proposes will benefit the people, we will act upon them.[93]

He inserted another Chinese quote into the winding up speech:

> ... I think it would be unwise for us to fall into the state of complacency of the last Empress Dowager of China who issued a decree, 'That by the accumulated wisdom of six successive sovereigns, our dynasty has succeeded in establishing a system based on absolute justice and benevolence which approaches very near to perfection.'[94]

The Government won the Lords debate and Jellicoe was through to a White Paper.

The coal strike got worse. A day or two before the union vote in which the strike was called off, Jellicoe met the miners' leaders. He was the first minister they had met since the strike began many months before. He re-established relations between them and the Government, which had totally broken down, and Heath placed Jellicoe in overall charge, according to the *Daily Express*, as 'Energy Supremo', to 'get the country moving again'. He threw himself into the huge effort and set up and chaired the Civil Contingencies Unit. This complex emergency structure of regional government in the event of a large-scale breakdown of energy supplies[95] was based on his experience of what had gone wrong and what worked best in coordinating different Government departments and agencies.[96]

Meanwhile, the European Communities Bill had been winding its way through Parliament. It came up from the Commons on 14 July 1972. The Prime Minister wanted no amendments to it since the House of Commons would soon rise. He did not want the Bill back in the Commons, in case it meant delaying the recess or bringing MPs back. More importantly, the Bill might receive a mauling and have to go back to the Lords again until final agreement was reached. Jellicoe was to get the Bill through, if possible, without a single amendment. The Lords were largely in favour of European entry[97] but to get it through without a single amendment was a tall order.[98]

Jellicoe wrote countless letters and got on his feet again and again to ensure success. Ten days later, the Bill had its second reading. The Opposition suspected he was under orders not to agree any amendments. Another marathon debate resulted in Contents 185 and Not-Contents 19. The Bill then went into committee stage.[99]

Several Opposition peers said that if the Government listened to their proposed amendments, they could hope for a useful and constructive committee stage of the Bill. But if, however, there were to be read out the kind of negative, prepared brief that they had heard so often 'during the unhappy Committee stage of the Industrial Relations Bill', then they would draw their conclusions.

Jellicoe avoided commenting. Considerable debate on the very technical and complicated Bill ensued. Lord Foot then queried

187

whether the Government were prepared to listen to argument and decide matters on merit or whether a decision had already been made to 'drive the Bill through this House without amendment of any kind, as it was driven through the other place'. They were entitled, he said, to be told by Lord Jellicoe whether such a decision had been made. If it had, then all the hours they were going to spend supposedly discussing various amendments on their merits would be a pure waste of time. The constitutional and revising function of the upper Chamber would be thwarted and their deliberations would be a prolonged farce. The House divided on the amendment resulting in Contents 49 and Not-Contents 154.[100]

To add to Jellicoe's difficulties, the Chief Whip, Michael St Aldwyn, had a heart attack. His deputy, Bertie Denham, took over. But being rather inexperienced, he banged on a three-line whip every night. So Jellicoe had to play a more active role.[101] On the second amendment, the House divided resulting in Contents 51 to Not-Contents 152. And so it continued, with each amendment being resisted on a vote by the Government. Lord Foot asked again whether the Government had already decided that they were not going to allow any amendments. If so, all talk of discussion on merits was mere hypocrisy. (Several noble Lords cried 'Hear! Hear!') Jellicoe said he had already made his position clear.

It was quite exceptional for the Lords still to be sitting in August. They sat unusually late, night after night, sometimes until 7 or 8 am the following morning. The Chief Whips had this kind of stamina – it goes with the job – and Shackleton at least was up to it. By 10 August, Jellicoe was still intervening where necessary with pronouncements like, 'I am entirely unpersuaded that this is in any sense an improvement to the Bill'. Finally, at the end of the committee stage, Lord Beswick said bitterly, 'If all my noble friends came along, those who are sick and those who for other good reasons are not here, we could not possibly muster 118. We just do not have 118; we do not have 100. My friends say that makes a mockery of this House and therefore decide not to interrupt their other affairs to come along here.'[102]

188

Jellicoe called a halt. Looking to mend fences, he thanked Beswick for the way in which he had helped through the usual channels to see that the business on the Bill was conducted. Shackleton was equally gracious, though he noted that it was certainly unique in his experience for a Bill to have passed the committee stage without a single amendment. The Bill was then reported – without amendment.[103]

On 12 September, it was still not plain sailing. Despite the Tory majority in the Lords, some were not in favour of entry while others wanted some amendments to be accepted. There was also a risk of total rebellion on grounds that the procedure was seriously unconstitutional. Jellicoe had to do quite a bit of talking during the report stage, causing Shackleton to observe, 'My Lords, we seem to be getting a lot of speeches from the Government tonight'.[104]

On 20 September, Jellicoe moved 'that the Bill now be read a third time'. Their debate that day marked the final stage of proceedings in Parliament on the Bill and indeed the final stage of consideration by Britain's Parliament of the question of its accession to the European Community. Jellicoe pointed out that the issue was not a party matter and time and time again the great majority of the cross-bench members had voted against the amendments moved to the Bill. He was forced therefore to conclude that 'noble Lords opposite have no justification for assuming that their amendments have been rejected on other than their strict merits'. Shackleton nonetheless had one final go at moving an amendment to the motion to add 'but this House deplores the insistence of Her Majesty's Government that this Bill should pass unamended through all stages, irrespective of the merits of amendments proposed, and deprecates the reliance of Her Majesty's Government upon their built-in majority to achieve this purpose'.[105]

It did no good. Jellicoe made a very optimistic winding-up speech on his view of the future in Europe. At 10.43 pm, the House divided on whether the Bill should now be read a third time, resulting in Contents 161 and Not-Contents 21. On 17 October, the Lord Chancellor notified the House that the Queen had signified her Royal Assent to three Acts, including the European Communities Act. It had passed without amendment and with an overwhelming vote in favour.[106]

Towards the end of 1972, following the White Paper on R&D, it was decided that one of Jellicoe's two Assistant Private Secretaries ought to be a scientist. The Establishment (Personnel) Officer for the CSD carried out the usual internal Whitehall trawl for suitable candidates; the front-runner was a young man from the Science Group called Malcolm Inglis.[107] The young hopeful duly presented himself for interview at six o'clock one winter evening. He waited until, at about twenty past six, he and Gerald Wilson, who had replaced Gilmore, were shown in together. Jellicoe greeted Inglis with, 'My God, I'm knackered! Do you want a whisky?' To which Inglis wisely said something like, 'That would be nice,' and got the job.[108]

Inglis's eyes were soon opened to the ways of ministers. At one meeting with the Civil Service unions, Jellicoe appeared to be studiously taking notes. At the end of the meeting, he beamed up at his departing interlocutors and said, 'Thank you *so* much. That was a most useful meeting.' Then, somewhat to the bewilderment of his audience, screwed up his notes and lobbed them into the waste paper basket.[109] Night after night Inglis would send Jellicoe off with four or five leather boxes full of submissions and reports. In the morning, they would all come back: submissions read and commented on, approval given or questions asked; reports read and important documents signed. Jellicoe's management style was considerate but autocratic. He expected them to get things right and was unimpressed when Inglis took him through the wrong entrance into an exhibition he was about to open. But once he had expressed his disapproval, the matter was forgotten.[110]

Civil Service negotiations were conducted rather differently. Before lunch, Jellicoe would usually have a sherry and offer one to Wilson. Jellicoe would then walk up and down, talking about his last meeting, glass in one hand and sherry bottle in the other, from which he liberally refilled both their glasses. A messenger called Albert used to bring fresh glasses every day and deal with the dirty ones.

Jellicoe sometimes deployed this pre-lunch drink strategically. On one occasion, the Civil Service unions' representatives came to see him as part of the annual ritual dance for pressing their case for a pay increase. 'Minister,' their leader began, 'I would like to discuss the following points about our members' pay and conditions.' He then enumerated a list of points, of such weight and import that others in the room wondered what on earth Jellicoe could say in response. Just as the Union Secretary paused to draw breath before launching into his first topic, Jellicoe said, 'Just a moment. Why don't we all have a drink while we're talking?' In came Albert, right on cue, with the glasses, sherry and a whole lot more besides. The meeting then descended into a welter of drinks requests and pouring while ice was clunked into glasses and the delegates jostled to get what they wanted. By the time the meeting resumed, the dynamics had totally changed and the Union Secretary had had the wind completely taken out of his sails.[111]

Jellicoe also knew his own mind. During a periodic blitz on public expenditure, the Diplomatic Service decided to make thirty people redundant; the question of compensation arose. The revised pension scheme had improved such payments. Herbecq thought the terms good enough but the DS wanted more. Jellicoe was sympathetic – he had been a diplomat himself. He got Herbecq in, listened carefully to his explanation of why the compensation was adequate and then looking straight at Herbecq said, 'But do you really mind?' It flashed across Herbecq's mind that this was rather offside. It was not a matter of whether *he*, a civil servant, *minded*. Then Jellicoe said winningly, 'Let's do it!' So the DS got their enhanced redundancy package.[112]

Another problem was Heath's pay freeze, which resulted in a situation where *retired* admirals' pensions exceeded the half pay of admirals of the Fleet, field marshals and marshals of the Royal Air Force. The fiction was still being preserved that these senior officers never actually retired – they simply came off the Active List and went onto half pay. So the pay freeze affected their *income* – whereas the *pensions* of retired officers remained intact. In the process of sorting out this anomaly Kenneth Baker got up in the House of Commons and gave an undertaking that no public servant's pension would be disadvantaged by the pay freeze. He then appeared in Jellicoe's office and said something like, 'Well, that seemed to go alright didn't it?' to which Herbecq replied he wasn't sure if Baker quite realized what he had done. This hostage to fortune led to the Pensions Increase legislation, which ended up being taken through the Commons on the very last day of the Heath Government.[113]

Jellicoe faced a tricky Whitehall turf battle when a huge row blew up about which Government department had to occupy a new building at the end of St James's Park. Because of all the steam over the matter, if Jellicoe could not resolve it, Cabinet would have to decide. So Jellicoe was under pressure to sort it out.

Herbecq arrived slightly late to find Jellicoe chairing a meeting of the Ministers of State of the involved departments. The Department of Industry and the Foreign Office both declared that there would be significant consequential implications for them if *they* had to move into the new accommodation. Robert Carr, the Home Secretary, was there in person. Chris Chataway had turned up for Industry and was dutifully reading from his brief. But he was seen off pretty quickly and treated with rather shocking contempt by the others. 'Right', he said with an air of fatalism, 'I've said what I was sent here to say so now I'll go.'

A lengthy and heated debate followed. Carr said that not being in Whitehall would mean that his department would be further from Parliament and No. 10. The prestige of being in Whitehall would also be totally undermined if he had to occupy the new premises. He definitely wanted to stay put. Then, imperceptibly at first, he started to stake out the consequences of such a move and what he and his department would need if they had to go. Jellicoe was very fly at this point. Though Carr appeared to resist, he was actually bargaining about the terms of surrender. Jellicoe was home and dry. The meeting eventually broke up with Carr stipulating all sorts of things that he would need if he had to go.

Jellicoe was hugely relieved. At four o'clock, he opened a bottle of whisky and poured himself rather more than half a tumbler and one for Herbecq. They went out onto the balcony overlooking the west front of the House of Lords to decompress. Herbecq later staggered back to his office as near drunk as he had ever been at work. There was a sequel to the episode. A week or so later, at some reception, Herbecq caught sight of Arthur Peterson, the Home Office Permanent Secretary, bearing down on him. It was too late to escape and Herbecq braced himself. To his surprise, Peterson was all bonhomie. 'I'm so glad to see you', he said. 'Thank you so much for letting us have that *marvellous* new building ...' So Carr had only been politicking after all.[114]

Towards the end of his time at the CSD, Jellicoe chaired a routine Cabinet Office meeting of the fledgling Civil Contingencies Unit. Herbecq turned up for his item on the agenda, spoke to his paper and excusing himself, headed for the door. To his surprise, Jellicoe leapt up and started tracking him down the other side of the long table. On reaching Herbecq, Jellicoe congratulated him on his promotion to Deputy Secretary. Herbecq was startled, as this was the first that he had heard of it. He was sent for the next morning by William Armstrong and had to exercise all his skills to look surprised when given the good news.[115]

On the last working day before Christmas, Jellicoe gave his usual office party. Herbecq always feared that civil servants signing off submissions would have approved anything going into the Minister's box in the short time left before they all drew stumps and went home for the holiday.

On New Year's Day 1973, Britain joined the EEC. Jellicoe, Michael Davies and the Speaker of the House of Commons flew from RAF Northolt to attend the first meeting of the European Parliament after British accession. Thereafter, the UK failed to follow up with any real involvement. Not surprisingly, the European Institutions were organized without much British flavour.

Meanwhile terrorism had moved onto mainland Britain. The IRA bombed 24 Whitehall – the first time a British Government building had been bombed since the Second World War. Jellicoe was in the Lords but immediately set off on foot up Whitehall to see what had happened to his people in the CSD. Inglis and the driver went via Birdcage Walk and round Trafalgar Square to pick him up.[116] Heath then asked Jellicoe to take responsibility for the security of all Whitehall Government buildings.[117]

The Industrial Relations and European Communities Bills had placed a great burden on Jellicoe. During the summer parliamentary recess he remained in London preparing for the special September session.[118] He was also conducting a number of difficult negotiations, one of which culminated in a major disruption to the Industrial Civil Service. And he was heavily involved in contingency planning for several successive public sector disputes. When the Home Secretary went abroad on holiday in August, he asked Jellicoe not only to cover for him but also to deal with the problem of the expulsion of Ugandan Asians by President Idi Amin.[119] Jellicoe could not leave London, even at weekends.

One hot August evening, he noticed some ads for Escort Agencies in *The Evening Standard*. On an impulse, he phoned one called *Glamour International* and using the name Jeffries arranged to meet a girl called Anne at his flat. He took the nicely spoken girl to *Annabel's* restaurant before dropping her off at her flat. A little while later, he contacted another agency, *Mayfair Escorts*. This time, a girl came to his flat. Over the next seven months, he made half a dozen bookings.

The seeds of his political undoing had been sown.

Chapter Thirteen

The Call Girl's Diary

London, 3.56 pm on Wednesday, 23 May 1973. A hushed House of Lords waited for their Leader to rise and speak.[1] Here and there around the chamber, order papers fluttered brightly among the red leather benches. Discreetly muffled coughs and the dull murmur of conversation died away in anticipation of an announcement.[2]

Ten years after the Profumo Affair, society still had a hearty and prurient appetite for sex gossip. And it was still said that when Labour were in power they tended to have their fingers in the till while the Tories were more inclined to a weakness for sexual proclivities.

At fifty-five, Jellicoe was still a strikingly handsome man. He had risen on many such occasions since he had become a Cabinet Minister. But today was different. Was it his imagination that the atmosphere was rather more tense than usual? Outside, the press hoardings in Whitehall blared 'Minister Resigns!' Rumours abounded that there might be more than one member of the Government involved.

Jellicoe mentally retraced his steps over the last twenty-four hours. The previous morning he had opened an exhibition of Muirhead's Ltd at the Commonwealth Club. He then walked back down Whitehall to deal with some papers in his Admiralty Buildings office. Returning to the Commonwealth Club, he sat at lunch between his host, Sir Ray Brown, and Michael Carey, the head of the Defence Procurement Executive. He exchanged

195

remarks with the Chief Scientist at the Ministry of Defence, sitting opposite him. Arthur Peterson, the Home Office Permanent Secretary, congratulated Jellicoe on having settled the rather tricky question of which department should occupy the Queen Anne's Chambers building. They talked briefly about the Hardman Report on the dispersal of Government offices outside London and Jellicoe said he hoped that neither Peterson nor the Home Secretary had ruled out dispersal of part of the Prison Department. All routine stuff.

Lunch was short. Jellicoe needed to be back in the House by Question Time at 2.30 pm. His temporary official driver, Isa, sped him quickly back to the Lords. He noticed the press headlines about a ministerial resignation. He thought no more about it, beyond idly wondering who it might be and why he was going.[3]

The Leader's office at the Lords, overlooking the west front of Parliament, was sombrely welcoming with its dark, red leather furniture and arched stone fireplace. The beautiful Pugin ceiling was restored to its original glory after Jellicoe had had some unsightly plasterboard removed.[4] He had a short meeting with young Lord O'Hagan, who had stupidly marked 'Bomb Enclosed' on an envelope and sent it to William Waldegrave in the No. 10 Think Tank. This had caused Black Rod and the House authorities a certain amount of trouble. Jellicoe told the young peer what a stupid prank this was. O'Hagan agreed and apologized profusely. Jellicoe then softened the reprimand by congratulating him on his good work in the UK's delegation to the European Parliament.

Jellicoe's private secretary, Gerald Wilson,[5] came in and asked if the Lord Privy Seal wished to attend a meeting which had been arranged with Lord Carrington, the Secretary of State for Defence, in the Leader's office. This was to discuss the precise formula – as far as the Ministry of Defence was concerned – for the Government announcement after the Whitsun recess on Government dispersal of offices. MOD officials queried whether a meeting was necessary, since Carrington and Jellicoe seemed to be in agreement. In view of the forthcoming recess, Jellicoe wanted to tie it up quickly. So he had a brief meeting in his office with Carrington and Herbecq. The two Ministers quickly disposed of the rather minor business in hand.[6]

196

Carrington stayed on for a chat, mainly to tease Jellicoe about the attitude he had taken in a recent meeting of the Chancellor's ad hoc group of ministers, consisting of Tony Lambton, Willie Whitelaw, Robert Carr, Jim Prior and Patrick Jenkin, on defence expenditure. Carrington joked that he knew what Jellicoe had said about industrial relations and rationalization and that he and others had pressed for bigger cuts in defence. They thought that Britain could not continue to spend more[7] on defence than her European allies. Carrington, however, took the line that he could not have stayed on in post if such cuts had been made. Jellicoe thought that the Government would have taken the Defence Secretary seriously and would not have wanted to find out whether or not he was bluffing.

The only other conversation that afternoon was a prescient chat with Michael St Aldwyn.[8] He had learned from his opposite number in the Commons, Francis Pym, that the minister who had resigned was Lambton, the Parliamentary Under-Secretary of State at the Ministry of Defence.[9] Details of a scandal were emerging. The *News of the World* had evidence that Lambton had been with two call girls and smoked cannabis.[10]

This exchange left Jellicoe with a vague sense of foreboding but he cut the conversation short. He and Philippa were going to a Covent Garden opera that evening. It was already 6.40 pm and Isa had said that they should leave themselves plenty of time since the traffic was bad, due to a practice Beating of the Retreat.

While he was being driven back to his flat in Onslow Square, Jellicoe cast his eye over the evening papers. The lead story, dramatically featured on the front page, was about an article due to appear in *Die Stern* on the involvement of an aristocratic British minister with an international call girl ring. Lambton's resignation was announced, not very prominently, on the back page. When Jellicoe reached the flat, he showed the article to Philippa. He suspected that the juxtaposition of the two stories might not be entirely coincidental.

They were held up by appalling traffic in the Mall and arrived a few minutes too late for the start of the performance. But thanks to the early break in the opera, *Lucia di Lammermoor*, they managed to slip into their seats after about fifteen minutes. It

197

was one of the most perfect performances Jellicoe could recall. Joan Sutherland as Lucia was superb among a magnificently balanced cast. He waved to Carla and Peter Thorneycroft, in the Royal Box with John Pope-Hennessy, one of the directors of Covent Garden.

At the end of the performance, Philippa insisted as usual on waiting for the encores. When they finally emerged in the still warm summer evening, they saw Robert Armstrong, the Prime Minister's Principal Private Secretary, standing near the main entrance.[11] Still enthralled by Lucia, Jellicoe asked Armstrong if he didn't think that this was one of the most marvellous performances he had ever attended. Armstrong unfortunately had not heard it. He had only just that evening got back with the Prime Minister from his talks with President Pompidou in Paris. He added that Heath was anxious to have a word at No. 10 straight away.[12]

Things then happened fast. It was hastily arranged that Jellicoe would go immediately with Armstrong in his car to No. 10. Philippa would be taken to the restaurant, San Frediano in the Fulham Road where Jellicoe would rejoin her. Armstrong's official car was parked nearby and his waiting driver took them to it. They had a long wait while a number of Covent Garden lorries blocked the traffic. It was probably only five minutes but it felt longer because then, for the first time, Jellicoe felt pangs of concern at why the Prime Minister should have sent for him so suddenly. Could it be connected with Lambton's resignation? Perhaps it meant a minor Government reshuffle on which Heath might need his urgent advice. Did he want Jellicoe, for example, to suggest a junior minister from the Lords to take Lambton's place? Optimistic speculations ran pell-mell through his mind. But he could not escape also the sense of foreboding. Could there be some connection between Lambton's resignation and the fact that his own private life was not entirely blameless? Could he himself be involved in some way?

On the way to No. 10, Jellicoe made desultory conversation with Armstrong. They discussed the Prime Minister's recent win in his yacht, *Morning Cloud*, and his astonishing physical stamina. After a virtually sleepless night, he had been picked up at

198

Thorney Island and flown to Paris for a briefing and dinner at the Paris embassy. Jellicoe asked about the discussions, which had gone well. Armstrong told him about the fantastic car, a Citröen/ Maserati, which had been placed at President Pompidou's disposal by the French Government. Jellicoe mentally contrasted it with the rather shop-worn official No. 10 Rover.

Armstrong knew Jellicoe well. He was unassuming and easy to get on with, yet a very effective Leader of the Lords. He had frequent meetings with the Prime Minister and was on the Cabinet legislative committee. The last thing that Heath wanted was another resignation on top of the Lambton affair and to have to find another Leader of the Lords. Yet Jellicoe's access to all Cabinet papers, and the echoes of the Profumo affair, meant that a possible national security angle had to be taken seriously, particularly given the other investigation that was already underway.[13]

At No. 10, Armstrong left Jellicoe in the Westminster Room sitting at the little round table outside the Cabinet Room. After a few minutes, Armstrong emerged from the Cabinet Room and asked him in. Again, a moment of increased apprehension. Normally, Heath would have received him in his sitting room upstairs. Jellicoe sat down beside the Prime Minister who asked if he would like a drink. He accepted and Armstrong busied himself with the decanter in the corner of the room.

'Soda water, Lord Privy Seal?'

'Soda', Jellicoe replied.

While they waited, Jellicoe told Heath what a marvellous performance of Lucia he had just enjoyed. Heath listened politely and then gave Jellicoe a brief account of his talks with Pompidou. The blocking tactics in which the French were then indulging in Brussels had not been reflected in Pompidou's own attitude. Armstrong poured a whisky and water for the Prime Minister and brought their drinks over to them. He sat down beside Heath who turned to Jellicoe. Heath apologized for sending for him so suddenly and for Philippa being left waiting at the restaurant. And then, speaking slowly and quietly, perhaps a little hesitantly, he also apologized for the fact that the matter he wanted to discuss with Jellicoe concerned his private affairs.

At that moment, Jellicoe's sense of foreboding was confirmed. Some time ago, according to Heath, facts had been brought to his attention that suggested one of his ministers might be involved with a call girl ring. Since matters of national security might conceivably be at stake, he had thought it right to authorize a security investigation. During the enquiry, the man who had made the allegations had claimed to have pictures in his possession. These showed the minister in compromising circumstances with a woman. No particular credence had initially been attached to these allegations. However when the minister (Heath did not mention his name) had been shown the photographs he had immediately agreed that they were of him. The young woman involved was Norma Levy.

Heath explained that unfortunately, allegations had also been made that Jellicoe too might be involved in some way. The investigators had been inclined to discount these stories. But the fact that the allegations had proved to be only too true in the case of one minister meant that they had to be taken seriously. He then asked Jellicoe if he had been subjected to any blackmail pressure. Jellicoe said immediately that, apart from the story in the evening paper, this was the first that he had heard about the whole affair. He certainly had not received any blackmail threats. And he had never heard of Norma Levy. He repeated these assertions several times while Heath listened impassively.

Jellicoe could not tell how long this conversation lasted: it was probably about fifteen minutes. At the end of it, having seen that Jellicoe's glass was refilled, Heath said he thought it right to inform him of the position without delay. The *Die Stern* article was due to appear the following day. He did not think that Jellicoe's name would feature in it but all kinds of press rumours had been circulating and he did not wish his colleague to be in any way taken by surprise. Jellicoe asked him more than once about the precise nature of the allegations being made against him. But the Prime Minister was either unable or unwilling to provide details. Jellicoe then took his leave of Heath, saying that he was of course at his disposal should he wish to see him further in connection with the matter.

Armstrong walked with the somewhat sober Lord Privy Seal to the door of No. 10 and asked his chauffeur to drive him back to South Kensington. As they crossed the black and white chequered hall, Armstrong mentioned that he did not think the name Norma Levy was, of itself, of any particular significance. Jellicoe took this to mean of any particular significance as far as he was concerned.

The No. 10 Rover took Jellicoe to San Frediano's. He was concentrating too hard on briefing the driver to get to the restaurant quickly to have much time to think. The man tried to turn up Beauchamp Place instead of down Walton Street but Jellicoe corrected him just in time. He was worried about Philippa being left for so long on her own in the crowded restaurant. They stopped outside San Frediano on the left-hand side of Fulham Road. Philippa looked up as Jellicoe made his way towards her and gave a cheery wave. As he sat down, the proprietor appeared. In view of the late hour, he and Philippa had taken the precaution of ordering Jellicoe some cold prawns, asparagus with vinaigrette and a bottle of Valpolicella. But the kitchen was still open and further orders were possible. Jellicoe demurred and immediately downed a good big glass of Valpolicella.

He then had not one moment's hesitation in putting Philippa completely in the picture and discussing, at very great length, the course of action he should follow. He gave her, straight and without gloss or embellishment, as accurate an account as he could of his talk with Ted Heath. He had given true and straightforward answers to the questions put to him but had not volunteered information about matters on which he had not been questioned. He then went on to say that on rare occasions he had invited a call girl to their flat in Onslow Square. Though women were attracted to him, he had not been looking for any long-running secret affairs.[14] He had not used his own name on these infrequent occasions but, since the Jellicoe name appeared at the entrance to the flats, some might have put two and two together and passed on the information to the press and No. 10. The Profumo affair and Peggy Dunne's experience as Profumo's constituency chairman was very much in their minds.

Philippa's immediate reaction was that she considered herself in large measure to blame. She had devoted too much time to their three small children in the country, leaving Jellicoe too much to his own devices in London. He told her it was ridiculous for her to blame herself in any way. For her part, marriage to Jellicoe had been exciting and exhilarating, though she much preferred her country life to life in London.[15] And so the Jellicoes closed ranks. Many wives would have been less staunch. Philippa's second and typically forthright reaction was to say that the sooner Jellicoe told Heath everything the better. The moral of the Profumo débâcle had been that once people were onto things, lack of forthrightness led to wild speculation. She was therefore strongly in favour of his informing Heath of everything with the least possible delay.

Jellicoe was inclined to consider the matter further. He had no idea what No. 10 knew. It did not cross his mind then, or indeed until he read it in the newspapers, that his telephone might have been tapped. Perhaps the linking of his name with the Lambton affair was no more than a rather obvious and crude guess. Looking around the Cabinet, there were only a very few possible candidates.[16] The allegations to which the Prime Minister had referred might be no more or less significant than completely unsupported surmise.

On the other hand, Jellicoe could not dismiss the possibility that there was hard evidence against him in the possession of the authorities and the press. He had not taken elaborate precautions to cover his traces and some girl could well have talked. Nevertheless, no whisper of a rumour had reached him and no pressure of any kind had been brought to bear on him. Was it not stupid therefore and quite unnecessary for him to tell No. 10 things which Heath might not want to know? Why lead with his chin? Was not the sensible thing to await developments?

So, after a long, frank and open talk, they decided to sleep on it. They walked to Philippa's Lancia (Isa had left her at the flat and she had picked it up there) and drove back to Onslow Square at about one o'clock in the morning. They half wondered whether some newspaper reporters might be waiting outside. There was no one.

Jellicoe slept fitfully until about five o'clock and then got up to tackle a couple of boxes. He went through them thoroughly. He was to have a meeting that morning, with representatives of the Royal Mint's employees about redundancy conditions. The details were exceptionally complicated and he found it more than usually difficult to master them. He also looked at a redraft of a speech he was due to make that evening to open a Viking exhibition at the National Maritime Museum at Greenwich. He thought of a number of additions and amendments and decided that it would perhaps be better to omit a reference to the beauty of Viking women. He could not have been concentrating fully on his work because he forgot to look through some copious briefing on the statement which John Davies was due to make that afternoon in the Commons on the latest round of negotiations in the Council of Ministers and which he, Jellicoe, would make simultaneously in the Lords. The papers had not arrived in time to be included in his normal boxes and had been handed to him separately as he was leaving the House the evening before.

At around quarter to eight, the usual full set of morning newspapers arrived. Jellicoe scanned them quickly before going back to the bedroom to wake Philippa. She was only half asleep. From even a cursory glance, the papers were blowing the Lambton affair up into a major event. Any pretence that his resignation was due primarily to health reasons or a recent controversy over his courtesy title had vanished. The call girl association was out in the open. It was also clear that a major police and security investigation into the whole business had been under way for some time.

Jellicoe shaved quickly and had a cold bath. He decided to shelve an idea of going early with Philippa to the Chelsea Flower Show. Instead, he had a brief telephone conversation with Matthew Ridley about the Water Bill, which he had introduced in the Lords on Monday. He and Philippa then discussed the position calmly over breakfast. It was clear that whatever they had thought the previous evening, a new situation had now arisen. A political scandal of major proportions was blowing up and a press campaign of real intensity was under way. There was, apart from anything else, evidence of at least one other minister being involved. Jellicoe did not know what was known about him. As they talked, it became clearer and clearer to him that there was only one course of action really open to him. That was to tell Heath with the least possible delay about his occasional association with call girls.

One factor in all this was a realistic calculation of the risk of exposure. But this was not the dominating impulse. He realized that his political career was in grave jeopardy. And therefore one thing became clear above all other, namely that if all else was lost he was determined not to lose his personal honour. In those few crucial moments he was in a highly emotional state and close to breaking down. He was determined that whatever else people could say about him he would not lay himself open to the accusation of having acted with dishonour. He felt that he must be able to look his colleagues, with whom he had worked so closely both in Opposition and in Government for ten years or more, in the eye. He felt this above all about Ted Heath.

After about half an hour, he decided to telephone Heath and ask to come and see him forthwith. But it took a few minutes' inner struggle before he could pick up the telephone and dial the number. There was an agonizing delay. At first, the Treasury did not reply. When he eventually got through to No. 10 and asked to speak to Armstrong, he had not yet arrived. So he asked to be put through to the Prime Minister. At first he too was not available. The telephonist thought that he was having a bath. Jellicoe was about to hang up when the operator asked him to hold on. Then Heath came on the line.

Jellicoe explained very briefly that he had been thinking over their conversation of the night before and had discussed matters with Philippa. He thought it would be a good thing if the Prime Minister could spare the time to see him early that morning. Heath asked if half past nine would suit; by then it was already half past eight. Jellicoe agreed and asked if he should come in at the Downing Street entrance. Heath thought it might be better to use the Cabinet Office entrance. Jellicoe rang off.

While being driven to his Private Office at the CSD, Jellicoe realized he had forgotten the briefing papers on the Community negotiations statement and was furious with himself. He arranged for Isa to pick them up from the flat during the morning. At the office, he dealt quickly with one or two mundane matters and then Isa drove him, with Gerald Wilson, over to the side entrance of the Cabinet Office. The door through from the Cabinet Office to No. 10 opened for him, which Heath must have arranged.

Almost immediately, he was shown into the Cabinet Room; it was a minute or two after nine thirty. The meeting was brief. Jellicoe said that he recognized from reading the morning papers that a major scandal was breaking. He therefore thought that he should ask himself, in the Prime Minister's presence a question that had not been put to him the previous evening. The question was a simple one. Had he ever, since being a member of Heath's administration, had any association with call girls? The answer was frankly that he had, intermittently, at his flat. He explained that he had always used an assumed name but could only suppose that someone had seen his name at the entrance to the flat and put two and two together.

Heath listened politely, intently and gravely. He thanked Jellicoe with noticeable warmth for coming to see him so promptly. He asked only two questions. Had Jellicoe seen a call girl recently? The answer was not in the past month or two. Was any one of the girls with whom he had associated part of any sort of 'ring'? (There was a current preoccupation with the idea of criminal 'rings'.) Jellicoe concurred; he had more than once telephoned a so-called agency called 'Mayfair Escorts'. His talk with Heath lasted ten minutes at most. Before he got up to leave, Jellicoe made clear that he would naturally take whatever action the Prime Minister felt would, in the circumstances, be least harmful to his administration. He also asked if he should carry on quite normally as a member of the Government for the time being. Heath said this would be the right thing to do.

Outside the Cabinet Room at about quarter to ten, Jellicoe turned to Armstrong and asked, point-blank if, in his personal view, he had been right in asking to see Heath and spilling the beans. He would not easily forget his reply. 'Yes, George,' said Armstrong. 'You were a thousand-fold right.' Then he added, 'I do not think that I have ever admired you so much as I do this morning'. Armstrong remembered that what had sunk Jack Profumo was telling lies.[17] It took Jellicoe a few moments to get his emotions under control. Then he walked back to John Davies's

205

office in the Cabinet Office. On the way, he tried to telephone Philippa at home from the telephone in the lobby but the number was engaged. He went in to see Davies.

Davies had just flown in from Brussels, where the Council of Ministers' meeting had ended at 4.30 in the morning. The French had been isolated in a discussion on energy policy, but were quite adamant and seemed determined to force a breach. However, he was unaware of the outcome of the Prime Minister's talks with Pompidou. Jellicoe asked Davies if he could possibly use the phone to ring Philippa. He tried twice; the number was still engaged. In the Cabinet Office briefing room with their officials, the two ministers slightly amended Davies's draft statement and ran over the supplementary briefing. Jellicoe and Wilson then walked down the corridor to the CSD to meet the delegation from the Royal Mint at eleven o'clock. There followed a very long, involved and complicated discussion. It was 12.20 by the time he managed to bring the meeting to a close.

Back at his CSD office, Jellicoe found that Wilson had contacted Philippa and she was joining him for lunch in the Lords at 1.00 pm. He dealt with one or two papers and dictated the final version of the Viking exhibition speech. Then he was driven, via the Horse Guards arch, back to his office in the Lords. He and Philippa lunched in the Lords' dining room. Neither had much appetite. At 2.30 pm, Jellicoe went into the House for Questions, intervening once or twice in order to curtail over-long supplementaries,[18] before going back to his office in the Lords.

Now it was nearly four o'clock and he was on his feet. With his usual slow, deliberate style, he delivered the Government statement on the EEC Council of Ministers' meeting. After listening politely, their Lordships asked questions. Jellicoe answered all their points without much difficulty. After some twenty-five minutes' discussion and in response to a question from Lord Avebury about the House needing to have access to information at least before it appeared in the national press, Jellicoe made his closing intervention. It was his last as a Minister of the Crown.

My Lords, I accept the point made by the noble Lord, Lord Avebury. The trouble is that one has to move at the speed of light to keep up with the speed of leaks in Brussels.[19]

When he reached his office, No. 10 had been on the phone. They wanted to know where he would be because the Prime Minister might want to have a word with him later in the day. Jellicoe was driven over to the Treasury for a meeting of the Cabinet Counter Inflation Committee chaired by the Chancellor of the Exchequer, Anthony Barber. The doorway to the Chancellor's office had a dark wooden surround built over it, rather like a church lych-gate, attesting to the importance of its occupant.

The group discussed the Government's stance towards the substantial price increases being sought by a number of nationalized industries. Jellicoe sat beside Jim Prior and John Peyton and opposite Peter Carrington and Tom Boardman, Minister for Industry at the DTI. The only non minister present was Dick Ross of the Think Tank, which had put in a short paper on the subject.

Boardman made the running as far as the nationalized industries were concerned and the group had no great difficulty in reaching a consensus. Jellicoe knew that it was easy to be over anxious but opposite him Carrington seemed to avoid catching his eye and Barber went out of his way to seek his opinion. Jellicoe left the meeting early. He had to be in the Lords by 5.30 pm to meet Philippa and drive down to Greenwich to open the Viking exhibition. Isa drove them down with Wilson in the front beside her. Partly to distract his mind and because he had not been able to give his speech the usual amount of attention, Jellicoe read it over to Philippa, who pronounced it excellent.

They arrived at Greenwich a little ahead of time, immediately behind the Swedish ambassador, and were greeted by Jellicoe's cousin, Admiral Sir Charles Madden, a trustee of the National Maritime Museum.[20] He showed Jellicoe into the library and produced a welcoming whisky soda. They went upstairs to be shown round the exhibition by the director of the Stockholm Museum.

A short welcome by Basil Greenhill, the Director of the Maritime Museum, and a longer speech by his Swedish counterpart, was followed by about five minutes from the Swedish ambassador. Then came a few nice words of introduction for Jellicoe from Madden, and then Jellicoe's own speech. It went down pretty well but he was very aware as he occasionally caught

Philippa's eye that this was probably his last public appearance as a minister. But he was determined that if he was to go out it should be with a bang.

While Jellicoe was speaking, Wilson was called to the telephone. It was Christopher Roberts, one of Heath's Assistant Private Secretaries, at No. 10. The Prime Minister wanted to see Jellicoe that evening. Up to that point Wilson had had no idea what was going on. He then realized that Jellicoe must be involved in the ministerial crisis and that he, Wilson, had been talking in the car rather insensitively about the references to Lord Lambton in the evening papers.[21] A member of the Museum staff gave Jellicoe a scribbled note; one of the Commons' Press Gallery wanted him urgently. Wilson went to investigate. The man claimed to be a personal friend. Jellicoe then took Wilson aside and told him in confidence that he might be caught up in the Lambton affair.

The Jellicoes then drove back to London. It was a quick return through traffic-free streets. The telephone in the car rang once on the way back but Isa did not understand how it worked and by the time Jellicoe got hold of it the line was dead. He assumed it was No. 10. Back at the flat, at around 8.30 pm Jellicoe telephoned the Sutherlands[22] and cancelled a meeting with them. While he was bathing and shaving before changing into his dinner jacket, the telephone rang. It was Robert Armstrong. Could Jellicoe go round to No. 10?

'What time?' Jellicoe asked. Armstrong suggested around 9.00 pm.

'Yes, of course', Jellicoe replied. Neither of them could have known it was already 8.45.

Jellicoe had asked Isa to wait, half-expecting that he might need her, and set off for No. 10.

It was not quite dark as they drove along Hyde Park. He couldn't help noticing the beauty of the horse chestnut trees in the twilight. It had rained heavily that evening and the park looked fresh and clean. He asked Isa to drop him at the Foreign Office steps, fearing that there might be a crowd of press outside No. 10. Nobody was in sight. He walked up the steps and was ushered in with the usual greeting from the policeman on duty.

He sat down at the familiar small table outside the Cabinet Room and waited for his summons to see Heath. He was fairly convinced under the circumstances his resignation was about to be accepted. But he was not quite certain. He glanced at the clock below the rather poor picture above the mantelpiece. Twenty minutes past nine. He assumed that Heath would ask to see him forthwith. But no summons came. The minutes ticked by.

He tried to occupy himself. He memorized the décor of the room. The paintings – the one above the mantelpiece, the Samuel Scott, or semi-Samuel Scott, view of London and the flower picture on the wall opposite the mantelpiece. He tried to read the weeklies laid out on the little round desk – the *Illustrated London News*, with a banal article about the Queen, the *Spectator* and the *New Statesman*. It was impossible to concentrate. More minutes ticked by. Nine forty-five. He wondered what could be the cause of the delay. Was the Prime Minister talking to some of his (and Jellicoe's) closest colleagues? Was he poring over the latest security service and police reports? Did this mean that his future might still be in the balance? He tried not to think about the possibilities. He telephoned Philippa to say that he still had yet to see Heath. She was surprised too.

Still no summons. The silence downstairs at No. 10 was total. It seemed eerie. The ticking of the grandfather clock. Nothing, save the occasional departure of a messenger. His nerves were extraordinarily strained, tense. Forever he would recall those sixty-five to seventy minutes of waiting. It was no good doing nothing so he composed a paragraph of a draft letter of resignation.

It was nearly ten thirty when Armstrong arrived. He apologized for having kept Jellicoe waiting for so long and said the Prime Minister was ready. They went straight up to the study, which Jellicoe had got to know so well during the past three years, with its Renoir, the rather good painting by Churchill (so much nicer than the one which Clementine and the family had presented to Chequers) and the one of *Morning Cloud*.

Heath treated Jellicoe kindly, almost affectionately. He walked over to the sideboard. 'Lord Privy Seal, what would you like to drink?' Jellicoe settled back on the sofa opposite him holding the whisky soda. Armstrong pulled up a chair. Without further ado, save to remark with a wry grin that it had been a hell of a day, Heath told Jellicoe of the latest developments. Charges concerning drugs (cannabis and amphetamines) were being brought against Lambton and there were other possibilities (he mentioned boys) in the background.

As far as Jellicoe was concerned, there were no embarrassing pictures. There was no question of drugs, let alone any other criminal charge. However, there had been some independent corroboration of Jellicoe's involvement with a call girl, or call girls. And it appeared from the enquiries which the police had made, even with due discretion, that the press, or at least some newspapers, had got hold of his name.

The Prime Minister totally understood. But Jellicoe's political career was in the balance. Heath talked about Jellicoe's service to the Government and said that he had been casting about for ways in which he could keep him on as a member of his administration. As he spoke, and as Jellicoe felt for him a personal liking and sympathy, which he had never felt before, he became convinced that he had to come out of his corner. So he said, point blank, that it was crystal clear to him that he must resign. Heath did not demur. But nor did he there and then accept the resignation. He said the time had come for Jellicoe to consult his lawyer, Arnold Goodman.[23] Just possibly, that ingenious man could think of some miracle that would allow Jellicoe to be kept on in the Government. In any event, he thought that Jellicoe should see Goodman without delay. This was in Jellicoe's own interest since it might be important for his future that as clean a distinction as possible be drawn between his possible resignation and that of Lambton. Robert Armstrong immediately offered to contact Goodman.

Jellicoe did not know how long he stayed with the Prime Minister. They discussed the question of his possible successor in the Lords. Jellicoe said that if Carrington was excluded – and he thought that this could only be a temporary expedient because he already had far too much on his plate – his own clear preference, if he could be spared from the Home Office, was David Windlesham. Heath asked Windlesham's age. Jellicoe said, rather speculatively, that he was in his forties, or perhaps a little

210

older. Armstrong went to consult *Who's Who* and reappeared saying that Windlesham was only forty-one. Jellicoe suggested a couple of other possibilities.[24]

At that moment, his hitherto pent up emotions of sadness, shame and regret began to get the better of him. He apologized to Heath for this show of feeling, thanked him for the many kindnesses which he had shown him and said that he hoped he would take for granted his regret for the embarrassment he was causing to him, the party and the administration. He then took his leave. He knew that he would always, always feel that Heath, who was dealing with a set of circumstances that must have been quite awful for him and probably well outside the range of his personal experience, treated him with a remarkable degree of consideration. Curiously, in those moments of pain and anguish, Jellicoe felt that he had never really known Heath before. They had been about half an hour together.

Jellicoe and Armstrong went down to his office next to the Cabinet Room to telephone Arnold Goodman. They finally located him at his flat in Portland Place. Jellicoe asked if he could go round to see him immediately. Typically, Goodman said 'of course' and Isa drove Jellicoe there. He explained the position and they agreed that Philippa should join them. Jellicoe also rang Shackleton who was his typically generous and kind-hearted self. That evening Janet Morgan had joined a group, including Shackleton, seeing a revival of *No, no Nanette*. They were having a drink in his rather poky flat just off Chester Square, when the call came through. Shackleton was stunned.

'George has resigned,' he said, as he slowly replaced the receiver. He was moved not only by the bombshell of the resignation but also by the circumstances. Jellicoe had been foremost in helping able women to progress in their careers. He could not imagine why Jellicoe had been involved with call girls.[25]

Goodman's first reaction was that resignation might not be necessary. Indeed, to resign might be held to be rather absurd. They agreed that it would be sensible to consult Armstrong, to whom Goodman could speak with complete frankness. Armstrong arrived shortly after Philippa and went to talk alone with Goodman in another room. Armstrong made a mental note of how excellent Goodman was and that if ever he was in trouble himself Goodman would give all the time, careful consideration and wise compassionate judgment one could wish for.[26] Meanwhile, the Jellicoes talked in Goodman's pleasant, rather dark, sitting room, admiring his very good Bandinis while Jellicoe consumed rather more of Goodman's whisky than a well-mannered guest should.

After about forty minutes, Goodman and Armstrong re-appeared. They had come to the firm conclusion that resignation was inevitable. Jellicoe agreed, adding that he had thought so since early that morning and now he wanted to get it over with as quickly as possible. The Prime Minister was due to make his statement in the Commons at 3.30 in the afternoon (by now it was after midnight) and the resignation letter ought to reach No. 10 in plenty of time for it to be announced on the one o'clock news.[27]

Goodman and Armstrong had produced a draft. They and Jellicoe agreed it should be short, frank and factual and devoid of ambiguity. The first draft was very much along the lines that Jellicoe had in mind. But he was anxious to include a final paragraph, which he had already roughed out on paper at No. 10, saying that his wish had been to serve his country as a member of Heath's administration and that it would always be a matter of infinite regret that his idiotic behaviour had made this impossible. Goodman persuaded him to delete the word 'idiotic'.

They moved into his library next door to finish the letter and discuss the general lines of Heath's reply. The only issue of what turned out to be a very long drafting session – with Goodman on his very best form – was a discussion of how Jellicoe should 'top and tail' his letter. They agreed on 'My Dear Prime Minister' and 'Yours ever'. Armstrong said that Heath's reply would almost certainly be in warm terms and along 'Dear George: Yours ever, Ted' lines. For some inexplicable reason, this gave Jellicoe considerable comfort in his, by then, rather emotional state.

But Jellicoe did not know what had changed Goodman's original view that resignation might not be necessary. Goodman said that because Jellicoe had told Heath the facts it was impossible for the Prime Minister to bluff his way out. He used Watergate as an analogy – Nixon's position would, in the end, have proved untenable if, in fact, it turned out that he *had*, all along, known the facts. But Jellicoe wondered if this might just have been Goodman's rationalization and if Armstrong had divulged facts known to the authorities which Heath had not revealed but which, if published, would force the resignation. He just did not know.

The die was almost cast. But Goodman suggested that before Jellicoe took any irrevocable decision, it would be wise to contact a close friend, abreast of the facts, on whose judgment he could rely. Philippa and Armstrong agreed. Carrington was the obvious person and they telephoned him at around 2.00 am Jellicoe apologized for ringing at such an appalling hour and said that he assumed that he knew the position. Carrington did. Jellicoe relayed the events of that evening and the conclusion that there was nothing for it but to resign and quickly. Rather wearily, but with great kindness and immense regret, Carrington said he saw no other way out. Jellicoe agreed, thanked him and rang off. There was nothing else to say.

The little group talked for another twenty minutes or so. They had sent Isa away about two hours before. The Jellicoes offered to run Armstrong back to No. 10 but his official car was still outside. They went down in the lift together. As they emerged into the hall, Philippa broke down for the first time. Until then she had been coolness and composure itself. Jellicoe was too overwrought, too spent and too constrained himself to comfort her. Armstrong put his arm around her and patted her on the shoulder. He told her that she had been quite marvellous, that he and all her friends were full of admiration and that she had shown quite extraordinary courage. Jellicoe turned away as he could not restrain his own tears. They both managed to pull themselves together, thanked Armstrong and said goodbye to him in the, by now, deserted Portland Place. Just after they got back to the flat at 2.30 in the morning, Goodman telephoned. On reflection he felt the proposed letter of resignation was almost too explicit about Jellicoe's 'casual associations'. They arranged to meet again at Portland Place at about 9.30 am.

213

It had been a long night. Philippa cooked some eggs (they had had no dinner) and he slept fitfully beside her until five or six in the morning. He got up at about 6.30 – much later than usual. He scanned through his boxes, conscious that it was the last time that he would do so. He signed about twenty papers and began a round of telephone calls to family and close friends to ensure that they heard the news before it broke on television and radio. Prudy was not at home so he spoke to a very calm Billy. Alexa was reassuring (she was in the middle of buying a mantelpiece) and Zara was asleep. He could not reach Nicky. He then looked at the press. It was full of Lambton's resignation. There was no mention of drugs but a lot about a police investigation authorized by the Prime Minister to follow up some concerns beforehand. For the first time it dawned on him that his telephone might have been tapped and that other ministers might be involved.

The Jellicoes breakfasted and concluded that whatever ideas they might have had before about telling Heath everything, the general tenor of the press confirmed the wisdom of doing so. In fact, the decision the day before had not, in the end, been a matter of finely balanced calculation. It was much more an instinctive, almost compulsive, feeling on Jellicoe's part that he owed it to himself and his personal honour to come as clean as possible.[28] The awful and inescapable consequences of Profumo's fabrication ten years before had also helped Jellicoe to resolve to tell the truth.

The next morning, on the way to see Goodman, Jellicoe spoke to Wilson on the car telephone and asked him to break the news of his resignation to Kenneth Baker. Jellicoe also told Isa; she tried to dissuade him, saying how sad she thought William Armstrong would be. Jellicoe's lack of concentration on the road meant that Isa took him by a rather roundabout route and he reached Portland Place a little late, at about 9.45. Goodman was breakfasting in a voluminous dressing gown and Jellicoe joined him over eggs and bacon. Goodman had already consulted counsel and they discussed the resignation letter that Armstrong had sent over from No. 10. It seemed to play down the seriousness of the matter and they decided to strengthen the last paragraph. One of the corrections that Goodman insisted on was to substitute 'affaires' for 'affairs'. He thought it typical of the 'innocence of those at No. 10' that they would not know how to spell 'affaires'. They then sent the letter to be typed by his secretary. Kenneth Baker telephoned and was very supportive.

Goodman told Jellicoe that the press were considering two other names, including a member of the Shadow Cabinet.[29] He hoped they would not come out. They discussed practical matters. Jellicoe was inclined to stay in London and face things but Goodman dissuaded him. There was bound to be a major press campaign and he should let things die down.

Armstrong rang a couple of times during the morning. He was anxious that at the same time as the resignation was announced Goodman should issue a statement making it clear that there was no question of any criminal charge, no possible breach of national security and no exposure to any kind of blackmail or pressure. Since this was all true, Jellicoe agreed. Armstrong read over to Goodman the Prime Minister's proposed reply to the resignation letter. It was more or less as they had roughed it out in the early hours of the morning. Armstrong was anxious to know when Jellicoe's letter would reach No. 10. The precise wording, as announced, was not quite as the original. 'Affairs' still stood!

There was little more to be done. Jellicoe signed the letter at about 11.30. It did not reach Downing Street until shortly before midday because of traffic hold-ups. Goodman was off to attend Noel Coward's memorial service and feared that he might be late so they went down in the lift together. Jellicoe thanked him for all his help and really meant it; Goodman had given unstintingly of his time.

'I've never heard such nonsense', was his reply. They said goodbye in the hall at Portland Place.

'God bless you,' said Goodman and advised Jellicoe to leave a few minutes after him. Isa drove Jellicoe round to Peggy's flat in Eaton Square to rejoin Philippa. When he arrived at about 11.50, Wilson had just telephoned to say that the news of the resignation was on the tapes.[30]

That morning, Inglis went into the office and Wilson said simply,

'He's resigned.' They were both stunned.

'How did he ever have time for call girls with all those boxes?' said Inglis. It was a common reaction to the news.

'How ever did he find the time?' repeated the secretaries in the Lords, with whom Jellicoe was immensely popular.[31] The story seemed to reinforce Jellicoe's rakish reputation. One cartoon in a national daily newspaper showed a four-poster bed, with a coronet on each corner and curtains closed. In front of it stood a scantily clad lady of the night brandishing a whip, while the caption read, 'Now I know the meaning of the expression "belted Earl"!'[32] But no call girl ever attempted to blackmail Jellicoe, though it would have been easy and profitable.

Gloom descended on the rest of the CSD. It was so sad; and such a waste. But Jellicoe's judgment was thought sound. Instead of blustering and trying to cling onto office, his decision to go defused gossip. His name had often been in the press, though few knew about his wartime career. He was known for being sound and sensible.[33]

The Lords were deeply shocked and distressed. This was not just any member of the House, but their Leader. Their general view too was that Jellicoe's reaction to his disgrace was typical of him – own up, don't tell lies, and take the punishment like a man. In a way, he was too honest – the opposite of Profumo.[34] With heavy hearts, Michael Davies and his wife accepted two tickets that would have been the Jellicoes' to see *Die Zauberflöte* on Friday, 1 June at Glyndebourne.[35]

To Malcolm Inglis fell the sad task of returning the Privy Seal. The Seal is the size of a man's hand and Inglis took it in a box over to Goodman's office at lunchtime. It was a poignant mission, rendering up this tangible symbol of ministerial power.[36] Jellicoe's Private Office staff were all scheduled to watch Trooping the Colour from his office windows. They still did so but the occasion was very flat.[37] Jellicoe's successor, Windlesham, was perfectly competent but life in the Lords without Jellicoe was infinitely duller.[38] Nobody was sorrier than the Prime Minister.[39] Heath wrote his old friend a long, very warm letter saying that his decision to stand down accorded with the best traditions of British public life. The real pressure for Jellicoe's resignation was that his association with call girls came to light

216

in the context of the Lambton enquiry, which made his position untenable.

Afterwards, Wilson got the impression that his CSD colleagues were giving him a wide berth, almost as if he had known something about what Jellicoe had been up to. The Security Commission held an enquiry, at which Goodman represented Jellicoe and Wilson was called to give evidence. It found that there had been no risk to security. However, concerned that Jellicoe had had classified files in his flat and that call girls might have been able to see them, the Commission recommended that all Cabinet Ministers should have combination safes installed in their homes – at the taxpayers' expense. Windlesham's sitting room floor had to be reinforced to take the weight. The thought that Jellicoe would have fiddled around putting papers into a safe and twiddling the combination lock to get them out was hard to believe. And, bearing in mind that Cabinet Ministers did not stay in office all that long, the costs were prohibitive while ensuring a good supply of business for security companies.[40]

The Jellicoes stayed at Eaton Square to escape the press. Peggy was very steadying and down to earth. Initially, she did not think the scandal a resigning matter. But having supported Profumo through the aftermath of his resignation crisis, she knew the ropes. That afternoon, the Jellicoes drove down to Herefordshire to stay with Philippa's brother Thomas[41] at Gatley Park.[42]

The press would not give up. They came into Tidcombe Manor at the back and even tried to get into the house from the front, where Daisy was on the terrace with her doll's pram. But Barbara Hunt planted herself squarely in their way, ignoring their pleadings of 'Oh *please* let us see their boudoir'.[43]

While the Jellicoes were at Gatley, the press rang. Martin Dunne, Philippa's other brother, told them that Jellicoe was in Ireland with his sister. Jellicoe was in the garden when a helicopter swooped low over the house. He immediately took cover but it was only the Midland Electricity Board inspecting their power lines. He was very stressed and for the only time in his life took sleeping pills. The Jellicoes then headed for Scotland. Since they needed fresh clothes, Tony Hunt packed some for them, giving the press the slip as he headed for the motorway.[44]

Two hours later, the press knocked on the door at Gatley. *The News of the World* wanted to upstage a story by one of their rivals by bringing Christine Keeler to be photographed at the bottom of the drive. They had discovered that during his Secret Intelligence Service days Jellicoe had had a fictitious name on his London flat door.

Opinion was divided among Jellicoe's friends and colleagues as to whether or not he should have resigned. About half of the people I interviewed thought that he should not – and that Heath should not have accepted it. This is easy to say with hindsight. The standards and mores of 1973 and the memory of the Profumo Affair, probably made it inevitable. Ten months later the Heath Government failed to win the General Election so Jellicoe was spared another five years in Opposition.[45]

It was some time before Jellicoe found out the background to his resignation. Lambton had been paying a call girl called Norma Levy (née Russell) by cheque. She was one of a ring of fifteen prostitutes who would take only millionaires and 'top people'. Her husband, alleged drugs trafficker Colin Levy, had taken pictures at her flat in Maida Vale of Lambton in bed with two girls and smoking cannabis, with a view to blackmail.[46] She was worried about what would happen to Lambton, given his position as a Defence Minister. She told the wife of the owner of the nightclub-cum brothel where she worked, who in turn told one of her customers with political connections – Joseph Nickerson[47].

'Look Mr Nickerson', she said one evening when they were having a drink while he recovered from his earlier exertions, 'I'm very worried about one of my girls, Norma'. She explained the problem and said that Levy was married to a villain who was getting dangerous. They agreed that this could be serious for Lambton. Nickerson then told James Prior, who was close to Heath.[48]

Ministers had dithered over how to deal with the affair. The Home Secretary, Robert Carr said having a mistress was not a crime and there was no proof that either Lambton or drugs were involved. The Foreign Secretary, Sir Alex Douglas-Home, Lambton's cousin, was asked to confront him but the Attorney

General blocked the idea lest any future police inquiry be prejudiced. Carr was even asked to examine the grainy photographs of the man in the bed to see if he thought it was Lambton. The police interviewed Lambton and after 1 oz of cannabis was found in his flat, he went that afternoon to see Pym. Lambton was adamant that he had not been blackmailed and there was no risk to national security. But because of his liability to criminal charges he wished to resign immediately. Levy told police that he had other photographs of prominent people in compromising situations.[49] Interviewed by Robin Day, Lambton said he could not understand what all the fuss was about since surely all men used prostitutes. But another BBC journalist present saw the continual interruptions to filming while Lambton recovered his composure, suggesting that the modern day Lord Byron had more humanity than met the eye.[50] Lambton also told MI5's investigator, Charles Elwell, that pressure of work, the futility of his job (idle hands) and the controversy over his father's title had made it impossible for him to read and had driven him to frantic activity, including seeing prostitutes. There were real fears that Lambton might commit suicide under all the pressure.[51]

In the course of the Security Commission investigation, various call girls' notebooks had been examined and the word 'Jellicoe' found in one. The police machine had then swung into action and, putting two and two together to make five, interpreted this supposed evidence as proof of assignations between Jellicoe and prostitutes. Very much later, it turned out to mean not Jellicoe himself but Jellicoe Hall, a community centre in Drummond Way, north London, named after Jellicoe's second cousin the Reverend Basil Jellicoe. A colourful character with huge charm and energy, he rode around north London in the 1930s on an open cart with a wind-up gramophone playing church bells. He had dedicated his short life to a major ministry to homeless people in the area, setting up the first housing association and even a Christian pub, becoming nationally influential before he died in 1937.[52] There is some kind of irony in the fact that Jellicoe should have been caught out because of the good works of this distant kinsman.

The Special Branch also had other evidence, probably through phone tapping, of contact between Jellicoe and a current girlfriend, which seemed to them to support their interpretation. It was this combined information that had prompted Heath to send for him. After the scandal had died down, the Metropolitan Police invited Jellicoe to a lunch, presumably to salve their consciences over the mistaken connection they had made, since they had no other reason to put on a lunch for him.[53]

At 2.30 pm on Tuesday 5 June, the House of Lords reassembled after the Whitsun recess. Following prayers led by the Lord Bishop of Hereford, Shackleton congratulated Windlesham on his appointment as the new Leader of the House and Lord Privy Seal and Lady Young (one of Jellicoe's protégées) on her 'meteoric career and on becoming a Parliamentary Under Secretary'. The next twenty minutes were taken up by tributes to Jellicoe, led by Shackleton, from various peers, amid cries of 'Hear, hear!' They 'bitterly regretted his resignation', noting that 'in Lord Jellicoe's concern for Members of the House of Lords and for our conditions he was the best shop steward the House of Lords ever had' and that 'the outstanding record of his achievement will not be dimmed'.

It fell eventually to his successor to acknowledge these tributes on Jellicoe's behalf, pointing out, 'My noble friend Lord Jellicoe, as we all know, has a light touch. He would prefer: "No flowers, by request" and to move on to the next business.'

To quote Crossman in *The Times*, 'The Government had lost one of the bravest, most competent and most humane of men in their company'.

Chapter Fourteen

Trade, Aids and Anti-terrorism

The Tories' loss of the General Election was a great shock. Heath had gambled and lost on the question of who rules. It was too soon to curb the power of the unions in the way that Margaret Thatcher did later.

Gradually, the Jellicoes came to terms with the change in their personal circumstances.

'Poor George', Peggy Dunne confided to her diary, 'both feel he needn't have resigned. Philippa worries because she feels she advised him to do so ... but it would be very different if he *hadn't* – he'd be worried and hounded by the Press.'[1] Jellicoe had no such thoughts. He joined the boards of SG Warburg, Smiths Industries, Morgan Crucible and Sotheby's.

The Sotheby's Chairman, Peter Wilson – the fastest gavel in the west – was a dashing 6 feet 4 inches. An entrepreneur and risk-taker who ran his auctions wearing black tie, he had a reputation for intrigue. He had worked for MI6 during the war, using the agent number 007. His friend Ian Fleming probably used Wilson to depict James Bond.[2]

In autumn 1974 Jellicoe joined forces with Lord Llewellyn-Davies and Nigel Thompson of Ove Arup,[3] to back British firms bidding to provide hospitals for the Shah.[4] Cementation International (part of the Trafalgar House Group) carried the commercial risk.[5] Jellicoe and the British ambassador at Teheran, Sir

Anthony Parsons, were personal friends of Hoveida, the Iranian Prime Minister. Friendship with such a VIP was not without its perks, especially given the Iranian fondness for giving gifts as a mark of regard. Back in the UK, Parsons and Thompson had lunch at Tidcombe. While they were eating caviar, Jellicoe said, 'Philippa. Where's the other tin? You know; the stuff that Hoveida gave me.' She made a face and said, 'It looked bad; so I threw it away'. It was the best golden caviar – the only kind the Shah ever ate.[6]

The Jellicoes employed an Italian butler called Oberdon. He was a sort of Passepartout character who had been valet to Ciano, Mussolini's Foreign Secretary, from which he had acquired a certain grandeur he had never quite laid down. He was not a proper butler and employed a mock obsequiousness. Gay and engaging, he had endearing kleptomania, often taking things and waiting to see if anyone noticed their disappearance.

One harsh winter, Tidcombe was snowbound. Oberdon needed to get to London so he and the Jellicoes broke out through the snow to the car to make it to the next village. Oberdon was making rather heavy weather of carrying his large suitcase. So in the end Jellicoe said, 'Here, let me have it', to which Oberdon readily agreed. When they got to the car, Jellicoe plonked the suitcase down heavily on the bonnet. It burst open scattering large quantities of the Jellicoes' silver. Oberdon was not at all discomfited, insisting coolly that the silver had to be taken back to London so that it could be properly cleaned.

On another occasion, Jellicoe went to his Onslow Square flat and was met at the door by Oberdon wearing his – Jellicoe's – pyjamas. Jellicoe was so astounded he said nothing and drove straight back to the country, where he blamed Philippa for Oberdon's presumptuousness. When he next appeared at Tidcombe, Philippa tackled him on the subject in the broken French that was their only common language. Failing to get much reaction, she said how cross Jellicoe was. 'Monsieur était furieux, vous savez ...' she said, to which Oberdon replied indignantly, 'Et pourquoi? J'étais très fatigué moi. J'avais travaillé toute la journée, toute la nuit. J'avais besoin de dormir....'[7] At the end of these protestations, Philippa ended up apologizing to *him*.[8]

222

In Iran, Jellicoe, Thompson and the Ove Arup chairman, Sir Jack Zunz, had a meeting with Parsons. Eventually, Zunz asked the ambassador, 'How do you think things will turn out in Iran?' to which Parsons replied smoothly, 'The conventional wisdom is that Persia is the one third world country that might make it – providing the Iranians don't fuck it up.' Zunz was very shocked at this uncouth statement from such an elegant Englishman.[9]

The hospitals were in Iranian Azerbaijan: Tabriz, Ardabil and Rezaiyeh and one in the east at Birjand. They cost about £100 million each at 1975 prices.[10] But as the Shah threw money at things it just disappeared. Corruption was rife and members of the large Imperial family also siphoned it off. Even the Shah's amazing fixer, Sir Shapur Reporter, who owned a house in Rutland Gate and probably a British passport too, could not stop it.

In 1978 the Shah was deposed, the Ayatollah Khomeini returned to Iran and things began to go awry for British companies. Iran defaulted on the hospitals contract. The Export Credit Guarantee Department (ECGD) stumped up but the British group still needed to recover the money to repay them. Cementation went to Switzerland, France and The Hague to try to get the £1 million that Iran owed. At the same time, Trafalgar House discovered that the Iranian Government had significant shares in Krupps. At the threat of a writ, the Iranians rushed round to Trafalgar House with suitcases stuffed full of money to protect their shareholders.[11]

In 1978, Jellicoe accepted the chairmanship of Tate & Lyle. The big institutional investors were worried about the company's declining profits. Tates and Lyles, who were simply not up to it, occupied most board positions. Jellicoe took this family company of Tates and Lyles and turned it into a modern competitive company.[12] Jellicoe brought Neil Shaw, responsible for Tate & Lyle in North America, over to London to help.[13]

While Tate & Lyle were in Iran buying sugar cane, the Iranians accused them of displacing Iranian businesses. Things began to look decidedly sticky. Thompson had lunch with two Tate & Lyle directors, who said, 'Look, we've got to leave rather hurriedly. Our private jet's waiting. Do you want a lift?'

'Great', replied Thompson, collected his eight year-old daughter Nim from school and flew back to England. That was Tate & Lyle pulling out of Iran.

Before long, Jellicoe's eye for potential lighted on a young graduate trainee, not long out of Oxford, Colin Moynihan, who became his PA.[14] Jellicoe set a punishing pace. He never wore a watch, having thrown it away at the end of the war. His position at the centre of Tate & Lyle, Warburgs and Smiths Industries made him very influential in the City.[15] His remit was truly global. On one visit to Nakambala, he returned from a party at 1 am and then decided to pay another visit to the factory. As his host said goodnight at 2 am, Jellicoe reminded him to be punctual in the morning. He was sitting waiting when the car arrived at 6 am.[16] On a 1980 visit to the Tate & Lyle Yonkers refinery, on the Hudson River near New York, he and Shaw dined at an Italian restaurant. Jellicoe was soon in animated discussion about the war with the Italian proprietor. Gradually, they identified where they had both been and when, and even in which actions they had been engaged. Finally realization dawned. 'Hey!' shouted the restaurateur, jumping up. 'You sink-a my ship!'[17]

In May 1981, addressing the New York Sugar Club, Jellicoe referred to his 'cookie-pusher' days as a Washington diplomat. He told them the US was the exemplar of responsible free enterprise. This meant a lot to Tate & Lyle. They had, after all, had to fend off a strong post-war Labour Government bid to nationalize them, an era epitomized by a throwaway remark of Churchill's. One evening, he followed Prime Minister Attlee into the House of Commons lavatories but hesitated to take his place beside him. Puzzled, Attlee asked him why. 'The trouble is Clem,' said Churchill, 'whenever you see something big and important, you want to nationalize it.'[18]

In 1982, Jellicoe and Shaw went to see the Prime Minister, Margaret Thatcher. The miners' strike had reached an impasse. The purpose of the visit was to warn Thatcher that Tate & Lyle were going to close their Liverpool sugar refinery. The Prime Minister was appalled. 'George', she remonstrated. 'You just can't do this to me.' The timing was very bad. The recession had bottomed and there was mass unemployment. The Prime

Minister held Jellicoe's feet to the fire and did all she could to make him change his mind. But he was adamant; the refinery had to close. He came away from the meeting having stuck to his guns, steady under fire from the iron lady.[19]

On one business trip to Athens, Jellicoe and Shaw were in animated discussion in a taxi when they stopped at traffic lights. Without even turning his head the driver let out a great shout:

'Yellicoe!'

'Zacharias!' Jellicoe shouted.

They both leapt out of the car and hugged one another, wartime comrades reunited.[20] At a post-Falklands war dinner presided over by Margaret Thatcher in the Guildhall, Jellicoe and Thomas Dunne bumped into Anders Lassen's wartime driver, Stephenson. Looking at the seating plan, Dunne found himself sitting next to Lassen's brother. When the meal was over, Dunne introduced Lassen to Stephenson. Both burst into tears.

Moynihan holidayed with the Jellicoes at Reintraid, bumping down the steeply descending, stony track in a beaten up, brake-less, Land-Rover. Jellicoe was fond of Moynihan and when he took a girlfriend about whom he was potentially serious to stay at Tidcombe, it was definitely thumbs down. Moynihan resolved *not* to take the girl he eventually married to stay with the Jellicoes until *after* the wedding.[21]

Jellicoe stood down as Chairman of Tate & Lyle in 1983. On retirement, the chairman has his portrait painted – it comes with the rations. Jellicoe sat for Derek Hill, who paid frequent visits to Tidcombe but spent more time taking the Jellicoes out to local restaurants than he did painting his sitter. The result was a disaster, portraying Jellicoe in an open-necked shirt and five o'clock shadow looking as though he'd just tossed a hand-grenade. Tate & Lyle declared the portrait unsuitable for their boardroom. Philippa came to the rescue with an elaborate scheme to have the portrait unveiled at the Jellicoe's flat in Onslow Square while the Tate & Lyle premises were being decorated. It worked and the artist never discovered that his work would not hang at Tate & Lyle.[22] At about this time, Jellicoe had a son with Sara Harrity, whom he had known for many years. Jellicoe remained deeply attached to his son, David Lloyd, a charming and intelligent young man.

Within two years, Jellicoe became chairman of Davy Corporation, the largest international engineering contractor in the world, with Roger Kingdon as chief executive.[23] In 1977, Jellicoe accepted the chairmanship of the Council of King's College London. Times were hard for academia and Jellicoe helped Kings to bid for Government money.[24] In 1986, he established an annual book prize award under the aegis of the Anglo-Hellenic League, naming it in honour of his former tutor and long-serving League chairman, Sir Steven Runciman. Jellicoe also maintained his link with Trinity College, Cambridge, often attending the Annual Fellowship Dinner with Runciman, he in a very palatial room and Jellicoe in one the size of a lavatory. Runciman preferred dining with royalty; if possible, Balkan.

Jellicoe's family ties with Southampton remained strong.[25] In 1984, he took over from Eric Roll as Chancellor of the University of Southampton. Jellicoe saw to it that the Wellington archive moved to Southampton on a (very long) loan. He enjoyed conferring degrees, awarding an Honorary Fellowship to a kneeling Shackleton – the one exception to the rule that Jellicoe followed Shackleton in public offices. Jellicoe paid so much more attention to the young women graduating than the men that the Student Union sent a deputation to the Vice Chancellor, Sir Gordon Higginson, asking if he could ensure a better balance of the Chancellor's attention.

When money was needed for computers, Jellicoe with a team of seven, including Waldegrave, Baker, Gordon Higginson and Ernie Harrison, the chairman of the private sector communications company Racal, went to see the Prime Minister, Margaret Thatcher. It was the day of the Falklands invasion, so they did not expect to see her. However, she gave it her slightly bullying attention for an hour and half before excusing herself. Their success launched a whole Information Technology bandwagon, led by Baker.[26]

Apart from his Science Ministerial role, Jellicoe, a non-scientist, had pursued a successful overseas strategy for Davy, chaired several scientific forums and was a longstanding member and president of the Parliamentary and Scientific Committee.[27] So it was no surprise when in 1982 he was mooted as chairman of the Medical Research Council (MRC).

News filtered through from the Department of Education and Science to the MRC's Chief Executive, Sir James Gowans, that the Lord President of the Council was approaching Jellicoe. Jellicoe rang Gowans to discuss the offer and they met at Brooks's.

Gowans had spent twenty-nine years fiddling, as only a truly eminent scientist can, in a lab in Oxford. He had qualified as a doctor but studied in Oxford under Florey, who had turned an Alexander Fleming lab curiosity into penicillin during the war.[28] Jellicoe and Gowans sat in Brooks's foyer while Gowans talked about the MRC. But Jellicoe was not listening. He got out a miniscule diary and consulted it with an air of anxiety.

'Oh', thought Gowans. 'I've lost my audience already!'

'Oh dear,' said Jellicoe. 'I'm going to be in the most frightful mess now. I'm supposed to be seeing my mother-in-law!'

He then told Gowans all about Peggy. So Gowans learned a lot about her, not Jellicoe.[29] It was typical Jellicoe self-effacement.

The MRC has a sort of cachet that other research councils lack and Jellicoe accepted. Gowans would brief Jellicoe before Council meetings, in his Onslow Square flat at 8.30 am where champagne was served. Jellicoe chaired the Council's meetings, mastering difficult briefs and pulling out the key issues for discussion and decision. He was political without being party political, had an excellent sense of consensus and knew what to do if there wasn't any. An avid and assiduous reader with a seemingly insatiable appetite for medical knowledge, he also had a terrific sense of occasion and could enliven dry, technical discussions.[30]

At one Council meeting, he dealt with the preliminaries and the apologies but before turning to item 1 on the agenda, he announced, 'I'm just back from Bangkok. I've seen my quack (this to the eminent assembled practitioners) and the quack says I've got toxoplasmosis. What is it?' The whole of the Council looked at their boots. None of them could remember. One of the microbiologists eventually hazarded that it was some sort of parasitic disease. 'Aha!' said Jellicoe in triumph. 'You don't know, do you?'[31]

At the annual dinner of the Royal College of Surgeons, he rose to give the after dinner speech. 'I don't really know why I'm here,' he said, holding out his arms expansively. 'It reminds me,' he said, 'of an occasion after the war. General de Gaulle was due to give David Stirling and me our French gongs. As he came along the row towards me, with an aide carrying a velvet cushion with the medals, I realized that by the time it reached me it was going to be empty. When de Gaulle got to me, he said, "Monsieur, je regrette infiniment. Je n'ai rien pour vous."[32]

'I feel the same tonight!' said Jellicoe. 'I've got low back pain, high back pain, foot rot *and* I've got toxoplasmosis. And you don't know what that is, do you!'

But it was not all fun. In 1983, while staying with his daughter Zara near San Francisco, Jellicoe became aware of the horror of Aids.[33] Victims were dying in California while in the UK Aids was virtually unknown and neither the medical profession nor the Government was coordinating any coherent action. Jellicoe discovered that just three cases of Aids had been confirmed in the UK. There was no mention of it in the press.

He went to see Margaret Thatcher at No. 10 to persuade her to warn those at risk and make resources available to care for sufferers. It was very hard going. Aids was seen as limited to gay people and intravenous drug users and therefore not a risk to the heterosexual population. A wall of prejudice seemed set against Aids victims. Despite his cool reception by the Prime Minister, Jellicoe knew it was an important first step towards getting the ear of Government.

Gowans went off to warn Sir Keith Joseph, Secretary of State at the Department of Education and Science, of an impending disaster if nothing was done. It was so serious Gowans asked if the officials could leave the room. Joseph agreed. Gowans then explained how homosexuals contracted Aids. The description was, perforce, rather anatomical – it was hardly drawing room talk. A long silence ensued. Joseph was horrified and embarrassed. He buried his face in his hands and, gradually parting his fingers, peeped through them like one of Michelangelo's angels. Seizing the moment, Gowans emphasized that Joseph, as Secretary of

State, needed to know about the situation and that he – Gowans – as Chief Executive of the MRC, needed money for research. He also brought the Government's Chief Medical Officer, Sir Donald Acheson up to speed. Jellicoe later made a speech saying that most research was taking place in America (which it was) thereby annoying one or two small-scale UK Aids researchers.[34] Certainly in the early days, the Government was reluctant to coordinate, leaving it to a hotchpotch of Government departments and voluntary organizations to coordinate their own activities. Only later did the Government develop a concerted policy.[35]

Jellicoe's role was also to secure Government funding for the MRC. The Thatcher years were truly awful for the Research Councils. Under the notion of 'annuality', they had to bid every year, whereas the pace of science was from three to five years. There was no flexibility. HM Treasury said that the Councils must have 'priorities' – their favourite word. So Jellicoe and Gowans went to see Sir Keith Joseph to talk about their dire financial situation. Joseph was very close to Margaret Thatcher. Yet he seemed strangely vulnerable as Gowans outlined the situation, concluding, 'Really, Secretary of State, it's an awful mess financially'.

'Yes. I know,' was all Joseph could say. So Jellicoe decided that they must see the Prime Minister herself.

They met at No. 10, upstairs in one of the larger rooms. It was full of Cabinet Ministers, including Tebbit, Fowler and Kenneth Clarke. The whole thing was rather like a mini theatre performance with rows of straight-backed seats and a stage set with chairs for the key actors. Eventually, the curtain rose and the performance began. Gowans and Thatcher had met before and she immediately pounced on him. 'Ah, yes,' she said. 'You're the man who gave monoclonal antibodies to the Americans aren't you?' Gowans was immediately overawed, only realizing later that he had not: the work had been published in 1975 whereas he had only gone to the MRC in 1977. This was the effect she had on people.[36]

Thatcher then said something like, 'Why are you here?' Jellicoe launched into a grand introduction. 'Prime Minister,' he began. 'The House of Lords Science and Technology Committee has been making a detailed study of the Science Base and is deeply concerned about our capacity to maintain our academic excellence. The present funding limitations and current commitments ...'

But at this point the Prime Minister interrupted him. 'But George,' she said. 'The House of Lords is just a nuisance.'

Gowans, who had to produce the funding arguments, had boned up enormously. As if sensing this readiness to do battle, Thatcher got to the edge of her sofa. The most difficult thing in engaging her was her total lack of blink reflex. After several exchanges, she resorted to her Mrs Beeton approach to public policy. 'Dr Gowans', she said, 'if you want more money, you should be like a good housewife – save up!'

Gowans parried that there was no point because money could not be carried over from one financial year into the next. The Prime Minister, immediately on the defensive, wheeled around and said accusingly, 'But Defence always carries money over from one year to the next'. She fixed her eyes on some poor chap from the Ministry of Defence who looked as though he saw his career hanging in the balance before him. There was an almost palpable sense of the power she wielded through holding all their careers in the palm of her hand.

The meeting continued for an hour and a half, during which Gowans and Thatcher interrupted each other to the point of rudeness. He thought her the world's greatest interrupter, so that it was impossible to carry on a logical dialogue. At one point, Gowans told her she was talking nonsense and from the expression on the face of Robin Nicholson, the Chief Scientist, thought that he might have gone too far.[37]

When the meeting drew to a close, the atmosphere mellowed slightly. Talking through her smile, the Prime Minister said that she really appreciated all the wonderful work that the Medical Research Council did. One day, when the UK was a rich country, they would be able to do much more. Gowans thought it was the other way round – when the UK did more research it would be a much richer country. Afterwards, he felt he could have done better. So he was surprised and touched to receive a handwritten note from Jellicoe in Greece full of holiday news but also thanks for his contribution.[38]

The Aids battle continued. After six months, Jellicoe saw Margaret Thatcher again. The Government had finally got the wind up. Since their first meeting, news had reached the UK that Aids could affect heterosexual people too. Some time in 1984, the British High Commissioner in Zambia had sent a dispatch with the evidence. Robert Armstrong immediately sent it to Acheson. They swiftly advised the Prime Minster that unless something was done the consequences might be disastrous.[39] Whatever the reason, when Jellicoe saw the Prime Minister again, she was much more disposed towards taking action. With a General Election on the horizon, she needed to avoid giving any impression that the Government was prejudiced against Aids sufferers.[40]

Gowans went to give evidence to the Cabinet Committee on Aids in one of the Lords' committee rooms. When he emerged, Jellicoe was outside. 'Come on,' he said. 'We're going to see Willie'. Jellicoe wanted money for MRC research. Whitelaw was surprisingly forceful, unlike his television appearances and his chairmanship of the Cabinet Committee where he had been quite avuncular. There were three men in that room and Gowans (at six feet five inches tall) felt himself to be the little man. Whitelaw was upfront. 'Gowans,' he said, 'you'll get your money for Aids research, unless those buggers at the Treasury cock it up'. Then he added, somewhat haggard-faced, 'But you know it is *frightfully* difficult talking to Margaret about condoms'.[41]

Finally, the Government ran a powerful national media campaign with two hard-hitting TV advertisements featuring falling tombstones and condoms. It was criticized for being in poor taste but it raised awareness of Aids overnight. At the meeting to approve the TV ads, Armstrong noticed that the blows of the chisel carving the letters AIDS on the tombstone were falling in time with the tune of the Catholic hymn *Dies Re* from the Mozart and Verdi requiems about divine judgment. He pointed out that this might send entirely the wrong message but he was overruled on the grounds that he would probably be the only one who knew the hymn.

231

The UK went on to have the smallest increase in Aids of any major European country. Jellicoe joined the Aids Trust led by Margaret Jay[42] and supported the work of the voluntary organizations.[43] He was after all the original architect of the partnership between them and Government. Diana, Princess of Wales, was among the first to respond. She showed a genuine interest in the MRC's work and Jellicoe accompanied her to visit Aids patients. It was extraordinarily moving as she let them see her heart for them without embarrassment or focusing attention on herself. Her ability to listen revealed a remarkable touch at a time when the disease was seen as certain death.[44]

On 28 June 1988, the Royal Society made Jellicoe, a non-scientist a Fellow. Samuel Pepys, Eddie Shackleton and Margaret Thatcher are others.[45] In 1983, Jellicoe became chairman of the British Overseas Trade Board. Promoting British exports was hard and unrewarding work (exporters are usually ungrateful and importers wonder why they are being importuned). The Foreign Office and DTI squabble over the way work and money are divided (these rows date back to 1870 at least and continue today – one of the longest running bureaucratic turf battles anywhere). So it was a slightly thankless task. He inherited The Duke of Kent as his vice chairman and before long had roped in Nigel Thompson.[46]

BOTB seminars were something of an art form. On one occasion, just after lunch, during the Mogadon slot, the lights were dimmed so that those still awake could see the slides. Jellicoe, who was sitting between the Duke of Kent and Thompson, appeared fast asleep. HRH and Thompson exchanged glances, as if to say, 'What do we do now?' Just as the speaker was going into his winding up spiel, the slumbering Jellicoe suddenly opened his eyes and fired off a series of penetrating questions.[47] On another occasion, he dozed off *after* asking a question and in December 1984 was pictured in *The Times*, apparently having a nap while Mikhail Gorbachev was making a speech at a major lunch at the Savoy Hotel. Gorbachev seemed not to notice the somnolent Earl, or if he did, made no comment. Jellicoe then got up and delivered a polished response.[48]

In early 1983, Jellicoe appointed a new BOTB Chief Executive, Christopher Roberts.[49] He sent for Roberts, who was responsible for international civil aviation, ostensibly to discuss how one could best fly from West to East Africa. Their conversation ranged all over the place while Jellicoe weighed up the unwitting candidate. Roberts got the job.[50]

The BOTB was in its heyday. It had been set up early on in the Heath administration on the basis that *business* would run the export promotions campaigns. Jellicoe did not need much contact with DTI Ministers Cockfield and Channon. He seemed to expect everyone to love him and most of the time they did. He was still very open, probably too much for his own good.[51]

Howard Fisher, the DTI's Exports Director for the south-east region, organized Jellicoe's factory visits, mainly to promote the BOTB's services to business and to give him a feel for export problems. Jellicoe was amenable as long as boring visits were leavened with more interesting ones – like Aston Martin at Milton Keynes. Milton Keynes was still new, with empty glass-walled office blocks set among leafy trees, soft landscapes and roads that petered out into fields. At the Milton Keynes Development Authority, Jellicoe was welcomed by a large gathering of architects and engineering executives, presided over by Lord Chilver. Presentations were followed by fulsome speeches praising Milton Keynes. Jellicoe was bored. 'Right,' he said. 'Which one of you buggers lives here?' There was an awkward pause. None of them did.

In summer 1985, Jellicoe went to Rome to visit Fiat and meet Agnelli. British Leyland's distributor in Rome provided a fleet of Rover 3.5 litres to take Jellicoe and his party around in style. But Leyland had been slow off the mark as far as diesel was concerned so the cars all had Italian engines. Jellicoe took with him some British businessmen, including a self-made businessman in engineering from the West Midlands.

While they were being driven from Rome airport to their hotel, Jellicoe sought to break the ice with the West Midlands man.

'Ah', he said. 'Is that a Guards tie you're wearing?'

'I don't really know,' said West Midlands man. 'I've got them all'. Silence in the back of the car. Then Jellicoe roared with

233

laughter. After that Jellicoe and West Midlands man got on famously.

Next morning, after visiting Fiat in one of the hybrid cars, a Bedford brewer called John Wells took Jellicoe to a beer trade festival in Milan. Wells had been making inroads with a *Biero Rosso* while another firm had been doing well with brewed lager. Jellicoe had just settled down with a glass of wine when Fisher dragged the British brewer with his prized ale over to Jellicoe.

'Do taste this beer sir,' said Fisher. 'It's doing very well here.'

'Yuk', replied Jellicoe, making a face. 'Never touch the stuff.' Bang went the planned photo shoot. There were limits to what Jellicoe would do for British overseas trade.[52]

In November 1985, he made a high profile visit to Iraq, attending the 22nd Baghdad International Trade Fair. Iraq was at war with Iran. Britain was not supplying arms or any goods that could be used to prolong or exacerbate the war but the British ambassador at Teheran, Sir Terence Clark, wanted to revive Britain's wider commercial interests. But British Ministers were afraid to visit. Jellicoe filled this gap, despite the fact that Ba'ath Party Ministers were not easy to deal with.[53]

Jellicoe met Taha Yassin Ramadhan, Saddam Hussein's powerful Deputy Prime Minister.[54] After the Iraq war in 2003 Ramadhan became the Ten of Diamonds in the coalition pack of cards issued to American soldiers to familiarize them with the wanted men. US forces captured him at Mosul on 19 August.[55]

In 1987, after standing down from the BOTB,[56] Jellicoe became chairman of Davy Corporation and chairman of the East European Trade Council (EETC). Its director, James McNeish,[57] a swashbuckling ex-army officer in the Royal Ulster Rifles, 'had a very good leg for a boot'.[58] They travelled to Russia, Mongolia, Poland, Bulgaria, Hungary, Czechoslovakia and the German Democratic Republic. Occasionally Jellicoe left things behind. Once they rushed back for a forgotten briefcase. At Onslow Square, they had difficulty getting past police cordons because of a suspicious briefcase outside number 97.

In the East German Republic, Jellicoe was a hit at the Leica camera factory near Leipzig, where he spoke in German. At the Cecilienhof, where the Potsdam Treaty had been signed and he had stayed with the Crown Prince and Fritzi, their guide was an awful little East German with sandals, an anorak and goatee beard. 'Wonders of Stalin, Churchill thrown out . . .' he intoned. The visitors stood looking mutinous and Jellicoe said, 'Bloody Russians! Show us the Crown Princess's study. It was always done up like a transatlantic liner.'

At the Leipzig Fair, in a meeting with the Industry Ministry, one official was very rude about Davy, saying, 'You didn't come back to us . . .' at which Jellicoe declared, 'Well. If Herr Schmidt would be kind enough to let me finish, any outstanding answers will be delivered to him first thing tomorrow morning.' They were. The Ministry had received the answer six months before.

At the Moscow trade fair Jellicoe bumped into Margaret Thatcher, who had taken four or five senior businessmen all hoping to get contracts. She came back to the embassy with the ambassador, Bryan Cartledge, and said to the magnates, which included Sir Norman Wooding, then representing Courtaulds, 'Well, you gentlemen will have to sharpen your pencils. You'll have to match the Germans' prices'.

'For goodness' sake Maggie,' Jellicoe retorted, 'stick to what you know'. At this, she became kittenish and said, 'Well, what do we do then?'

The Jellicoes went to China with Daisy, who was learning Chinese. A Chinese official practising his English asked Jellicoe how much he earned. Jellicoe told him and the chap was totally crushed. Daisy was absolutely furious.

The Gobi desert was freezing cold at night. One icy pass with freezing streams presented a crossing problem. They waded through the stream after Jellicoe who then did starbursts. His feat was only surpassed by the wife of the Swedish ambassador who must have had the blood of Gustavus Adolphus flowing in her veins as she hitched up her mini skirt and waded through the floating ice.

They went to Bulgaria for a skiing weekend and promoted the MRC at the same time. Their guide at Borovetz was a cardiologist who ran his stethoscope over the Bulgarian leadership once a week and smoked a villainous pipe. No slogging up the slopes for him. He went up in a tracked vehicle.[59]

235

In 1992, the impending launch of the European Single Market and the chill wind of competition meant that companies needed help. A new company called European Capital, providing independent and confidential financial advice, made Jellicoe their chairman.[60]

Jellicoe and one of the directors, Andrew Winckler, dined with Bertie Denham, who was about to retire as Lords Chief Whip. Denham wrote novels about foxhunting and took snuff during meals. They shared a taxi home and as they jogged along, Jellicoe said in the dark back of the cab, 'How's the Government doing then Bertie?'

'Very well of course,' replied Denham.

'Aren't the country getting a bit tired of this lot?' said Jellicoe.

'Actually,' said Denham, 'that's exactly what I said to the PM – and that's why I'm retiring!'[61]

In March 1982, after initial hesitation, Jellicoe agreed to review the Prevention of Terrorism Act 1976. He hesitated. Eddie Shackleton had reviewed it just three years before. With the job came the role of Secretary to the Cabinet's Anti-Terrorism Committee.[62]

Jellicoe began with the police. Metropolitan Police Special Branch officers briefed him at Scotland Yard and while staying with Whitelaw, Secretary of State in Northern Ireland, he interviewed inmates at the Maze prison. He talked to political leaders, including the Reverend Ian Paisley. He examined controls at Heathrow, Gatwick and other airports, and how well the legislation worked at ports with direct air or sea links with Northern Ireland.[63] He looked at anti-terrorism arrangements in Germany and France, both countries with considerable experience of the problem, and examined detention conditions.[64]

After nine months, Jellicoe was convinced of the continuing need for the legislation. The most notable trend in the UK had been the increasing threat posed by *international* terrorism.[65] The 1980 Iranian Embassy siege, the 1982 hijacking of a Tanzanian airliner at Stansted Airport and the June 1982 attempted murder of the Israeli ambassador were by no means the only incidents. Since 1978, mainland police had dealt with as many acts of terrorism *un*related to Northern Ireland as acts related to

Republican or Loyalist causes. Jellicoe pointed out that the *number* of incidents was only a very approximate measure of terrorist threat, which took no account of the scale or seriousness of each event. Acts of terrorism carried out by groups associated with the Middle East had led to fewer casualties than those perpetrated by the Provisionals *but* 'one should not underestimate the seriousness of the international terrorist threat in the UK'. It was a prescient conclusion.[66] Thus he drew attention to the need for a fundamental change of focus on the preventive measures needed to protect the country. On the administrative side, he suggested improvements to the technical workings of the Act.[67] As a result, Jellicoe became an IRA target and had special protection – and automatic outside lighting fitted at Tidcombe.

After resigning as Leader of the Lords, Jellicoe had seldom attended but still pushed for its reform.[68] On 14 February 1990, the Lords passed a motion to have a select committee to scrutinize all Bills.[69] Introducing the report, Jellicoe began, 'My Lords, I remain in my simple, hereditary way as I was back in 1968, a Reformer at heart ...'.[70]

The House appointed a committee to review its own select committee work with Jellicoe as chair and Michael Pownall, the Clerk of Committees in the Lords, as secretary. It became known as the 'committee on committees'. Jellicoe suggested that it could look at the existing Lords committees, consider their reform and extension and compare them with those of the Commons.

Jellicoe was popular and able, so the committee members felt they would be associated with success – a key Jellicoe leadership factor. And he was fun. In January 1992 he took a delegation of members to Brussels to discover what the EU Institutions thought of the Lords' reports on the EU and to see Jacques Delors, President of the European Commission. That night in the freezing Gran' Place in Brussels, Jellicoe looked up at a familiar looking building and realized that he had lived there in the 1950s.

Jellicoe's committee recommended that a permanent committee should scrutinize all bills to ensure that the delegated powers sought by ministers were appropriate and subject to the right degree of parliamentary approval. The result was the Delegated Powers Committee. It has been very successful. High powered and effective, its recommendations are almost always accepted on the floor of the House. Its teeth come by way of a provision known as a 'Henry VIII clause'. Put simply, this means the power to change primary legislation by passing secondary legislation. Such clauses give enormous power to the executive and the House is generally wary of agreeing them. These improvements increased the standing of the House of Lords.

Jellicoe's association with Greece remained important. It had begun with the sort of Byronic romantic attitude that some Englishmen have for Greece. But from the moment in 1942 when he first saw Crete through the submarine viewfinder during the SAS raid and risked his life fighting for its people, his love had become steadfast.[71] He had led a powerful Trade Mission to Greece and was made a Freeman of Athens.[72]

He went to extraordinary lengths to help his Greek causes. In 1987, he rang William Waldegrave. 'How would you like to give the Onassis Lecture on the Environment in Athens?' Waldegrave declined. Within ten minutes, Jellicoe was back on the phone. 'How would you like to give the Onassis Lecture on the Environment in Athens *and* spend the weekend with Paddy Leigh Fermor?' Waldegrave accepted – a good example of how Jellicoe achieves his objectives.

Jellicoe had never talked about the war. But as the Waldegraves and the Jellicoes drove from Athens to Leigh Fermor's house in the Mani, he described the momentous advance through the Peloponnese to Athens. Leigh Fermor had demijohns of retsina and for the next thirty-six hours they heard the story of the Dodecanese Campaign.[73]

Of all Jellicoe's Greek friendships, the one with Christodoulos Tsigantes, Commander of the Greek Sacred Squadron, was perhaps the most special. After the war, they lost touch but years later met again by chance at Athens Airport. Tsigantes took the Jellicoes on a ten-day trip in a beautiful schooner, round the Peloponnese. Calling in on Leigh Fermor, who had just started building his house, Jellicoe jumped overboard and swam ashore.[74]

As President of the SAS Regimental Association from 1993, Jellicoe actively refreshed relationships with the French, the Greeks and the Belgians, which over time had tended to become a little distant. He went to every funeral of the old and bold, comforted their families and encouraged remaining wartime members of special forces.[75] As chairman of the Crete Veterans Association, he went with Mather and Hastings to the Dodecanese Islands and Crete in April 1998. He and Leigh Fermor attended the packed 50th and 60th Anniversaries presided over by the Duke of Kent[76] while he made two trips to Rhodes with Sutherland, including in 2001 the major official commemoration of the fiftieth anniversary of its liberation.

Jellicoe was active on Greece's behalf in England too. In 1978, he became chairman of the Anglo-Hellenic League. Steven Runciman had been its chairman for many years while its vice chair, Katie Lentakis, had been in the Greek underground movement in occupied Athens and had seen Jellicoe liberate Athens on his bicycle. The outgoing chairman, Sir Robin Hooper, told its secretary, Nan White-Gaze that his replacement was Jellicoe.

'Will I like him?' she asked. Hooper's wife immediately perked up and said, 'Oh yes. You'll like him!'[77]

When Jellicoe took over, White-Gaze thought she had died and gone to heaven. When she had a real problem, she would ring up Jellicoe at Tate & Lyle. 'Right,' he would say, 'I'll send the car round.' Once she told him they were being turned out of their premises. 'Never mind darling,' he said and the problem was sorted. If a crisis occurred in the afternoon, he would have her taken to the Lords where they would resolve it over tea – or champagne.

Jellicoe persuaded Prince Michael of Kent to be a patron. In 1992 he unveiled a plaque in the thronged St Sophia Greek Cathedral in Moscow Road, in memory of the Greeks and Allies who fell in the Second World War. Jellicoe had Lassen in his mind.

When Jellicoe retired, saying it was time to rotate the crops, he was close to tears at his farewell party when Lentakis presented him with a miniature bicycle and some personal letters she had found between King George V and Admiral Jellicoe.[78] His friendship once pledged is forever.[79] By now Jellicoe was heaped with Greek honours.[80]

Tsigantes frequently stayed at Tidcombe, still a larger than life character. One evening, he sat on the sofa next to a very attractive woman, smoking his big cigar. When the Jellicoes left the room, overcome by his Greek passion, Tsigantes moved to embrace her. She remonstrated vigorously and in the fracas the cigar set the sofa ablaze. The Jellicoes rushed in to find Tsigantes beating out flames.[81]

When Tsigantes became ill, Jellicoe visited him in hospital. He asked Jellicoe to promise that as long as the Greek colonels who had taken over Government in Greece were in power he – Tsigantes – would not be buried in his beloved Greece but in St Michael's churchyard at Tidcombe. When Jellicoe visited Tsigantes at the London Clinic, the night before he died, he reminded Jellicoe of the promise. So Tsigantes was buried in the tiny English churchyard. The Greek ambassador and the Greek archbishop were present as the Commander of the third Greek Sacred Squadron was laid to rest. When the Colonels' day was over, Jellicoe saw to it that Tsigantes was reburied in Athens.[82] Another major service was held at St Michael's. The new Greek President, Balasteros, sent a Dakota with half a platoon of Evzones and other dignitaries. The sight of the Evzones in an English country village etched itself vividly onto Jellicoe's memory. The headstone to Tsigantes still stands in that Wiltshire churchyard, a bit of England that will be forever Greece.[83]

Three main activities kept Jellicoe busy in his later years: the SAS Regimental Association; helping to launch Hakluyt, a secret commercial intelligence company; and the Royal Geographical Society.

In 1992, the SAS's founder David Stirling died. He and Jellicoe had remained close, always attending SAS reunions and reunions with Allied Special Forces in France. At his memorial service in the Guards Chapel, Fitzroy Maclean gave the address. Snow was falling softly through the bitter winter gloom and the chapel was packed. Then, a whisper, barely perceptible at first, rippled round the congregation that something had happened. The IRA had landed a bomb in the gardens of No. 10 Downing Street.

Jellicoe often visited Belgian, British and French special forces at Sennecy-le-Grand in Burgundy and saw as much as possible of

Georges Bergé. In 1994, they paraded together up the Champs Elysées to the Arc de Triomphe in the French celebrations for the fiftieth anniversary of the Normandy landings and had dinner with Jacques Chirac, then Mayor of Paris.

In 1995, Jellicoe helped to found Hakluyt – an intriguing enterprise run by an ex-SAS and MI6 officer, Christopher James. The firm was named after Richard Hakluyt, a 1580s priest in charge of Christchurch, Oxford, who became secretary to the British ambassador to France and was in the pay of Francis Walsingham, Britain's first Head of Intelligence. He was 'the secret man, seated in the dark corner, who is content to listen and remember'.[84] The company aimed to provide political intelligence for commercial ends on the basis that knowledge of local politics and personalities often matters more to a business than information about markets and economies.[85] Hakluyt's first chairman, Fitzroy Maclean, asked Jellicoe to join quarterly meetings to plan the company. Jellicoe accepted, but without remuneration.[86]

At one meeting, somebody suggested working in the US. There was a pause and then Jellicoe said, 'Let's get England done first'. Everyone listened – and agreed. Everything was done through personal contacts: there were no websites, mail shots, or cold calls. Jellicoe spoke to people he knew; doors opened and people listened. Henry Kissinger became a strategic partner. The firm went on to become masters of the great game in a commercial setting. By 2002 it had provided intelligence for over 25 per cent of the FTSE 100 companies and more than a dozen major US and European clients.

In June 1993 Jellicoe began a four-year stint as president of the Royal Geographical Society (RGS).[87] He helped merge it with the Institute of British Geographers, saw off a threat to the merger, appointed its first woman director, Dr Rita Gardner, and produced its first Strategic Plan. His presidency was one of the most important commitments of his life.

Gradually, friends with health less robust than his began to slip away. In summer 1994, Shackleton was far from well. Jellicoe visited him and his wife frequently in the country. On 22 September, Shackleton died and Jellicoe gave the address at

241

the memorial service in Westminster Abbey. He was not his usual confident self, turning over two pages together and momentarily losing his place.[88] He paid tribute to Shackleton's achievements, particularly his Leadership of the Lords, Fellowship of the Royal Society, presidency of the Royal Geographical Society, his contribution to reform of the Civil Service and his constant joking about Jellicoe always following him in various jobs.[89] Most of all, Jellicoe saluted his appointment to the Order of the Garter. After the ceremony at Windsor, Shackleton had arrived at Tidcombe wearing the Garter; all weekend it had held pride of place in their drawing room.[90]

In 1997, Jellicoe was diagnosed with prostate cancer. However, as Roy Jenkins said, 'You would never know because he never talks about himself'. He has kept it at bay. Patsy too has become a friend again and they meet from time to time. The three cavaliers of the 1941 desert war – Mather, Hastings and Jellicoe – were inseparable.

Tidcombe remains the focus for family and friends. The house has brought great pleasure to all seven children and now nine grandchildren. Apart from the trees framing the view from the front of the house, up the sweep of lawns to the hills beyond, only St Michael's church breaks the skyline. Just over the churchyard wall, Tsigantes's headstone is lichen-covered but the inscription is still legible. The Hunts have now been looking after the Jellicoes for forty-five years and are very much part of the family. They say they could not ask for better employers. Jellicoe sends them postcards even when he goes abroad for a weekend.[91]

Parliamentary life still plays a major role. Jellicoe remains in favour of Lords reform but feels it a great pity that the Government embarked on reform without really knowing where they wanted to go. He does not want to see an entirely elected House of Lords, resulting in the wrong kind of equality, favouring instead a partly elected House based very much on the regions.[92]

When the 1997 Labour Government decided that hereditary peers were to be abolished, Jellicoe was invited to put his name forward to be voted on as a life peer. He was on holiday in France with Philippa but would not have stood anyway. As an

242

ex-Leader of the House, he was made a life peer and continues to sit regularly. He remains strongly pro-Europe, still hoping that in the future, without committing ourselves to a totally federal Europe, Britain will play a leading role.[93]

When Parliament is sitting, the Jellicoes are usually in London from Tuesday to Thursday. At eighty-seven, he thinks nothing of driving up and down to London at the crack of dawn, from March to October taking a dip in the pool at Tidcombe before he goes. He is not remotely interested in writing but he reads a lot.[94] His keen interest in the Lords will keep him attending. His position there, as the longest sitting member since 1939, is another reason. Except that the House of Lords does not have quite the same concept as the House of Commons, he is the Father of the House.

Recognition has been slow – Jellicoe remains his unassuming self. He was born into privilege but has been a driving force for the underprivileged and for reform. He was utterly changed by the loss of his father at seventeen – and by the war – but the impact of these two events probably gave him the sympathy without which he would not have been in touch with himself and the issues he knew really mattered. It helped him to win the trust of soldiers and of Sultans; to liberate Patras and Athens but to keep order and save many lives; to lead the House of Lords, yet to lead the miners back to work after the bitter winter strikes of 1972; and to forge a real and lasting partnership between Government and voluntary organizations. His discretion and judgment admitted him to the secret club of the intelligence services. He is one of England's last great military commanders, statesmen and gentlemen.

He has been courageous in supporting controversial issues – his international outlook, particularly on Europe, has occasionally been too much for some members of his own political party and he took a risk with his early stance on Aids – but his loyalty, once pledged, is forever. A great supporter of women in public life, his Achilles' heel was a weakness in his personal dealings with them. It led him to two turning points in his life and two resignations – from the Foreign Office and from the Cabinet – but he faced them bravely and recovered quickly. There are streaks of ruthlessness and remorse: he never suffers fools gladly and, over the divorce and his resignation from Cabinet, he hurt both his wives.

Always Jellicoe has been full of intellectual vigour, full of fun and yet concerned to do what is right. But there is an inner Jellicoe we do not know: perhaps having such able parents and older sisters caused him to hold himself in check. We seldom know what he is thinking, or about his feelings, worries or fears if any. Had it not been for the resignation, would he have gone on to higher things in politics? If he had been asked, he would probably have accepted.

Still Jellicoe does not talk about himself. In November 2003, he went to Alexandria and Washington to receive from the US World War II Veterans Association the Sir Winston Churchill Allied Nations Award 'for noteworthy contribution to the success of the Allied victory in World War II'. It is awarded annually to one non-US citizen and Jellicoe is the second recipient. I found out about it quite by accident when I noticed a new award on the sideboard at Tidcombe.

Just inside the peers' entrance to the right, in the cloakroom, Jellicoe has a coat peg with his name on it. When making his way to the Chamber, he frequently decides to go up the steep stairs, despite his troublesome knees. Rounding the bend half way up, the first thing that meets his eye is his father. High up, above the stairs, is a small stained-glass window dedicated to him,[95] inscribed:

John, Earl Jellicoe
1918
Admiral of the Fleet.

There is for the son still 'more sadness than pride', bridging the gap of years. His father 'was a foundation on which to build, a comfort and a conscience'.[96] He is still the only single individual ever to hold the nation's future entirely in his hands. He delivered.

The son has done no less with what was entrusted to him. And had a great deal of fun doing it.

Notes on Sources

Chapter One: A Young Man's Fancy

1 He had retreated and established his main supply base at Tripoli.
2 Admiral of the Fleet Earl Jellicoe of Scapa and Commander-in-Chief, Grand Fleet.
3 Interview Lord Jellicoe, St George's Day, 23 April 2002, hereafter interview GPJRJ.
4 *The Times Atlas of the Second World War*, Times Books, 1989, p. 80.
5 Interview GPJRJ.
6 Who almost became the Duchess of Wellington. Interview GPJRJ.
7 His father, the Kaiser, was by now in Holland. Fritzi later married Lady Brigid Guinness while an exile in England during the war. After the war, he returned to Germany and drowned himself in the River Rhine.
8 Robert Rhodes James (ed.), *Chips: The Diaries of Sir Henry Channon*, Weidenfeld & Nicolson, 1967; Penguin, 1984, p. 137.
9 Interview GPJRJ. At this time Jellicoe also got to know Alan Phipps, son of the Ambassador Sir Eric Phipps, who was later killed in action on the Greek island of Leros.
10 Ibid.
11 She had other qualities too, being later lucky to survive after acting as a runner in the Hitler bomb plot of 20 July 1944. She and Cécile both married Americans. Christa became, and at time of writing still is, Mrs Hamilton Fish Armstrong of New York. Both ladies came to see Jellicoe in 1949 when he was in his second year in the British Embassy, Washington. He last met them when he was in Baghdad.
12 Interview GPJRJ.
13 Richard Hilary, *The Last Enemy*, Macmillan, London, 1942, p. 53.
14 Sir Carol Mather, MC, who later joined the Welsh Guards and served with Jellicoe in the Ski Battalion, No. 8 Guards Commando and the SAS, remained a life-long friend.
15 They were together two days before Runciman died in 1998.
16 Martin had been the inspiration for the lead character in *French Without Tears*, but Jellicoe found him rather demanding.
17 Interview GPJRJ.
18 'Coming out' had a very different meaning from that of today and meant the launching of a young lady into adult society.
19 Diary of GPJRJ, Monday, 3 July 1939.
20 Diary of GPJRJ, Thursday, 27 September 1939.
21 Diary of GPJRJ, Monday, 1 May 1939.
22 The Parliamentary Debates (Hansard) Official Report, Session 1938/39, Volume CXIV, Column 455.
23 As heir to an hereditary title he was allowed to sit on the steps of the throne to learn what went on.
24 Who Debo eventually married.
25 Diary of GPJRJ, Monday, 21 August 1939.
26 Diary of GPJRJ, Saturday, 26 August 1939.
27 Joe Wingfield, his sister Norah's future husband.
28 Diary of GPJRJ, Thursday, 31 August 1939.

29 Diary of GPJRJ, Friday, 1 September 1939.
30 Air Raid Precautions.
31 Diary of GPJRJ, 3 September 1939.
32 Diary of GPJRJ, 4 September 1939 and interview GPJRJ.
33 Diary of GPJRJ, 4 September 1939.
34 Diary of GPJRJ, 5 September 1939.
35 Ibid.
36 Diary of GPJRJ, 7 September 1939.
37 Diary of GPJRJ, 11–14 September 1939.
38 Diary of GPJRJ, 20 September 1939.
39 GPJRJ's underlining.
40 Diary of GPJRJ, 23 September 1939.
41 Interview GPJRJ.
42 Diary of GPJRJ, 26–27 September 1939.
43 MOD letter Ref DR2b/0237622-1/HEO dated 29/05/2002.
44 This entry is recorded on a blank page in GPJRJ's 1939 diary.
45 Interview GPJRJ.
46 Carol Mather, *When the Grass Stops Growing: a War Memoir*, Pen & Sword Books Ltd., Barnsley, 1997, p. 4.
47 Some of the volunteers were civilian expert skiers who had never even been in the armed forces before. Mather, op. cit. p. 6.
48 They had met very briefly at Cambridge before Stirling went mountaineering in the United States.
49 There were few non-commissioned officers or private soldiers at that time who had had the opportunity to learn to ski so the ranks had to be filled by officers who temporarily laid aside their commissions.
50 Interview GPJRJ.
51 Ibid.
52 Mather, pp. 10–12.
53 Mather, p. 15.
54 Mark Howard had joined the Coldstream Guards and probably because of this connection Jellicoe was commissioned into it.
55 MOD letter Ref DR2b/0237622-1/HEO dated 29/05/2002.
56 *The Times Atlas of the Second World War*, Times Books, 1989, p. 110. Eleven Commando units were formed within two months, each consisting of 500 volunteers.
57 Interview GPJRJ and MOD letter Ref DR2b/0237622-1/HEO dated 29/05/2002.
58 See also Lorna Almonds Windmill, *Gentleman Jim: The Wartime Story of a Founder of the SAS and Special Forces*, Constable & Robinson, London, 2002. Major 'Gentleman Jim' Almonds is the author's father. Jellicoe was to meet up with him and Riley again some sixteen months later when he joined the SAS. Together with two other men from 2 Troop, Bob Lilley and Jim Blakeney, Almonds and Riley had by then become known as the 'Tobruk Four'. Interviews GPJRJ and Major 'Gentleman Jim' Almonds, MM and Bar, Croix de Guerre, 7 December 2002.
59 Interview Major 'Gentleman Jim' Almonds, MM and Bar, Croix de Guerre, 7 December 2002.
60 But later on the training proved its worth in Italy when Almonds was on the run for thirty-two days in enemy territory as an escaping POW. It almost certainly helped to save his life. Interview Major 'Gentleman Jim' Almonds, MM and Bar, Croix de Guerre, 7 December 2002.
61 Note by Major 'Gentleman Jim' Almonds, MM and Bar, Croix de Guerre, written in 1945, author's possession.
62 PRO WO218/170. In 1917, Keyes had sent the *Vindictive* to Ostend, where her volunteer crew sank the ship across the harbour entrance, curtailing most German U-boat operations in Dover Command waters.
63 Later on he belied that particular nickname. Interview GPJRJ.
64 Dunne and his comrades were a generation older than Jellicoe and were part of the 'Whites Club group'. They were rather hedonistic – Dunne later said that he had found Jellicoe 'rather serious'.
65 Interview GPJRJ.
66 Wartime diary of Major 'Gentleman Jim' Almonds, MM and Bar, Croix de Guerre, 29 February 1941, author's possession.
67 South African Prime Minister and British Field Marshal. Jellicoe's father had known Smuts; the three had lunched together not long before John Jellicoe died. Interview GPJRJ.
68 Wartime diary of Major 'Gentleman Jim' Almonds, MM and Bar, Croix de Guerre, 19 May 1941.
69 On shore, at Halfya and Sollum, the 7th Armoured Division and 22 Guards Brigade were counterattacking Rommel's forces. The Allies were slowly retaking ground but the outcome was by no means certain. *Gentleman Jim*, p. 42.
70 See front jacket cover.

71 Mather, pp. 45–8.
72 Interview Sir Carol Mather, 29 June 2002.
73 This rather unpromising beginning for the future Commander of the Special Boat Squadron seems to have done nothing to dampen Jellicoe's enthusiasm for special boat operations. Interview GPJRJ.
74 Some years later, in about 1954 or 1955, there came an agonized cry from the caretaker of the contraband munitions. He was still in Alexandria, Nasser's police were searching foreign residents and what was he to do with this incriminating arsenal? Mather had some explaining to do as to why he, then an officer at the Guards Depot at Caterham, had a secret arms cache in Alexandria. Interview, Sir Carol Mather, 29 June 2002.
75 Loyd was a renowned leader of men. Sadly, he later became ill and died. Interview GPJRJ.
76 Interview GPJRJ.
77 MOD letter Ref DR2b/0237622-1/HEO dated 29/05/2002.
78 Brigadier Dudley Clarke, who was responsible for misinformation, had invented the imaginary First Special Air Service Brigade the previous September and persuaded David Stirling to name his initial small detachment of men accordingly.

Chapter Two: The Admiral's Son

1 Francis William Marten, CMG, MC, former Counsellor, Foreign and Commonwealth Office (always known as Tim).
2 Interview Tim Marten, 28 May 2002
3 Andrew Gordon, *The Rules of the Game: Jutland and British Naval Command*, John Murray (Publishers) Ltd, London, 1996. Interview Lord Waldegrave, 27 May 2002. The King and John Jellicoe certainly maintained a personal correspondence. Interview Nan White-Gaze, Secretary, The Anglo-Hellenic League, 5 June 2002.
4 Roy Jenkins, *Churchill*, Macmillan, London, 2001, p. 216.
5 Gordon, op. cit. Preface.
6 The Naval and Military Record, 9 April 1919. If Jellicoe had won an overwhelming victory, the Grand Fleet could have been disbanded and the men and resources used elsewhere in the Great War but the risks of losing far outweighed this possible advantage. The loss of life on both sides in achieving such a win would also have been horrific.
7 Which might be translated as 'brave heart' using a subsidiary meaning of 'joli' no longer in common usage.
8 Marrying wealthy and beautiful women seems to have been a Jellicoe family trait. Gwendoline Cayzer was also very well off when John Jellicoe married her. However, the Jellicoes seem at the same time also to have married for love.
9 Montagu Burrows, *The Family of Brocas of Beaurepaire and Roche Court: Hereditary Masters of the Royal Buckhounds with some account of the English Rule in Aquitaine,* Longman's Green & Co, London, 1886.
10 Shakespeare's Richard II, Act V, Scene VI, mentions 'the heads of Brocas'. The Brocas family owned lands from Eton to Winchester and there is a field at Eton which is still known as 'the Brocas'.
11 Admiral Sir Reginald Bacon, *The Life of John Rushworth, Earl Jellicoe*, Cassell & Co. Ltd, London, 1936, pp. 1–4.
12 John Winton, *Jellicoe*, Michael Joseph Ltd, London, 1981, p. 8.
13 Ibid. p. 9.
14 Also a Naval training ship.
15 Winton, op. cit. p. 51.
16 Letter from John Jellicoe to his mother, Tientsin, June 28 1900, Jellicoe papers at Tidcombe.
17 Interview GPJRJ.
18 While in this post, Jellicoe became acquainted with the deficiencies of armour and shell bursting power of British ships in comparison to those of the German Navy. Numerical superiority in terms of ships, which the Grand Fleet had at Jutland, was therefore crucial.
19 Admiral Sir R. H. Bacon, *The Life of John Rushworth Earl Jellicoe*, Cassell & Co. Ltd., London, 1936, p. 134.
20 Augustus Muir and Muir Davies, *A Victorian Shipowner*, Cayzer, Irvine and Company Limited, London, 1978, p. 29 ff.
21 The company eventually became Caledonia Investment plc, and then British and Commonwealth whose main business is now finance and administration.
22 Interview GPJRJ.
23 Bacon, op. cit. p. 152.
24 Winton, op. cit. p. 117.

25 Ibid., pp. 120–1.
26 'Prudy' was very competent. Had she been born later, she would have been very involved in public life. Interview GPJRJ.
27 Some have described it as more than prudence. Hankey's diary entry for 17 June 1916 says 'but Jellicoe is always rather a pessimist'. Stephen Roskill, *Hankey, Man of Secrets, Volume I 1877–1918*, Collins, London, 1970, p. 284.
28 Interview GPJRJ.
29 New Zealand's male population had been decimated by the First World War when it had lost more young men per head of population than Germany. The lack of a Wolf Cub pack might have been because there was no man available to lead one.
30 Interview GPJRJ.
31 Ibid.
32 He was not to return again until he went back to both the North and South Islands when he was Chairman of Davy Corporation in the late 1980s. Interview GPJRJ.
33 This problem began during the journey from New Zealand and only stopped completely when he went to University and had a room of his own.
34 Interview GPJRJ.
35 One of Lord Jellicoe's friends, Lord Selborne, who had been First Sea Lord in the latter part of the nineteenth century when Jellicoe was a senior officer at the Admiralty, was Warden of Winchester College. Tim Marten had gone to Winchester ahead of Jellicoe, who was known as Brocas, and was in Trant's House. Brocas was in Middle Part 3 of the college at three forms from the bottom, which was 'pretty good going' academically. Interviews Tim Marten, 28 May 2002 and Patrick McClure, Winchester College, September 2002.
36 Walker clearly also had a high regard for his pupil. He remained in touch, visiting the Jellicoes at their house in Wiltshire. On his death, he arranged for one or two favourite pupils, including the former Brocas, to be given the choice of some of his most cherished personal effects. Interview GPJRJ.
37 He continued to race competitively at Davos and Klosters up to the beginning of the Second World War.
38 Interviews GPJRJ and Patrick McClure, Winchester College, September 2002.
39 There were two Bird brothers in Freddies House; Edward, the elder, was killed in May 1940 serving with the 1st Battalion the Rifle Brigade in the defence of Calais. The younger brother, Tom, had a gallant war career and later became an architect.
40 The son of Field Marshal Wavell; he was killed in Kenya in the early 1950s. Pamela Wavell remained a lifelong friend.
41 Interview GPJRJ.
42 His maturity must also have been a factor in his handling of the situation. He was by now seventy-six.
43 Interview GPJRJ.
44 Ibid.
45 Lord Jellicoe's speaking engagement the following term at Winchester on the Royal Navy and the Battle of Jutland never happened, though his son fulfilled it many years later. Interview GPJRJ.
46 His mother's sister Constance had married Admiral Sir Charles Madden.
47 Interview GPJRJ.
48 Letter from Jellicoe to his cousin Elizabeth Madden, undated but written on the Thursday after his father's funeral. Tidcombe papers.

Chapter Three: The SAS Submarine

1 Interview GPJRJ.
2 Ibid.
3 Alan Hoe, *David Stirling: the Authorised Biography of the Creator of the SAS*, Little Brown, Great Britain, 1992, pp. 223–4.
4 Peter Stirling was attached to the British Embassy as a career diplomat and First Secretary.
5 Interview GPJRJ. In a long life since, it remains Jellicoe's view that he has seen many fine leaders but never anyone with the galvanizing leadership that David Stirling had, certainly in his SAS days.
6 Ibid.
7 Lorna Almonds Windmill, *Gentleman Jim: The Wartime Story of a Founder of the SAS*, Constable, 2001, pp. 97–106.
8 Interview GPJRJ.
9 Interview Sir Carol Mather, 29 June 2002.
10 The French equivalent Army rank to major in the British Army.

11 Language skills later became more formally part of the required proficiencies of the modern, four-man SAS team.

12 Speech to the New York Sugar Club, 13 May 1981.

13 Interview M. Augustin Jourdan, 9 November 2002.

14 Where it became the Suez Canal. Letter from Jack Sibard to the author dated 25 September 2002.

15 Under a Sergeant Kennedy. Letter from Jack Sibard to the author dated 25 September 2002.

16 Ibid.

17 They had passed the training that confirmed their selection into the SAS and were entitled to replace the cap badge of their original unit with that of the SAS.

18 A British brigade then holding the island had been developing Suda Bay as a refuelling base for the Royal Navy and the airfields at Maleme and Heraklion. The battle for Crete in May 1941 had been strategically important. Despite hard and bloody resistance by the Allies under the New Zealander, Major General Freyberg, the island had fallen. Just under half of the 28,000 British, Australian and New Zealand troops had been taken prisoner. Brigadier Bob Laycock, formerly Commanding Officer of No. 8 Commando, was commanding a last ditch Commando operation, accompanied by Evelyn Waugh as his Staff Captain.

19 Undated letter from GPJRJ to Lady Henderson, from Ditchley Park, probably in 1986 or 1987.

20 Jack Sibard, Récit Condensé: Mission Créte – Juin 1942, author's collection.

21 Ibid.

22 Ibid.

23 Interview GPJRJ.

24 Sibard, op. cit.

25 Ibid.

26 Ibid.

27 Interview GPJRJ.

28 Sibard, op. cit.

29 Antony Beevor, Crete: The Battle and the Resistance, Penguin, 1992, p. 269.

30 This was near a subsidiary entrance on the west side of the airfield; the main entrance was on the north side.

31 Interview GPJRJ.

32 Ibid.

33 On the competence of German sentries, see also Almonds Windmill, op. cit. p. 221.

34 Letter from Jack Sibard to the author dated 25 September 2002.

35 Sibard, op. cit.

36 PRO, WO 373/46, 5 Nov 1942, DSO.

37 Letter from Jack Sibard to the author, 25 September 2002.

38 Sibard, op. cit.

39 Letter from Jack Sibard to the author, 22 February 2004.

40 Beevor, op. cit. p. 262.

41 Interview GPJRJ.

42 Letter from Jack Sibard, 25 September 2002.

43 Ibid.

44 Letter from Jack Sibard to the author, 22 February 2004.

45 Sibard, op. cit.

46 The Cretan newcomer had sent his son on ahead into Tymbaki to the German garrison.

47 Sibard, op. cit.

48 Bergé ended up in Colditz with David Stirling.

49 Interview Colonel David Sutherland, 25 May 2002.

50 PRO, WO 373/46, 5 Nov 1942, DSO.

51 Interview Paddy Leigh Fermor, 25 July 2002. Leigh Fermor had originally enlisted in the Irish Guards and trained at Caterham. The SOE was a fighting part of the Secret Service, established in 1940 to support and stimulate resistance in occupied countries.

52 Undated letter from GPJRJ to Lady Henderson, from Ditchley Park, probably in 1986 or 1987.

53 Interview GPJRJ.

54 Leigh Fermor had in fact met Jellicoe briefly in 1942 with Stirling in Cairo and at the time of Rommel's advance when Jellicoe had been on leave there. Interview Paddy Leigh Fermor, 25 July 2002.

55 Barrie Pitt, Special Boat Squadron: The Story of the SBS in the Mediterranean, Century, 1983, p. 32.

56 Operation HARPOON, 14–15 June 1942.

57 Address by General (CR) G. Bergé, Heraklion, Greece, 13 June 1992.

58 They showed it by making him a member of the Légion d'Honneur and decorating him with the Croix de Guerre. Interview M. Augustin Jourdan, 9 November 2002.

59 PRO Cab/44/152 (Open) p. 62.
60 Founded by Brigadier Ralph Bagnold in 1941. 'G' patrols were drawn from the Brigade of Guards (originally equally drawn from Coldstream and Scots Guards and later from the Grenadier Guards); 'Y' patrols consisted mainly of English Yeomanry; 'T' patrols were New Zealanders, while 'R' patrols were made up of Rhodesians.
61 PRO Cab/44/152 (Open) p. 60.
62 Interview Sir Stephen Hastings, 3 June 2002.
63 Ibid.
64 Interview GPJRJ and *To War with Whitaker: The Wartime Diaries of the Countess of Ranfurly 1939–45,* William Heinemann Ltd, Great Britain, 1994. Hermione's husband Dan had been captured quite early on in the war and she had promised to remain working as a secretary in the Middle East until he was free, which she did.
65 PRO Cab/44/152 (Open) p. 62.
66 They had originally been ordered to move north-east and attack the four aerodromes at El Daba, accompanied by Y.2 Patrol, LRDG. However, last minute information from HQ Eighth Army that the counter-attack had begun required their target to be changed. Interview GPJRJ and PRO Cab/44/152 (Open) p. 62.
67 In which my father, 'Gentleman Jim' Almonds also took part.
68 Stephen Hastings, *The Drums of Memory: The Autobiography,* Pen & Sword, 2001, pp. 52–3.
69 Interview Sir Stephen Hastings, 3 June 2002.
70 Hastings, pp. 52–53 and interview Sir Stephen Hastings, 3 June 2002.
71 PRO Cab/44/152 (Open) pp. 68–69.
72 Ibid.
73 Interview Sir Stephen Hastings, 3 June 2002.
74 PRO Cab/44/152 (Open) p. 70.
75 PRO Cab/44/152 (Open) pp. 68–69.
76 The doctor might have been to see Rommel; it was rumoured that he was unwell at this time. Interview GPJRJ.
77 He subsequently escaped. For more on this story see Almonds Windmill, op. cit. pp. 139–41.
78 He had formerly been the Medical Officer attached to the 3rd Coldstream Guards and had treated Jellicoe's wounded shoulder.
79 Malcolm James, *Born of the Desert,* Collins, London, 1945, p. 173.
80 Interview Lady Henderson, 18 June 2002.
81 Supplement to the *London Gazette* of Tuesday 3 November 1942 and WO 373/46, LG 5 Nov 1942, DSO.
82 Captain G W Read, *Raiding Forces and the Levant Schooner Flotilla: a Story of an Independent Command in the Aegean 1943–1945,* July 1945, given to members of Raiding Forces on disbandment, author's possession.

Chapter Four: Commander of the SBS

1 Interview GPJRJ.
2 Either Sarah or Diana. Interviews GPJRJ and Lady Soames, 15 April 2003.
3 He was later succeeded by Bob Laycock.
4 John Peyton, *Solly Zuckerman: A Scientist out of the Ordinary,* John Murray, London, 2001, p. 37.
5 Ibid.
6 I can remember a ready supply of them being available during my childhood sailing days at the Naval Base Sailing Club, Sembawang, Singapore.
7 Interview GPJRJ.
8 G W Read, *A Story of an Independent Command in the Aegean 1943–1945: Raiding Forces and the Levant Schooner Flotilla,* No. 1 Public Relations Service, GHQ MEF, July 1945.
9 Both brothers had been born into the prosperous, cosmopolitan Greek world of Braila in the Danube Delta. They spoke voluble French and wore monocles, which gave them a dashing and worldly air.
10 Interview GPJRJ.
11 Interview Colonel David Sutherland, 25 May 2002.
12 Interview GPJRJ.
13 Alan Hoe, *David Stirling: the Authorised Biography of the Creator of the SAS,* Little Brown, Great Britain, 1992, pp. 223–4.
14 It became 1SAS again when the SAS Brigade was created on 1 January 1944.
15 Interview GPJRJ. Jellicoe was granted substantive rank of Captain and appointed temporary Major on 29 March 1943, MOD letter DR2b/0237622-1/HEO dated 29/05/2002.

16 David Sutherland, *He Who Dares: SAS, SBS and MI5*, Pen & Sword, 1998, p. 117.
17 Robin Hunter, *True Stories of the SBS*, Virgin, 1998, pp. 22–33.
18 The raid, like the first big SAS raid on the airfields at Timimi and Gazala, was timed for the night of 17/18 November in support of Operation CRUSADER which aimed to relieve besieged Tobruk and push Rommel back westwards out of Cyrenaica. Sutherland, op. cit. pp. 46–9.
19 Ibid.
20 Interview GPJRJ.
21 Hunter, op. cit. p. 156.
22 Interview GPJRJ.
23 Lorna Almonds Windmill, *Gentleman Jim: The Wartime Story of a Founder of the SAS*, Constable, 2001, pp. 118–19.
24 Fitzroy Maclean, *Eastern Approaches*, Jonathan Cape, London, 1949, pp. 264–73.
25 Interview GPJRJ.
26 Interview Colonel David Sutherland, 25 May 2002.
27 Ibid.
28 Interview GPJRJ.
29 For further possible modelling of himself on Mayne see chapter 6, footnote 51.
30 Interview Colonel David Sutherland, 25 May 2002.
31 Mike Langley, *Anders Lassen VC, MC, of the SAS*, Grafton, 1990, p. 147.
32 John Verney in Langley, op. cit. p. 164.
33 Interview Paddy Leigh Fermor, 10 January 2004.
34 Interview Colonel David Sutherland, 25 May 2002.
35 Read, op. cit. Author's collection.
36 Hunter, op. cit. p. 20.
37 Interview Colonel David Sutherland, 25 May 2002.
38 A useful Scots Guards officer and Oxford Rowing Blue who had joined the SAS in November 1942. James Hancock, *True Blue – He Rowed to Adventure*, interview with Ronnie Rowe shortly before his death in 1997, pp. 4–5.
39 Sutherland, op. cit. pp. 103–5.
40 Hancock, op. cit., interview with Ronnie Rowe shortly before his death in 1997, p. 5. On arriving in Cairo with his two prisoners, Rowe found GHQ closed for siesta so he took them for a cream tea at Groppis, an elegant Cairo café before handing them over!
41 Interview GPJRJ.
42 *Eastern Approaches*, Fitzroy Maclean, Jonathan Cape, London, 1949, p. 277–9.
43 He had also 'met' Rommel when he was wounded and captured on the great retreat close to the Egyptian border. Rommel noticed him and sent him off for medical attention, from which he promptly escaped. Barrie Pitt, *Special Boat Squadron: The Story of the SBS in the Mediterranean*, Century, 1983, p. 86.
44 Interview GPJRJ.
45 Interview Colonel David Sutherland, 25 May 2002.
46 Interview GPJRJ.
47 Anthony Kemp, *The SAS at War: 1941–1945*, Penguin, 1991, p. 99.
48 Interview GPJRJ. In Bari, Italy in September 1943, Popski managed to save a beautiful church from being destroyed by convincing the American army commander that the enemy was not using it for subversive activities. A monument to him still stands there.
49 Interview GPJRJ.
50 Leigh Fermor, Moss and others, dressed as Germans, held up Kreipe's car at one of his own roadblocks. They marched him over Mount Ida to be taken off by submarine from a beach near Rodakino for Egypt. Interview Paddy Leigh Fermor, 7 February 2004. In November 1944, Bury was shot in a caique off Salonika by Greek Royalists who mistook him and Lassen for Communists. Antony Beevor, *Crete: The Battle and the Resistance*, Penguin, 1992, p. 334.
51 Interview GPJRJ.
52 Interview GPJRJ.
53 Interview GPJRJ.
54 D. I. Harrison, *These Men are Dangerous: The Special Air Service at War*, Cassell, 1957, p. 27.

Chapter Five: Two Lords A-Leaping

1 Interview GPJRJ.
2 Ibid.
3 Barrie Pitt, *Special Boat Squadron: The Story of the SBS in the Mediterranean*, Century, London, 1983, p. 94.

4 Interview GPJRJ and Count Julian Dobrski's personal account, papers of Lieutenant Colonel Count J. A. Dobrski, OBE, MC, alias Lieutenant Colonel Julian Dolbey, King's College, London, Liddell Hart Centre for Military Archives, p. 2.

5 Interview GPJRJ and Dobrski, p. 2.

6 M. R. D. Foot, SOE: The Special Operations Executive 1940–46, BBC, London, 1984, frontispiece.

7 Interview the Countess Dobrska, 15 March 2003. Jellicoe knew Dobrski as Dolbey throughout this operation, hence the use of that name throughout the chapter.

8 Dick Mallaby was an SOE operator who was captured by the Carabinieri when he parachuted onto one of the Italian lakes. He ended up providing clandestine communications with the Allies for Italy's post-Armistice Prime Minister, Marshal Badoglio. Foot, op. cit. p. 230.

9 Dobrski, p. 1.

10 It was announced on 8 September 1943.

11 Dobrski, p. 3.

12 Dobrski, p. 5.

13 Ibid.

14 Dolbey's account refers to a Lancaster but the aircraft used had a jump hatch, whereas a Lancaster has a rear door. It is much more likely to have been a Liberator.

15 Dobrski, p. 5.

16 Ibid.

17 Ibid. The low cloud over the whole area would have made it impossible to see the island and rendered the 100 per cent navigation necessary for drops into enemy territory impossible.

18 Interview GPJRJ.

19 Interview GPJRJ and Dobrski, p. 7.

20 Ibid. See also footnote 14 above.

21 Interview GPJRJ.

22 Dobrski, p. 8.

23 The crew would have picked an 'initial point' (IP) on the coast and then followed a timed run on the correct heading towards it. From the IP, they would have approached the DZ with the aircraft straight and level at the correct speed and height. It must have been a static line drop, close together, at about 800 feet.

24 Interview GPJRJ and Dobrski, p. 8.

25 Dobrski, p. 8 and interview GPJRJ.

26 Ibid.

27 Dobrski, p. 9.

28 Dobrski, p. 10.

29 Ibid.

30 None of the Operation RODEL party had opened fire. The Italians had possibly been firing at each other by mistake.

31 Dobrski, p. 11.

32 Ibid.

33 Dolbey (alias Dobrski) says in his account that Jellicoe and Kesterton had in fact heard him shouting but had decided to remain in hiding in case he, Dolbey, had been captured and was being used to bait a trap. Jellicoe has no recollection of having heard him. Interview GPJRJ.

34 Interview GPJRJ.

35 Dobrski, p. 12.

36 Ibid.

37 Dobrski, p. 13 and interview GPJRJ.

38 In fact, it later transpired that there were multi-fractures to the bones in the leg, which Dobrski later referred to as like a 'skiing salad'. Interview the Countess Dobrska, 15 March 2003.

39 Dobrski, p. 13.

40 Dobrski, p. 15.

41 The Operation RODEL party had landed almost directly on top of this front line.

42 Dobrski, pp. 15–24.

43 Ibid and interview GPJRJ.

44 Pitt, op. cit. p. 90.

45 Dobrski, pp. 2–26.

46 Interview GPJRJ.

47 Interview GPJRJ and Dobrski, p. 26.

48 Interview GPJRJ.

49 He has been much criticized for cowardice but this is grossly unfair, given the situation. He was nevertheless handed over to the Graziani Government (Marshal Graziani remained loyal to Mussolini's Government in Northern Italy) and executed later.

50 Pitt, op. cit. pp. 92–3.
51 Dobrski, p. 29.
52 Interview the Countess Dobrska, 15 March 2003. Dobrski was awarded an 'Immediate' MC for his role in the Rhodes operation.

Chapter Six: The Last Seadogs

1 Ed. Julian Paget, *Second to None: The Coldstream Guards 1650–2000*, Leo Cooper, 2000, p. 172.
2 Interview GPJRJ.
3 David Sutherland, *He Who Dares: SAS, SBS and MI5*, Leo Cooper, 1998, pp. 115–17.
4 Barrie Pitt, *Special Boat Squadron: The Story of the SBS in the Mediterranean*, Century, 1983, p. 94.
5 Interview GPJRJ.
6 Crown copyright, from the report on the mission to Rhodes carried out on the night of 9 September 1943 by Major the Lord Jellicoe and subsequent operations. See also Pitt, op. cit. p. 96.
7 Pitt, op. cit. p. 97.
8 Interview GPJRJ and Crown copyright, from the report on the mission to Rhodes carried out on the night of 9 September 1943 by Major the Lord Jellicoe and subsequent operations. See also Pitt, op. cit. p. 97.
9 In English, 'It's looking bad; yes, it's bad'.
10 In English, 'It's worse'.
11 In English, 'But we have to keep going'.
12 Interview GPJRJ.
13 Sutherland, op. cit. p. 119.
14 Paget, op. cit. p. 173.
15 Robin Hunter, *True Stories of the SBS*, Virgin, 1998, p. 166.
16 Sutherland, op. cit. p. 121.
17 Interview GPJRJ.
18 Lieutenant Alan Phipps, RN, son of Sir Eric Phipps, HMA to Berlin before the war.
19 Hunter, op. cit. p. 168.
20 G. W. Read, *A Story of an Independent Command in the Aegean 1943–1945: Raiding Forces and the Levant Schooner Flotilla*, No. 1 Public Relations Service, GHQ MEF, July 1945, p. 15.
21 Interview GPJRJ.
22 Interview GPJRJ.
23 Phipps had also been in the RN destroyer which took Jellicoe from Kos to Alexandria. Interview GPJRJ.
24 Interview GPJRJ.
25 This contrasted with German behaviour when withdrawing from Greece, when there were many atrocities, including the murder of Italian soldiers in Cephalonia; interview GPJRJ.
26 Sadly, Phipps had already been killed. Interview GPJRJ.
27 Interview GPJRJ.
28 Hunter, op. cit. p. 169.
29 Of the four Allied infantry battalions engaged in the fighting, fewer than 250 men survived, while the graves of soldiers from both sides remain as a grim testimony; Pitt, op. cit. p. 120.
30 Residence of Richard G. Casey, an Australian diplomat and Liberal politician, Minister of State Resident in the Middle East and at that time a member of the British War Cabinet, Mary Soames, *Speaking for Themselves*, Black Swan, 1998, pp. 468 and 488.
31 Jellicoe had stayed at the Mena House Hotel as a child with his parents on the way back to England from New Zealand.
32 Interview GPJRJ.
33 Interview GPJRJ.
34 Letter dated 26 November 1943, from Winston Spencer Churchill to Clementine Spencer Churchill, by kind permission of Winston Spencer Churchill.
35 Jellicoe had known Woodhouse from Winchester where Woodhouse had been a couple of years senior.
36 Interview GPJRJ.
37 Countess Ranfurly, *To War with Whitaker: The Wartime Diaries of the Countess of Ranfurly 1939–45*, Mandarin, 1995, p. 198.
38 Ibid. p. 201.
39 Jellicoe hotly disputes these sightings!
40 Interview GPJRJ.

41 Interview Colonel David Sutherland, 25 May 2002.
42 Who had been in Persia before the war and who went on to be a prominent Irish MP and author. The author Anita Leslie also worked for him.
43 Interview Patricia, Countess Jellicoe 11 July 2002.
44 Ibid.
45 He managed to get off the island in September 1943. Moss married a Countess instead, in the English Cathedral in Cairo. Jellicoe was heard to say at the wedding that the bride and groom were 'the two most beautiful people he had ever seen'. Moss later wrote *Ill Met By Moonlight*. Interview Paddy Leigh Fermor, 25 July 2002.
46 Interview GPJRJ.
47 Lloyd Owen's diary in Julian Thompson, *War Behind Enemy Lines*, Sidgwick & Jackson, 1998, p. 358.
48 Sutherland, op. cit. p. 132.
49 Written message from GPJRJ to the 60th Anniversary of the founding of the Greek Sacred Squadron, 12 September 2002.
50 Interview GPJRJ.
51 It is possible that the young Dane had Paddy Mayne's daring achievements in mind. In the third failed SAS raid on Benghazi in September 1942, Mayne's job was to rob the bank. Almonds Windmill, op. cit. p. 147.
52 Hunter, op. cit. p. 170.
53 Ibid.
54 Mogens Kofod-Hansen, *Andy – A Portrait of the Dane Major Anders Lassen*, Narayana Press, 1989, p. 53.
55 Interview Colonel David Sutherland, 25 May 2002.
56 Hunter, op. cit. p. 172.
57 Ibid. p. 173.
58 Interview GPJRJ.
59 Mike Langley, *Anders Lassen VC, MC, of the SAS*, Grafton, 1990, p. 164.
60 Interview GPJRJ and Robin Hunter, p. 162.
61 Susanne Lassen, *Anders Lassen VC*, Frederick Muller, 1965, p. 119.
62 Antony Beevor, *Crete: The Battle and the Resistance*, Penguin, 1992, pp. 312–13.
63 Julian Thompson, *War Behind Enemy Lines*, Sidgwick & Jackson, 1998, pp. 291–2.
64 Ibid. pp. 291–2.
65 Read, op. cit. p. 51.

Chapter Seven: Liberating Athens on a Bicycle

1 Interview GPJRJ.
2 Interview GPJRJ.
3 Barrie Pitt, *Special Boat Squadron: The Story of the SBS in the Mediterranean*, Century, 1983, p. 162.
4 Robin Hunter, *True Stories of the SBS*, Virgin, 1998, pp. 177–8.
5 Interview GPJRJ.
6 Interview GPJRJ.
7 Interview GPJRJ.
8 A situation not unlike that in Iraq in 2005. Interview George Papoulias, 28 November 2002.
9 Pitt, op. cit. p. 167 and Julian Thompson, *War Behind Enemy Lines*, Sidgwick & Jackson, 1998, p. 356.
10 Interview GPJRJ.
11 Interview GPJRJ.
12 Pitt, op. cit. p. 171.
13 Interview Lord Waldegrave, 27 May 2002.
14 And the Distinguished Service Order! (Evenstoll seems not to have noticed the DSO.) According to GPJRJ's personal army records, he was promoted with effect from 9 October but clearly he had been invited to put up the higher rank some days before that.
15 *Diary of Hans Evenstoll*, Representative of the Swedish Red Cross in Patras, Athens, 1961, as quoted in The *Diary of Panayiotis Kanellopoulos, 31 March 1942–4 February 1945*, Edition 'Kedros', Athens, 1977.
16 *Diary of Hans Evenstoll*, 1961.
17 Interview GPJRJ.
18 Interview GPJRJ.

19 Interview GPJRJ.

20 Pitt, op. cit. pp. 170–1.

21 Evenstoll later published his memoirs in a Greek newspaper, which were later drawn on by Panayiotis Kanellopoulos, who had been sent back from Cairo in advance by George Papandreou's government in exile. *The Diary of Panayiotis Kanellopoulos, 31 March 1942–4 February 1945*, Edition 'Kedros', Athens, 1977, p. 2177.

22 *On the Eve of the Liberation*, Themistoclis D. Tsatsoe, with reference to the unpublished diary of Panayiotis Kanellopoulos, Ikaros, Athens, 1973, p. 277.

23 Mary Henderson, *Xenia – A Memoir: Greece 1919–1949*, George Weidenfeld & Nicolson, 1988, p. 61.

24 PRO AIR 23/8193 107595 dated 4 October 1944.

25 PRO AIR 23/8193 107595 dated 5 October 1944.

26 PRO AIR 23/8193 107595 dated 6 October 1944.

27 *The Diary of Panayiotis Kanellopoulos, 31 March 1942–4 February 1945*, Edition 'Kedros', Athens, 1977, p. 656.

28 Agreement of 26 September 1944 between the Greek Government and the guerrilla leaders of Greek political organizations, including ELAS and others.

29 PRO AIR 23/8193 107595 dated 7 October 1944.

30 PRO AIR 23/8193 107595 dated 8 October 1944.

31 PRO AIR 23/8193 107595 dated 8 October 1944.

32 PRO AIR 23/8193 107595 dated 8 October 1944.

33 PRO AIR 23/8193 107595 dated 9 October 1944.

34 MOD letter DR2b/0237622-1/HEO dated 29/05/2002.

35 Interview GPJRJ. Jellicoe had known Woodhouse from Winchester where Woodhouse had been a couple of years senior. They knew each other again later when Woodhouse was Parliamentary Under Secretary of State in the Home Office when Jellicoe was a Minister. Jellicoe became godfather to Woodhouse's son who is now his medical consultant.

36 For which there is no promulgation date in his personal army records and appears to have been authorized in the field.

37 PRO AIR 23/8193 107595 dated 9 October 1944.

38 PRO AIR 23/8193 107595 dated 11 October 1944.

39 PRO AIR 23/8193 107595 dated 11 October 1944. The date of 12 October conflicts with the diary account of Kanellopoulos which says that it was early in the morning of 12 October that Jellicoe and Macaskie appeared on the balcony of the Grande Bretagne hotel. Jellicoe was probably present for the advance party drop on 11 October.

40 Thompson, op. cit. p. 356 and interview GPJRJ.

41 Interview Lord Waldegrave, 27 May 2002.

42 Interview George Papoulias, 28 November 2002.

43 Interview GPJRJ.

44 Lieutenant Colonel Frank Macaskie DSO, MC and Bar, *The Times* correspondent in Athens, 1947, died 1952 at the age of thirty-nine, Mary Henderson, p. 99.

45 Interview GPJRJ.

46 *The Chronicle of Slavery 1942–1944*, Christos Zalocostas, New Hellenic Literature No. 177, Bookshop Estia, 1 d Kolarov & Co., pp. 386–7.

47 The French for 'Brigadier' is 'Général de brigade'.

48 Interview GPJRJ.

49 Tsatsoe, op. cit. with reference to the unpublished diary of Panayotis Kanellopoulos, Ikaros, Athens, 1973, pp. 187–8.

50 Interviews GPJRJ and George Papoulias, 28 November 2002.

51 Henderson, op. cit. p. 72 and interview GPJRJ.

52 Interviews GPJRJ and Lady Henderson (Mary Cawadias subsequently became Time-Life's post-war correspondent in Greece and married Sir Nicholson Henderson, British Ambassador to Poland, West Germany, France and the United States), 18 June 2002. Opinions differ as to how Sophia came to be on the balcony. She had probably either inserted herself into the scene or had been invited up there by Lassen. See also Henderson, op. cit. p. 83.

53 Interview George Papoulias, 28 November 2002. ELAS eventually led an uprising on 4 December.

54 Interviews GPJRJ and Lady Henderson, 18 June 2002.

55 Interview Lady Henderson, 18 June 2002.

56 Tsatsoe, op. cit. with reference to the unpublished diary of Panayiotis Kanellopoulos, Ikaros, Athens, 1973, pp. 187–8.

57 Interview GPJRJ.

58 Derived from '*les pompiers*', French for fire-fighters.

59 Interview GPJRJ and Mogens Kofod-Hansen, p. 62.

255

60 Interview Lord Waldegrave, 27 May 2002.
61 Countess of Ranfurly, *To War with Whitaker: The Wartime Diaries of the Countess of Ranfurly 1939–45*, Mandarin, 1995, p. 296. After Jellicoe left Athens however, the political problems continued and these marked the beginning of the civil war.
62 G. W. Read.
63 David Sutherland, *He Who Dares: SAS, SBS and MI5*, Pen & Sword, 1998, p. 172.
64 Interview GPJRJ.
65 Interview GPJRJ.
66 Particularly if they were not married prior to joining the Special Forces. For example, Paddy Mayne, who was killed driving his car in the mid-1950s after never really settling to a job in civilian life.
67 Interview GPJRJ. David Sutherland shares this view.
68 Interview GPJRJ and Ranfurly, op. cit. p. 363.

Chapter Eight: Washington and the Cambridge Spies

1 Interview GPJRJ.
2 Interview Patricia, Countess Jellicoe, 11 July 2002.
3 Interview Patricia, Countess Jellicoe, 11 July 2002.
4 Johnny Cooper, *One of the Originals: The Story of a Founder Member of the SAS*, Pan, 1991, p. 119.
5 Interview GPJRJ.
6 Interview GPJRJ.
7 Interview GPJRJ.
8 Interview GPJRJ.
9 Interview GPJRJ.
10 With which newspaper the Sulzberger family had close connections.
11 Sulzberger had married a close friend of Mary Cawadias, later Lady Henderson. Mary Henderson, *Xenia – A Memoir: Greece 1919–1949*, George Weidenfeld & Nicolson, 1988, pp. 44–6.
12 Interview GPJRJ.
13 Interview GPJRJ.
14 Interview GPJRJ.
15 Christopher Andrew and Oleg Gordiesvsky, *KGB: The inside story of its foreign operations from Lenin to Gorbachev*, Hodder & Stoughton, London, 1990, p. 167.
16 Ibid. p. 170.
17 He later had breakdowns in London and Cairo.
18 Interview GPJRJ.
19 Interview Patricia, Countess Jellicoe, 11 July 2002.
20 Marten had served with the Rifle Brigade in the Middle East during the war; he and Jellicoe had met occasionally in Shepheard's Hotel in Cairo. After the battle of El Alamein, Marten had gone back to the UK as an instructor at the School of Infantry, which was then at Barnard Castle in Yorkshire. Interview Tim Marten, 28 May 2002.
21 Sir Roger Stevens, later ambassador in Teheran, 1954–55 and subsequently Vice Chancellor of Keele University.
22 Interview Tim Marten, 28 May 2002.
23 Sir Nicholas Henderson. He went on to be ambassador at Warsaw, Bonn, Paris and Washington, to which he was brought back from retirement to play a crucial role in the politics of the Falklands War.
24 Speech as No. 2 Government Spokesman on Defence & Aviation, March 1961, Tidcombe papers.
25 FO 371/78860.
26 Speech as No. 2 Government Spokesman on Defence & Aviation, March 1961, Tidcombe papers.
27 Speech as No. 2 Government Spokesman on Defence & Aviation, March 1961, Tidcombe papers.
28 Andrew and Gordiesvsky, op. cit. p. 321.
29 Interview GPJRJ.
30 Interview Tim Marten, 28 May 2002.
31 Andrew and Gordiesvsky, op. cit. p. 161.
32 Abdul Aziz Ibn Saud became King of Saudi Arabia in 1922 when he established the Kingdom following the collapse of Turkish rule at the end of the First World War.
33 Andrew and Gordiesvsky, op. cit. p. 161.
34 Interview GPJRJ.
35 Interview GPJRJ.
36 Andrew and Gordiesvsky, op. cit. p. 321.

37 Philby would have had no legitimate reason to go regularly to New York to drop off information to Soviet contacts. Interview Chapman Pincher, 14 June 2003.
38 Interview GPJRJ.
39 Interview Patricia, Countess Jellicoe, 11 July 2002.
40 Interview Tim Marten, 28 May 2002.
41 Interview Tim Marten, 28 May 2002.
42 'Minister' is a senior Foreign Office official grade.
43 This story was common knowledge in the British Embassy at the time, the details of the story presumably coming from the Americans and the statements taken by the Interstate Highway Police. Interview Tim Marten, 28 May 2002.
44 Interview Tim Marten, 28 May 2002.
45 Ibid.
46 Alan Bennett, *Plays: An Englishman Abroad*, Faber & Faber, London, 1998, Introduction, p. x.
47 Interview Chapman Pincher, 14 June 2003.
48 Bennett, op. cit. Introduction, p. ix.
49 Andrew and Gordiesvsky, op. cit. p. 322.
50 Interview Tim Marten, 28 May 2002.
51 Interview Patricia, Countess Jellicoe, 11 July 2002.
52 Interview Tim Marten, 28 May 2002.
53 Interview Lady Henderson, 18 June 2002.
54 Sir Ronald Grierson, entrepreneur, merchant banker, financier and holder of many senior public appointments. They had, in fact, known each other by sight in the SAS.
55 Interview GPJRJ.
56 Interview Sir Ronald Grierson, 16 July 2002.
57 Ibid.
58 He was rescued after the Allied occupation of Belgium.
59 Which was later sold to Gina Lollobrigida.
60 Interview GPJRJ.
61 Undated speech while Lord-in-Waiting to the Anglo-Belgian Union, 1961, Tidcombe papers.
62 Interview GPJRJ.
63 Interview Sir Stephen Hastings, 3 June 2002.
64 Interview Tim Marten, 28 May 2002.
65 Interview GPJRJ.

Chapter Nine: Cold War Warrior

1 PRO CAB 163/8.
2 For example, the Berlin Blockade.
3 Interview GPJRJ. JIB was the forerunner of the present Defence Intelligence Staff (DIS).
4 They are 'retained' (withheld) under section 3(4) of the Public Records Act.
5 PRO CAB 163/8 and Peter Wright, *Spycatcher*, 1987.
6 Also formerly the Middle East Treaty Organization, a mutual security alliance of Turkey, Iran, Pakistan, Britain and Iraq founded in 1955 with its headquarters in Baghdad and from 1959 when Iraq withdrew and the US became an associate member known as the Central Treaty Organization (CENTO) and with its headquarters in Ankara until its dissolution in 1979 following the withdrawal of Iran.
7 Lord Aberdare, who later became Jellicoe's deputy when he was Leader of the House of Lords.
8 Interviews GPJRJ and PAJ.
9 Interview the Honourable Susan Baring, 12 August 2002.
10 She had been briefly married to Christopher Bridge, interview PAJ.
11 Interview the Hon Susan Baring, 12 August, 2002.
12 Interview GPJRJ.
13 Phillip Dunne had also been in the wartime SAS.
14 Interview PAJ.
15 Keith Kyle, *Suez: Britain's End of Empire in the Middle East*, Weidenfeld & Nicolson, London, 1991, p. 57.
16 Ibid. p. 58. The pack was called the Royal Harthiya and followers wore English hunting pink and rode with foxhounds imported from Dorset.
17 Her husband Max Mallowan was head of the British School of Archeology and she accompanied him on expeditions, drawing on them for many of the scenes and characters in her novels. Interview GPJRJ and Janet Morgan, *Agatha Christie: A Biography*, William Collins & Sons Co. Ltd, 1984, p. 280.

18 Each member country provided a Deputy Secretary General, with varying degrees of willingness and efficiency. The US, not being full members, did not. But the US secondee, with whom Jellicoe worked closely, was very effective.
19 Letter from Sir Terence Clark, HM Ambassador to Iraq, 1985–89, to *The Times* dated 1 March 2003.
20 Interview GPJRJ.
21 PRO FO/371/12/255, Letter from British Embassy Teheran to The Rt. Hon. Selwyn Lloyd, PC, CBE, MP, Foreign Office, London, SW1 and FO/371/121257.
22 PRO FO/371/121255, Letter from British Embassy Teheran to The Rt. Hon. Selwyn Lloyd, PC, CBE, MP, Foreign Office, London, SW1.
23 PRO FO/371/121255, Letter from British Embassy Teheran to The Rt. Hon. Selwyn Lloyd, PC, CBE, MP, Foreign Office, London, SW1.
24 Ibid.
25 Interview GPJRJ.
26 Interview GPJRJ.
27 Interview GPJRJ.
28 Interview GPJRJ.
29 Interview GPJRJ.
30 Interview GPJRJ.
31 There had been a misunderstanding about Lady Wright thinking that Jellicoe had arranged a job for Philippa in the Pact Secretariat. This totally untrue story might have got back to the Foreign Office but Jellicoe was unable to deal with it because it was never officially voiced.
32 Interview GPJRJ.
33 Interview GPJRJ.
34 Interview Sir Stephen Hastings, 3 June 2002.
35 Letter from Hoyer-Millar, Foreign Office, London, SW1, to Jellicoe, 5 March 1958, Tidcombe papers.
36 The company had approached Jellicoe at the end of the war but at that time he had preferred the Foreign Office.
37 Interview GPJRJ.
38 Interview GPJRJ.
39 Nuri had sponsored an Arab union with Jordan, hoping to persuade other Arab countries to join the Pact, assert leadership of the Arab unity movement and secure popular support in Iraq. But resentment against the West became too strong and too prevalent for the Pact to achieve such ends.
40 Interview GPJRJ. In the same year, the pact changed its name to CENTO, moved its headquarters to Ankara and the US became an associate member. The new Iraqi leadership was more enlightened than its pre-revolutionary predecessor's but the older political and military leaders resisted and embarked on an unpopular foreign policy. This included an alliance with Britain via CENTO and opposition to the United Arab Republic, the 'Free Officers'. After the fall of the Shah in 1979, Iran withdrew and CENTO was wound up. The Baghdad Pact/CENTO was never very effective.
41 Immediately after the war he had sat briefly on the Labour benches after going to see Clement Attlee at someone's request. Interview GPJRJ. He had taken the oath on 3 December 1957, Hansard, Session 1958–59, Vol. 214, Col. 207.
42 Article 3 of the pact in any case strictly forbade this.
43 Vol. 211, No. 100, Parliamentary Debates (HANSARD) House of Lords OFFICIAL REPORT, Monday 28 July 1958, 265–71.
44 Vol. 211, No. 100, Parliamentary Debates (HANSARD) House of Lords OFFICIAL REPORT, Monday 28 July 1958, 271–85.
45 Interview GPJRJ.

Chapter Ten: Whitehall Warrior

1 The Parliamentary Debates (Hansard) Official Report, Session 1957/58, 28 October 1958, Volume 212.
2 He congratulated the Government on its associated White Paper. Lord Shackleton spoke too, for the Opposition, thus beginning a friendship and political sparring relationship that was to endure for almost forty years. The Parliamentary Debates (Hansard) Official Report, Session 1958/59, Volume 214, Column 913–918. Jellicoe also spoke the following day, in the debate on the Address in reply to the Queen's speech, on aviation, roads and shipbuilding.
3 3 February 1960. The Parliamentary Debates (Hansard) Official Report, Session 1958/59, Volume 220, Column 895–903.

4 John Dennis Profumo. They had been close friends since their idyllic early childhood days in Warwickshire, interview PAJ, 23 June 2002.
5 Interview PAJ, 23 June 2002.
6 Interview, Tony and Barbara Hunt.
7 The famous photographer, writer and climber.
8 Interview Sir Carol Mather, 29 June 2002.
9 Interview GPJRJ.
10 General Agreement on Trade and Tariffs.
11 Edward Heath, *Travels: People and Places in my Life*, Sidgwick & Jackson, 1977, Chapter 6 Mr Europe.
12 The conference followed up a declaration on the 'Battle for the minds of men' adopted at its 6th Annual Assembly meeting in Oslo by the Atlantic Treaty Association, of which the British Atlantic Committee was a British Branch. Tidcombe papers.
13 School of Slavonic and Eastern European Studies. Tidcombe papers.
14 Letter to Jellicoe on Ministry of Aviation headed notepaper, dated 10 February 1961, signed 'Thorneycroft', Tidcombe papers.
15 Letter to Jellicoe from Harold Macmillan on Admiralty House headed notepaper dated 2 February 1961, Tidcombe papers.
16 The 'Rota of Waits' – the annual duty roster showing the dates on which Lords-in-Waiting were on duty – showed that Jellicoe would be 'waiting' in March and August. Letter to Jellicoe from Brigadier Sir Norman Gwatkin, Comptroller, dated 11 February 1961, Tidcombe papers.
17 Letter to Jellicoe from Tam Galbraith, Secretary of State for Scotland, dated 11 February 1961, Tidcombe papers.
18 Letter to Jellicoe from John Profumo (undated) from 3 Chester Terrace, Regents Park, Tidcombe papers.
19 Letter dated March 1961 to unknown correspondent, Tidcombe papers.
20 The UK's intercontinental ballistic missile, which was much in the news at the time.
21 Baroness Somerskill, one of a prominent group of educational, medical and social reformers.
22 Undated speech while Lord-in-Waiting to the Anglo-Belgian Union, 1961, Tidcombe papers.
23 Letter from John Profumo to Jellicoe, 8 June 1961, Tidcombe papers.
24 Letter from Sue Baring, dated 30 June 1961, Tidcombe papers.
25 Letter signed 'Evelyn', dated 19 July 1961, Tidcombe papers.
26 Letter signed 'Michael', dated 25 July 1961, Tidcombe papers.
27 Brooke authored several books and became involved with the BBC.
28 Interview GPJRJ.
29 Interview GPJRJ.
30 The report was published in February 1963 *Conference on Water Resources in the North West, HMSO, SO Code No. 75–11, February 1963, 4s 6d.*
31 Interview GPJRJ.
32 The formidable (and at the time the only female) Permanent Secretary.
33 Undated note from Henry Brooke, Tidcombe papers.
34 Letter signed 'Harold', dated 17 July 1962, Tidcombe papers.
35 Tidcombe papers.
36 Letter signed 'R. McWilliam', 2, rue de Spa, Brussels, dated 20 July 1962, Tidcombe papers.
37 A reference to the current hit weekly TV satirical show, 'That Was the Week that Was'.
38 Army Council Instruction, letter from John Profumo, dated 28 June 1962, Tidcombe papers.
39 Interview Baron Renton of Huntingdon, 17 June 2002. Renton also saw Jellicoe in late spring 1940, dancing in uniform at a ball in the Dorchester or Grosvenor hotel for 'debs' delights'. When Renton asked who the young man was, he was told that it was Jellicoe, the Admiral's son, wearing uniform because he was going into action and sailing to Norway the next morning. (Jellicoe might have broken his journey home with the 'Snowballers' from Chamonix to Glasgow to slip up to London for a night out.)
40 Interview, Sir Carol Mather, 30 June 2002.
41 Interview GPJRJ.
42 Furthermore, she claims that she and Ward were used as a smokescreen by the establishment, who wanted the media to focus on the racier aspects of the story in order to cover up a serious breach of British security.
43 *Daily Sketch, Daily Mirror, Daily Telegraph* and *Financial Times* of 6 June 1963.
44 Interview GPJRJ.
45 Tidcombe papers.
46 Letter from Patrick Corcoran dated 23 October 1963, Tidcombe papers.
47 Interview Lord Jenkins of Hillhead, 9 July 2002.
48 Interview Lord Carrington, 19 June 2002.

49 Letter from J. B. Caldwell, Naval Member, Canadian Joint Staff, London dated 19 October 1964, Tidcombe papers.
50 Tidcombe papers.
51 It was later changed again when the ministerial posts for the three armed services were combined.
52 Interview Sir Michael Davies, 5 September 2002.
53 Alan Clark, *The Tories: Conservatives and the Nation State 1922–1997*, Weidenfeld & Nicolson, 1998, p. 336 and Tidcombe papers.
54 Letter from J. B. Caldwell, Naval Member, Canadian Joint Staff, London dated 19 October 1964, Tidcombe papers.
55 Letter on Admiralty House, Devonport headed notepaper, from 'Nigel' dated 20 December 1964, Tidcombe papers.
56 Letter from the First Sea Lord, signed 'David', dated 12 November 1964, Tidcombe papers.
57 Letter from 'Michael', dated 16 October 1964, Tidcombe papers.
58 Letter from 'Antony', dated 22 October 1964, Tidcombe papers.
59 Letter from Sir Ian Orr-Ewing, dated 30 October 1964, Tidcombe papers.
60 Undated letter signed 'Ian', Tidcombe papers.
61 Letter from Sir Charles Madden, dated 20 October 1964, Tidcombe papers.
62 A view borne out by events. When Denis Healey became Secretary of State for Defence after the General Election, he cancelled much of the defence programme, including some of the aircraft carrier programme. Letter from Vice Admiral Sir Peter Cazalet, dated 27 October 1964, Tidcombe papers.
63 Letter from J. H. Hall, dated 25 October 1964, Tidcombe papers.

Chapter Eleven: Opposition and House of Lords Reform

1 David Harlech, long-time friend of President Kennedy and a former ambassador to Washington, would probably have had a major political career had not his wife been killed in a car crash, as was he a little while later.
2 Shackleton later succeeded Longford as Leader of the Lords.
3 Interview Lord Carrington, 19 June 2002.
4 He even made time to write to friends whose political careers were in decline, receiving on one occasion an appreciative reply from Sir Alec Douglas-Home. Letter from the Rt. Hon. Sir Alec Douglas-Home, dated 10 August 1965, Tidcombe papers.
5 Interview GPJRJ.
6 Interview the Rt. Hon. Sir Edward Heath, 20 July 2002.
7 The Parliamentary Debates (Hansard) Official Report, Session 1965/66, Volume 270, 11 November 1965, Address in Reply to Her Majesty's Speech.
8 The Parliamentary Debates (Hansard) Official Report, Session 1968/69, Volume 298, Column 305–307, 5 December 1968, Whitehall Redevelopment Plan.
9 The Parliamentary Debates (Hansard) Official Report, Session 1969/70, Volume 306, Column 980–982, 16 December 1969, Greece and the Council of Europe.
10 Later Lord Roll of Ipsden, KCMG.
11 At ninety-eight, he still works for SG Warburg and sits in the House of Lords. Born in 1907 just east of Slovakia in what is now Russia, Roll had, apart from his outstanding achievements in academic scholarship, already held a number of very senior and ministerial international public appointments. He too had had a distinguished career during the war. As an Under-Secretary at the Treasury on the Central Economic Planning Staff, he had gone on to act as Deputy Leader of the UK Delegation for negotiations on entry into the European Economic Community, before they were torpedoed by de Gaulle. Interview GPJRJ.
12 Interview Lord Roll of Ipsden, 22 July 2002.
13 And a great deal more later.
14 Interview Lord Roll of Ipsden, 22 July 2002.
15 Ibid.
16 Tunku Abdul Rahman, the Malay Prime Minister.
17 Letter from Lee Kuan Yew, dated 21 September 1965, Tidcombe papers.
18 Short biographical note dated 1973, Tidcombe papers.
19 Letter from John T. Hambley, dated 22 May 1965, Tidcombe papers.
20 Interview PAJ, 23 June 2002.
21 Jellicoe had to catch a plane that afternoon to Paris, on which he sat next to the French ambassador's wife.
22 Interview PAJ, 23 June 2002.
23 Interview Tony and Barbara Hunt

24 Interview Nikki, Countess Dobrska, 15 March 2003.
25 Interview Sir Stephen Hastings, 3 June 2002.
26 Interview Lord Gowrie, 29 August 2002.
27 Janet Morgan, *The House of Lords and the Labour Government 1964–1970*, OUP, UK, 1975, pp. 3–7.
28 *The Guardian*, 7 July 1966.
29 Later Sir Michael Wheeler-Booth, Clerk of the Parliaments, 1991–1997. The other Secretary was initially David Faulkner CB.
30 It met some forty times. GPJRJ, biography of Shackleton: Biog. Mems Fell. R. Soc. Lond. 45, 485–505 (199).
31 Interview Sir Michael Wheeler-Booth, Clerk of the Parliaments, 1991–1997, 9 August 2002.
32 Richard Crossman, *The Crossman Diaries, Volume 2, 1976*, The Estate of R. H. S. Crossman, Hamish Hamilton and Jonathan Cape, 1976, pp. 532–5.
33 Ibid, pp. 589–90.
34 Ibid, pp. 589–90.
35 Ibid, pp. 640–1.
36 Morgan, op. cit. p. 181.
37 Crossman, op. cit. p. 737.
38 Ibid, p. 757.
39 Ibid, p. 767.
40 Ibid, pp. 21–2.
41 Ibid, p. 51.
42 Morgan, op. cit. p. 144.
43 Crossman, op. cit. Volume 3, p. 221.
44 Morgan, op. cit. p. xx
45 Ibid, p. 205.
46 Ibid, p. 206.
47 The Parliamentary Debates (Hansard) Official Report, Session 1968/69, Volume 297, Column 658, 'Reform'.
48 The Parliamentary Debates (Hansard) Official Report, Session 1968/69, Volume 297, Column 659, 'Reform'.
49 The Parliamentary Debates (Hansard) Official Report, Session 1968/69, Volume 297, Column 660, 'Reform'.
50 *The Daily Mail*, 24 March 1969. Their Lordships average attendance had in fact increased from 131 to 225 in four years. *The Daily Telegraph*, 28 March 1969.
51 Crossman, op. cit. Volume 3, pp. 392–3.
52 Interview GPJRJ.
53 Colloquial name for a House of Commons Order – a Timetable Motion – limiting the time spent discussing a Bill or sections of a Bill.
54 Crossman, op. cit. Volume 3, p. 396.
55 The Parliamentary Debates (Hansard) House of Commons Official Report, Session 1968/69, Volume 777, 'House of Lords Reform'.
56 Interview GPJRJ.
57 Who subsequently became Lady Balfour of Burleigh.
58 Interview Janet Morgan, Lady Balfour of Burleigh, 7 November 2002.

Chapter Twelve: Sons of Heroes

1 Nicholas Henderson *Old Friends and Modern Instances*, Profile Books, London, 2000, p. 105 and interviews GPJRJ and PAJ.
2 An historic office of state often held by a member of Government. The holder is sometimes invited by the Prime Minister to undertake specific departmental responsibilities and a more general role, for example as leading Government Spokesman in the House of Lords.
3 Interview GPJRJ. Carrington had in fact told Heath about the drink-driving incident.
4 Speech to the CPSA Conference, Margate, 10 May 1972, Tidcombe papers.
5 Interview Sir Michael Davies, Clerk of the Parliaments 1997 to 2003, 13 June 2002.
6 Interview Brian Gilmore, 19 June 2002.
7 Interview Tony and Barbara Hunt,
8 He was Lord President of the Council, Leader of the House of Commons,
9 John Campbell, *Edward Heath: A Biography*, Jonathan Cape, London, 1993, p. 377.
10 Interview Brian Gilmore, 19 June 2002.
11 Interview Lord Carrington, 19 June 2002.

12 Interview the Rt. Hon. Sir Edward Heath, 20 July 2002.
13 Interview Brian Gilmore, 19 June 2002.
14 Interview Sir Michael Davies, Clerk of the Parliaments 1997 to 2003, 13 June 2002.
15 In 1979, Churchill's son-in-law Christopher Soames came into the same office to take up post as Lord President. His eyes filled with tears. 'This was my father-in-law's office', he said. But, mercurial as ever, he soon emerged from reverie to say: 'But you've moved the desk. Have it put back so the daylight comes from the right as he had it.' 26 February 2004, email from James Buckley, who had been a Principal working in the Public Sector Pensions Division of the CSD. He went on to become Principal Private Secretary to Fred Peart, Christopher Soames and Janet Young, the first woman Leader of the House of Lords (and one of Jellicoe's protégées).
16 No relation to Robert Armstrong, Sir William Armstrong became Edward Heath's principal advisor.
17 'RED TAPE', Tidcombe papers.
18 Interview Brian Gilmore, 19 June 2002.
19 Interview Lord Waldegrave, 27 May 2002.
20 Kenneth Rose, Elusive Rothschild: The Life of Victor, Third Baron, Weidenfeld & Nicolson, 2003, p. 174. He also turned down several other 'safe' nominees put forward by civil servants. Interview Lord Waldegrave, 27 May 2002.
21 Interview Lord Waldegrave, 27 May 2002.
22 Rose, op. cit. p. 186. Not long afterwards, Heath with Jellicoe and Shackleton opened the new Civil Service College at Sunningdale which helped to improve civil servants' skills.
23 His wife, Rosalind, was a Treasury official, the Gilmores being known as 'the star couple of the Civil Service'. Interview Malcolm Inglis, 6 December 2002.
24 Interview Malcolm Inglis, 6 December 2002.
25 Interview James Buckley, Chief Executive, Baltic Exchange, 11 December 2002. See note 5.
26 Ibid.
27 Interview Brian Gilmore, 19 June 2002.
28 Interview Sir Gerald Wilson, 30 March 2003.
29 Subsequently, Sir John (Edward) Herbecq, KCB.
30 Interview Sir John Herbecq, 3 August 2002.
31 Ibid.
32 Herbecq worked on superannuation for six and a half years. He was to make major changes in the last two years, which a successor to him after four years with no previous experience would not have been able to do. Interview, Sir John Herbecq, 3 August 2002.
33 Ibid.
34 Interview Sir Michael Wheeler-Booth, Clerk of the Parliaments, 1991–1997, 9 August 2002.
35 In addition to being the Opposition front bench spokesman, he had been a former General Secretary of the Inland Revenue Staff Federation.
36 Interview Sir John Herbecq, 3 August 2002.The trades unions would have liked what they called 'parity', so that someone who had retired in the past would have received a pension as if he or she were currently retiring. This would have created a link with pay and resulted in a 20–30 per cent increase in pensions. But it was never likely because the State old-age pension is linked to inflation, not pay.
37 It lives on – and will outlive most of us. When in 2002, civil servants were offered alternative options, over 80 per cent of them chose to stay with the original scheme, which is now closed to new members. The removal of retirement dates could mean the last pension will begin in 2050, or even a bit later. With increasing longevity (and because widows and disabled children receive lifetime benefits) it could go on being paid 100 years after that. Jellicoe's scheme will have endured nearly 200 years. Interestingly, the Civil Service replaced the original scheme with one that had enhanced benefits, including faster accruals. But in 2003 it started planning for an increase in retirement ages and realized that the new scheme would need changing, to reduce the accrual rate. A reversion to something closer to the Jellicoe original scheme now seems likely.
38 Interview Ivor Lightman, 16 August 2002.
39 An experience shared by his biographer, who fortunately has the benefit of Army training in interrogation skills! Interview Lord Peyton, 29 July 2002.
40 Speech to a Youth Leaders' Community and Youth Service dinner at the Guildhall in Salisbury on 8 May 1971, Tidcombe papers.
41 Lord Windlesham, Politics in Practice, Jonathan Cape, London, 1974, pp. 60–4.
42 Ibid, pp. 69–70.
43 Interview Sir Michael Wheeler-Booth, Clerk of the Parliaments, 1991–1997, 9 August 2002.
44 Interview GPJRJ. Shackleton's war had been spent with RAF Intelligence and the Anti U-Boat campaign, flying long hours in Sunderland flying boats and earning several distinctions for improvements to U-Boat intelligence. An MP during the first Wilson Government, he had been

made a life peer in 1958. He became Minister of Defence for the RAF in 1964 before being made Deputy Leader in the Lords under Lord Longford in 1967 and Leader in 1968.

45 However, he told me he found Jellicoe 'much cleverer than Shackleton, or Carrington'. Interview Lord Jenkins of Hillhead, 9 July 2002.

46 He sent Shackleton a copy of the first Annual Report of the Civil Service College (which Shackleton had helped to establish as part of the implementation of the Fulton Report recommendations). It had only recently been decided to publish the report and to do so annually thereafter. House of Lords Record Office, Shackleton papers, October 1972.

47 Shackleton letter to Jellicoe dated 23 December 1971, House of Lords Record Office, Shackleton papers.

48 Interview Sir Michael Davies, Clerk of the Parliaments 1997–2003, 13 June 2002. This was the Ministerial and Other Salaries Act 1971. Lords members were not paid for attending but could claim expenses, whereas members of the Commons received both.

49 Interview Brian Gilmore, 19 June 2002.

50 Interview Lord Gowrie, 29 August 2002.

51 Ibid. Gowrie was Opposition spokesman on economic affairs from 1974–1979, Minister of State at the Department of Employment from 1979–1981, Deputy Secretary of State at the Northern Ireland Office from 1981–1983 and Minister for the Arts from 1983–1985.

52 Tidcombe papers. Malcolm Inglis's daughter, then two, still has her 'Jellicoe dress' to pass on to her own daughter.

53 Interview Lord Gowrie, 29 August 2002.

54 PRO PREM 13/342 in response to a note dictated by the Labour Prime Minister at 11.45 pm on 11 February 1970 after Vic Feather had been to see him.

55 Under the Emergency Powers Act (EPA) 1920, as amended by the EPA 1964, The Parliamentary Debates (Hansard) Official Report, Session 1970/71, Volume 311, Column 730, 16 July 1970, Docks Strike.

56 Tidcombe papers.

57 The Parliamentary Debates (Hansard) Official Report, Session 1970/71, Volume 316, 25 March 1971, Industrial Relations Bill.

58 He was present for 126 out of 141 sitting days that Parliamentary Session, letter from Michael Pownall, Reading Clerk, dated 29 August 2002, author's possession.

59 The Parliamentary Debates (Hansard) Official Report, Session 1970/71, Volume 317, Column 4, ff, 4 and 5 April 1971, Docks Strike.

60 Ibid, 6 April 1971.

61 Bodies set up in the mid-1960s to deal with appeals against industrial training levies, and more recently redundancy payments disputes.

62 Conciliators later operated under the aegis of the Advisory, Conciliation and Arbitration Service (ACAS).

63 On constitutional grounds they did not usually vote on Second Reading.

64 The Parliamentary Debates (Hansard) Official Report, Session 1970/1971, Volume 317, 6 April 1971.

65 Ibid.

66 Ibid.

67 The Parliamentary Debates (Hansard) Official Report, Session 1970/71, Volume 318, Column 348, 4 May 1971, Industrial Relations Bill.

68 The Parliamentary Debates (Hansard) Official Report, Session 1970/71, Volume 318, Column 1197, 13 May 1971, Industrial Relations Bill.

69 Ibid.

70 The Parliamentary Debates (Hansard) Official Report, Session 1970/71, Volume 320, Column 24–25, 18 June 1971, Industrial Relations Bill. Here, Jellicoe was really explaining why the existing, informal bodies were the right ones to take on this new role.

71 The Parliamentary Debates (Hansard) Official Report, Session 1970/71, Volume 320, Column 930, 20 July 1971, Industrial Relations Bill. 185 and 169 amendments had been made during the Committee and Report stages respectively.

72 The new branch of the High Court called the National Industrial Relations Court presided over by the then Sir John Donaldson was abolished and has never been resurrected.

73 The term 'employment rights' implies that it was the Unfair Dismissal proposals that Labour were opposed to in the 1971 Bill and which caused the long debates. In fact, such measures were included in their own 1970 Industrial Relations Bill and subsequently adopted by the Conservatives.

74 Alan Clark, *The Tories: Conservatives and the Nation State 1922–1977*, Weidenfeld & Nicolson, 1998, p. 342.

75 Interview the Rt. Hon. Sir Edward Heath, 20 July 2002 and interview GPJRJ.

76 Interview Lord Peyton, 29 July 2002.
77 Jellicoe's continuing interest and contacts in defence and aerospace were also well known. He had also attended the Concorde Rockwell International dinner on 21 May 1972. Tidcombe papers.
78 Interview Sir Ronald Grierson, 16 July 2002.
79 At their own private expense.
80 The retiring British Ambassador in Tokyo.
81 *The Sun*, (Australian edition), 22 June 1972. Nobody actually bought a Concorde, although Iran and China nearly did.
82 *Britain and the European Communities: An Economic Assessment*. Comd 4289.
83 The Parliamentary Debates (Hansard) Official Report, Session 1969/70, Volume 308, Column 1007, 17 March 1970, Britain and the European Communities.
84 The Parliamentary Debates (Hansard) Official Report, Session 1969/70, Volume 308, Column 1007, 17 March 1970, Britain and the European Communities.
85 The Parliamentary Debates (Hansard) Official Report, Session 1969/70, Volume 308, Column 1007, 17 March 1970, Britain and the European Communities.
86 Interview GPJRJ and The Parliamentary Debates (Hansard) Official Report, Session 1970/71, Volume 321, Columns 991–2, 7 July 1971, European Communities and the United Kingdom.
87 The Parliamentary Debates (Hansard) Official Report, Session 1971/72, Volume 324, Columns 942–52, 28 October 1971, the United Kingdom and the European Communities.
88 Interview GPJRJ. His successor, Lord Windlesham, did not carry this responsibility.
89 Interview Sir John Herbecq, 3 August 2002.
90 Interview Ivor Lightman, 16 August 2002.
91 A public consultation paper.
92 Interview Ivor Lightman, 16 August 2002.
93 The Parliamentary Debates (Hansard) Official Report of the House of Lords, Session 1971/72, Volume 328, Column 832, Debate on 'Government Research and Development'. In fact, Lord Bessborough opened the debate with a short speech, probably because Jellicoe was not there, but Jellicoe followed later with a major oration.
94 The Parliamentary Debates (Hansard) Official House of Lords Report, Session 1971/72, Volume 328, Column 1080, Debate on 'Government Research and Development'.
95 Campbell, op. cit. p. 571.
96 Letter from Brian Gilmore dated 19 February 2004.
97 Interview the Rt. Hon. Sir Edward Heath, 20 July 2002.
98 And indeed, very rare, as Shackleton was to remark later.
99 The Parliamentary Debates (Hansard) Official Report, Session 1971/72, Volume 333, Column 1223, 25 July 1972, the United Kingdom and the European Communities.
100 The Parliamentary Debates (Hansard) Official Report, Session 1971/72, Volume 334, 3 August 1972, the United Kingdom and the European Communities.
101 Interview Sir Michael Davies, 5 September 2002.
102 The Parliamentary Debates (Hansard) Official Report, Session 1971/72, Volume 334, Column 1426, 8 August 1972, the United Kingdom and the European Communities.
103 The Parliamentary Debates (Hansard) Official Report, Session 1971/72, Volume 334, Column 203-320, 10 August 1972, the United Kingdom and the European Communities. Actually, the Bill probably needed amendment so as to be able to provide for proper Parliamentary scrutiny. Interview Sir Michael Wheeler-Booth, 9 August 2002.
104 The Parliamentary Debates (Hansard) Official Report, Session 1971/72, Volume 335, Column 329, 13 September 1972, the United Kingdom and the European Communities.
105 The Parliamentary Debates (Hansard) Official Report, Session 1971/72, Volume 335, Column 1145, 20 September 1972, the European Communities.
106 Interview the Rt. Hon. Sir Edward Heath, 20 July 2002.
107 Inglis had joined the Scientific Civil Service in 1964 after reading engineering at St Edmund Hall, Oxford and was working at the National Gas Turbine Establishment, undertaking control system research for aero-engines.
108 Interview Malcolm Inglis, 2 December 2002.
109 Ibid.
110 Interview Malcolm Inglis, 6 December 2002.
111 Interview Gerald Wilson, 30 March 2003.
112 In the Ministerial and Other Salaries Act 1971. Interview Sir John Herbecq, 3 August 2002.
113 Interview James Buckley, Chief Executive, Baltic Exchange, 11 December 2002.
114 Interview Sir John Herbecq, 3 August 2002.
115 Ibid.
116 Interview Malcolm Inglis, 6 December 2002.

117 He was already in charge of their restoration, which had included raising money for Westminster Abbey and Chequers. The US ambassador had been a major contributor to both historic buildings. Interview GPJRJ.
118 The Reform of Local Government Bill had also gone through Parliament during 1972.
119 For a while, the idea was to put 75,000 of them onto an island to create a sort of new 'Hong Kong' of businessmen and professionals. The Seychelles, Bermuda and the Solomon Islands had been considered but had refused. And so the policy focused instead on changing public opinion to accept them in Britain and arranging for their reception. Interview GPJRJ.

Chapter Thirteen: The Call Girl's Diary

1 This chapter draws on a 10,000 word, handwritten contemporaneous account by Jellicoe covering the events from lunchtime on Tuesday 22 May 1973 to lunchtime on Thursday 24 May 1973. I have been able to enhance its usefulness by cross-referencing from it to the Official Record of Parliamentary Debates (Hansard) and to records in the National Archives (formerly the Public Record Office). Hereafter referred to as GPJRJ 'The account of events last week'.
2 It was being made simultaneously in the House of Commons by John Davies, the Chancellor of the Duchy of Lancaster, who is usually a member of the Government who may or may not have specific departmental responsibilities, and often a member of Cabinet. At this time it was John Davies.
3 He could not later, in the absence of being able to consult his engagement book, recall the rest of the afternoon, save that he had no loss of business himself. GPJRJ 'The account of events last week'.
4 Interview Sir Michael Davies, Clerk of the Parliaments 1997–2003 and Principal Private Secretary to the Lord Privy Seal and Leader of the House of Lords, 1971–2, 14 June 2002.
5 Gerald Robertson Wilson. He went on to have a highly successful Civil Service career.
6 GPJRJ 'The account of events last week'.
7 As a percentage of GNP.
8 Lord St Aldwyn, responsible to the Leader and Lord Chancellor, the Speaker of the House of Lords for arranging the timetable of the Government's business in the House, with due regard to the needs of the Opposition, 'Whip' being derived from the 'whippers-in' or 'whips' employed by a hunt to look after the hounds and keep them together in the field.
9 Viscount Antony Claud Frederick Lambton, son of the 5th Earl of Durham who died in 1970. Lambton had disclaimed the peerage for life but was allowed by Mr Speaker Lloyd to continue to sit in Parliament using his former courtesy title of 'Lord'.
10 Unknown to Jellicoe, Stradling Thomas MP had written to Pym, copy to the Prime Minister on 14 May saying that Rupert Murdoch had a 'Profumo' type story on the stocks *with* photographs about a junior minister and sexual orgies. The official car was involved and the story was about to break. PRO, PREM 15/1904.
11 Later Lord Armstrong of Ilminster.
12 Sir Edward (Richard George) Heath, KG.
13 Interview Lord Armstrong of Ilminster, 4 July 2002.
14 Interview GPJRJ 3–5 May 2002.
15 Interview Philippa, Countess Jellicoe, 23 June 2002, hereafter interview PAJ.
16 'The account of events last week' includes names that cannot be disclosed because the people concerned are still living.
17 Interview Lord Armstrong of Ilminster, 4 July 2002.
18 There is no real equivalent in the House of Lords to the Speaker in the House of Commons. All members of the Lords are equally responsible for ensuring that business progresses smoothly. The presiding officer, who has no powers to compare with those of the Speaker in the Commons, is the Lord Chancellor. The Leader of the House of Lords therefore played a role where necessary in regulating the conduct of business.
19 The Parliamentary Debates (Hansard) Official Report, Session 1972/73, Volume 342, Column 1221, 'EEC Council of Ministers' Meeting'.
20 His mother, Constance, was old Lady Jellicoe's sister.
21 Email from Gerald Wilson, 18 March 2003.
22 David Sutherland, 'Dinky' of SBS days.
23 Lord Goodman, who represented Jellicoe at a security investigation after the resignation.
24 Delicacy prevents their being mentioned.
25 Interview Janet Morgan, Lady Balfour of Burleigh, 7 November 2002.
26 Interview Lord Armstrong of Ilminster, 4 July 2002.
27 Somehow, Jellicoe also found the time to phone Gerald Wilson at around midnight to tell him about the resignation.
28 GPJRJ's contemporaneous record, 'The account of events last week'.

29 Names not able to be disclosed because they are still living.
30 GPJRJ's contemporaneous record, 'The account of events last week'.
31 Interviews Malcolm Inglis, 6 December 2002 and Michael Wheeler-Booth, 9 August 2002.
32 Tidcombe papers.
33 Interview Sir Carol Mather, 29 June 2002.
34 Interview Sir Michael Wheeler Booth.
35 Interview Sir Michael Davies, Clerk of the Parliaments 1997 to 2003, 13 June 2002.
36 The Seal would normally go back to the Privy Council Office in Whitehall direct but on this occasion Jellicoe's lawyer Lord Goodman offered to arrange for its return.
37 Interview Malcolm Inglis, 6 December 2002.
38 Interview Sir Michael Davies, Clerk of the Parliaments 1997 to 2003, 13 June 2002.
39 Interview the Rt. Hon. Sir Edward Heath, 20 July 2002.
40 Interview Gerald Wilson, 30 March 2003.
41 Daisy stayed with the nanny at Tidcombe. Tony Hunt took the other two children to Herefordshire. Interview, PAJ, 23 June 2002.
42 He was, and is, Lord Lieutenant of Hereford and Worcestershire (the senior Lord Lieutenant).
43 Interview, Tony and Barbara Hunt, 31 August 2002.
44 Ibid.
45 Heath subsequently made no mention of Jellicoe in his biography, which was odd. Heath had worked closely with Jellicoe, particularly during their early days in office, very much relying on him in a number of key areas. Perhaps he did not want to draw attention to the resignation.
46 The Scotsman, 1 January 2004.
47 Later Sir Joseph Nickerson, who founded Rothwells Seeds in Lincolnshire.
48 Interview Chapman Pincher, 18 June 2003 and Chapman Pincher, Inside Story: A Documentary of the Pursuit of Power, Sidgwick and Jackson, London, 1978, pp. 2723.
49 These include three whose names are still withheld in the file released to the National Archives in 2004, presumably because they are still alive, PRO, PREM 15/1904.
50 Mary Sweeting, Tatler, Autumn, 2003.
51 The Scotsman, 1 January 2004.
52 Interview GPJRJ.
53 Interview GPJRJ.

Chapter Fourteen: Trade, Aids and Anti-terrorism

1 Diary of Peggy Dunne, 18 July 1973, Tidcombe papers.
2 In 1978, Wilson's great 'find', in Hungary, was the Sevso Silver, a collection of Roman artefacts and coins. In preparing to auction it off, Sotheby's notified all the countries that had been occupied by the Romans and several nations claimed ownership, beginning a controversy that has raged ever since. Interview GPJRJ.
3 Now Sir Nigel Thompson, KCMG, CBE, deputy chairman of Ove Arup.
4 Interview Sir Nigel Thompson, 13 August 2002.
5 Which became Trafalgar House plc, for whom Mark Thatcher later worked, and was involved in a contentious bid for Northern Electric in 1995.
6 Interview Sir Nigel Thompson, 13 August 2002.
7 In English, 'Lord Jellicoe was furious you know. And why so? I was very tired. I had been working day and night and I needed to sleep.'
8 Interview GPJRJ and PAJ.
9 Interview Sir Nigel Thompson, 13 August 2002.
10 Ibid.
11 Ibid.
12 Interview Lord Haslam, 9 September 2002.
13 Interview Sir Neil Shaw, 10 January 2003.
14 Interview Lord Moynihan, 12 June 2002.
15 Ibid.
16 Letter from Jamaica Sugar Holdings, Tidcombe papers.
17 Interview Sir Neil Shaw, 10 January 2003.
18 Speech to the New York Sugar Club, 13 May 1981, Tidcombe Papers.
19 Interview Sir Neil Shaw, 10 January 2003.
20 Ibid.
21 He named his second son, George, after Jellicoe. Interview Lord Moynihan, 12 June 2002.
22 In due course Jellicoe was painted by June Mendosa for Tate & Lyle. His successor as chairman was Lord Haslam.

23 Based on the size by value of the projects it was handling outside of the UK. Davy was a global company, supplying developing countries with plant and engineering to help develop their primary industries. Interview Roger Kingdon, CBE, Chief Executive Davy Corporation, 1987–90, 15 June 2002. At this time also, Jellicoe was just completing his successful chairmanship of the BOTB.
24 King's was then a quarter of the size it is now.
25 Jellicoe roped in John Peyton to become chairman of two Southampton charities, extracting money from him for Red Nose day and for a charity for children with fibrosis. For the last ten years Peyton has gone every year in Jellicoe's car to the home in Southampton. Interview Lord John Peyton, 29 July 2002.
26 Interview Sir Gordon Higginson, 7 July 2002.
27 He only stepped down in 1983. Parliamentary and Scientific Committee Annual Report 1976, Tidcombe papers and interview GPJRJ. Jellicoe is still a member and a member of the House of Lords Committee on Science and Technology.
28 For which Fleming and Florey had shared a Nobel Prize.
29 Interview Sir James Gowans, 3 June 2002.
30 Ibid.
31 Ibid.
32 In English, 'I am most awfully sorry. I'm afraid I have nothing for you'. They were attending another medal ceremony at which Stirling had thought they would receive their medals, which were eventually presented on another occasion.
33 Interview Zara Jellicoe Banghart, 10 March 2004.
34 Interview Sir James Gowans, 3 June 2002.
35 Ibid
36 Ibid.
37 Nicholson said later that he had never heard anyone talk to Mrs Thatcher like that. Interview Sir James Gowans, 29 February 2004.
38 Interview Sir James Gowans, 3 June 2002.
39 Interview Sir Donald Acheson, Chief Medical Officer 1983–1991, 10 March 2004.
40 Ibid.
41 Interview Sir James Gowans, 3 June 2002.
42 Later Baroness Jay.
43 Interview GPJRJ.
44 Some years later, on a trade visit to Russia, Jellicoe offered the Health Minister everything that the UK had learned about Aids. But the Russians turned it down, saying that they had no problem and no need of it. Interview GPJRJ.
45 The supporting statement cited Jellicoe's work on Aids, the Human Fertilization and Embryology Bill, his presidency of the Parliamentary and Scientific Committee and his presidency of the amalgamation of King's College London with Queen Elizabeth and Chelsea Colleges, as well as his chairmanship of the Medical Research Council. Jellicoe carried on as MRC chairman until 1990 but Gowans retired as chief executive in 1987.
46 Interview GPJRJ.
47 Interview Sir Nigel Thompson, 13 August 2002.
48 Jellicoe spoke on behalf of the London Chamber of Commerce and Industry, the CBI, the British Soviet Chamber of Commerce and the BOTB.
49 An Assistant Secretary in the DTI, Roberts had been Private Secretary to Prime Minister Edward Heath.
50 Interview Sir Christopher Roberts, 25 June 2002.
51 Ibid.
52 Interview Howard Fisher, 21 February 2003.
53 Interview Sir Terence Clark, HMA Baghdad 1985–1989, 20 June 2003.
54 Curiously, there was no Prime Minister: Saddam as executive President played that role himself.
55 Interview Sir Terence Clark, HMA Baghdad 1985–1989, 20 June 2003.
56 In 1986, as Jellicoe left the BOTB, he suggested that it should be more closely integrated with the Foreign Office overseas and with the regions. Years later, exactly that happened with the creation of Trade Partners International.
57 Interview James McNeish, 10 June 2002. McNeish had been a senior manager in John Lewis Partnership before joining the London Commodity Exchange and had military, business and policy experience. He was director of the East European Trade Council from 1980 until 2000 when it was wound up as a result of a Government review.
58 According to Peggy Dunne. Interview PAJ, 23 June 2002.
59 Interview James McNeish, 10 June 2002.
60 Interview Andrew Winckler, chairman, Regulatory Practice Financial Services, Ernst & Young, 18 June 2002.

61 Winckler had been Private Secretary to the Chancellor and remembered the marked contrast between Heath's resignation acceptance letter to Jellicoe and to Lambton. Interview Andrew Winckler, chairman, Regulatory Practice Financial Services, Ernst & Young, 18 June 2002.

62 Rt. Hon. Earl Jellicoe, DSO, MC, *Review of the Operations of the Prevention of Terrorism (Temporary Provisions) Act 1976*, Tidcombe papers, and interview GPJRJ. He was helped by an excellent young principal from the Foreign Office, Howard Webber.

63 Ports serving international destinations were also important because although passengers could be stopped under the Prevention of Terrorism Act, questioning had to be carried out by immigration officials under the Immigration Act.

64 London had special arrangements. A National Joint Unit, staffed by the Special Branch of the Metropolitan Police and provincial Special Branches, handled hard-line terrorist incidents. Interview GPJRJ.

65 Jellicoe, op. cit. paragraph 25, Tidcombe papers.

66 Ibid, paragraph 33.

67 Including an anomaly that left section 11 open to misuse. It was an offence under s.11 to withhold information of material assistance in preventing an act of terrorism or in catching those who had committed an offence involving an act of terrorism. But it had not been Parliament's intention to alter the well-established legal principle that no one should be compelled to incriminate himself. Jellicoe concluded that s.11 was of significant value to the police but that they could operate without it. He recommended that it should be used only where the public suspected that relevant information was being withheld. Police everywhere had told Jellicoe that their primary use of s.11 was to help them get information from those on whom they already had intelligence, but not admissible evidence suggesting deeper involvement in terrorism than the mere possession of information. Jellicoe therefore recommended that an officer's reasonable suspicion that someone was guilty of an offence under s.11 should no longer be sufficient grounds for arrest under s.12 and s.11 itself should be amended to make it clear that the information which it was an offence to withhold should relate only to third parties, thereby removing the risk of misuse.

68 Unlike the House of Commons, committees in the Lords focussed almost entirely on the scrutiny of EU legislation and science and technology. The EU committee had a fine reputation and was one of the most effective examples of EU scrutiny by a national parliament. Lord Roll of Ipsden still sits on it.

69 The Parliamentary Debates (Hansard) Official Report, Session 1990/91, 14 February 1990, Legislative Scrutiny Proposal.

70 Hansard, HoL 11 June 1992.

71 Interview Lady Henderson, author of *Xenia – A Memoir, Greece 1919–1949* and Jellicoe's longstanding personal friend, 18 June 2002.

72 He attended meetings of the prestigious Onassis Foundation, of which he was already a trustee. This honour was subsequently closed to non-Greeks.

73 Interview Lord Waldegrave, 27 May 2002. The stories are in chapters 6 and 7.

74 Interview GPJRJ.

75 Interview Viscount Slim, 23 February 2004.

76 HRH The Duke of Kent was also involved with Jellicoe in Crete and the Crete Veterans Association.

77 Interview Mrs Nan White-Gaze, 5 June 2002.

78 Annual Report, The Anglo-Hellenic League, London, 1985, 12 February 1986. The correspondence was about Jellicoe's christening, at which the King was Godfather.

79 Jellicoe was the only chairman to become a patron and do even more things for the League than before. Interview Mrs Nan White-Gaze, 5 June 2002.

80 The Hendersons said that every time they got invited to the Greek embassy it was because Jellicoe was getting another medal. Interview Lady Henderson, 18 June 2002. In 1988, he became chairman of the Greece Fund and in 1992 received the Greek Grand Commander Order of Honour.

81 Interview GPJRJ.

82 Where there is a memorial to him and Greek Sacred Squadron, Hieros Lokos.

83 Written message from GPJRJ to the 60th anniversary of the founding of the Greek Sacred Squadron, 12 September 2002.

84 Professor Walter Raleigh, *The English Voyages of the Sixteenth Century*, Glasgow, 1904.

85 Interview Christopher James, 13 June 2002.

86 Ibid.

87 Subsequently the Royal Geographical Society (with the Institute of British Geographers).

88 Interview Sir Michael Wheeler-Booth, Clerk of the Parliaments, 1991–1997, 9 August 2002. At the request of the Royal Society, Jellicoe wrote a short biography of Shackleton: Biog. Mems. Fell. R. Soc. Lond. 45, 485–505 (1999).

89 When Labour regained power in 1974, they tried to get Shackleton back again but by that time he had what he called a proper job with Rio Tinto Zinc and said he couldn't afford it. Interview Malcolm Inglis, 6 December 2002.

90 His daughter was soon to lay his Garter Banner down in Christchurch Cathedral, Port Stanley as a token of Shackleton's undying loyalty to the Falkland Islands. Jellicoe later wrote a short biography of Shackleton for the Royal Society.

91 Interview Tony and Barbara Hunt.

92 Interview GPJRJ.

93 Interview GPJRJ.

94 Interview Sir Nicholas Henderson, 18 June 2002.

95 All military novel creations had such a window dedicated. Interview Michael Pownall, House of Lords Reading Clerk, 3 July 2002.

96 Letter from Jellicoe to his cousin Elizabeth Madden, undated but written on the Thursday after his father's funeral. Tidcombe papers.

Bibliography

Almonds Windmill, Lorna, *Gentleman Jim: The Wartime Story of a Founder of the SAS and Special Forces*, Constable & Robinson, 2002

Andrew, Christopher and Oleg Gordiesvsky, *KGB: The inside story of its foreign operations from Lenin to Gorbachev*, Hodder & Stoughton, 1990

Bacon, Admiral Sir R. H., *The Life of John Rushworth, Earl Jellicoe*, Cassell & Company Ltd., 1936

Beevor, Anthony, *Crete: The Battle and the Resistance*, Penguin, 1992

Burrows, Montagu, *The Family of Brocas of Beaurepaire and Roche Court: Hereditary Masters of the Royal Buckhounds with some account of the English Rule in Aquitaine,* Longman's Green & Co., 1886

Campbell, John, *Edward Heath: A Biography*, Jonathan Cape, 1993

Clark, Alan, *The Tories: Conservatives and the Nation State 1922–1997*, Weidenfeld & Nicolson, 1998

Cooper, Johnny, *One of the Originals: The Story of a Founder Member of the SAS*, Pan, 1991

Crossman, Richard, *The Crossman Diaries, Volume 2, 1976*, The Estate of RHS Crossman, Hamish Hamilton and Jonathan Cape, 1976

Diary of Hans Evenstoll, Representative of the Swedish Red Cross in Patras, Athens, 1961, as quoted in *The Diary of Panayiotis Kanellopoulos, 31 March 1942–4 February 1945*, Edition 'Kedros', Athens, 1977

Foot, M. R. D., *SOE: The Special Operations Executive 1940–46*, BBC, 1984

Gordon, Andrew, *The Rules of the Game: Jutland and British Naval Command*, John Murray (Publishers) Ltd., 1996

Harrison, D. I., *These Men are Dangerous: The Special Air Service at War*, Cassell, 1957

Hastings, Stephen, *The Drums of Memory: The Autobiography*, Pen & Sword Books Ltd., 2001

Heath, Edward, *Travels: People and Places in my Life*, Sidgwick & Jackson, 1977

Henderson, Mary, *Xenia – A Memoir: Greece 1919–1949*, George Weidenfeld & Nicolson, 1988

Henderson, Nicholas, *Old Friends and Modern Instances*, Profile Books, 2000

Hilary, Richard, *The Last Enemy*, Macmillan, 1942

Hoe, Alan, *David Stirling: the Authorised Biography of the Creator of the SAS*, Little Brown, 1992

Hunter, Robin, *True Stories of the SBS*, Virgin, 1998

James, Malcolm, *Born of the Desert*, Collins, 1945

Keegan, John, ed., *The Times Atlas of the Second World War*, Times Books, 1989

Keeler, Christine, *The Truth At Last: My Story*, Pan, 2002

Kemp, Anthony, *The SAS at War: 1941–1945*, Penguin, 1991

Kofod-Hansen, Mogens, *Andy – A Portrait of the Dane Major Anders Lassen*, Narayana Press, 1989

Kyle, Keith, *Suez: Britain's End of Empire in the Middle East*, Weidenfeld & Nicolson, 1991

Langley, Mike, *Anders Lassen VC, MC, of the SAS*, Grafton, 1990

Lassen, Susanne, *Anders Lassen VC*, Frederick Muller, 1965

Maclean, Fitzroy, *Eastern Approaches*, Jonathan Cape, 1949

Mather, Carol, *When the Grass Stops Growing: a War Memoir*, Pen & Sword Books Ltd., 1997

Morgan, Janet, *Agatha Christie: A Biography*, William Collins & Sons Co. Ltd., 1984

— *The House of Lords and the Labour Government 1964–1970*, OUP, 1975

Muir, Augustus and Muir Davies, *A Victorian Shipowner*, Cayzer, Irvine & Co. Ltd., 1978

Paget, Julian, ed., *Second to None: The Coldstream Guards 1650–2000,* Leo Cooper, 2000

Peyton, John, *Solly Zuckerman: A Scientist Out of the Ordinary,* John Murray, 2001

Pincher, Chapman, *Inside Story: A Documentary of the Pursuit of Power,* Sidgwick and Jackson, 1978

Pitt, Barrie, *Special Boat Squadron: The Story of the SBS in the Mediterranean,* Century, 1983

Raleigh, Professor Walter, *The English Voyages of the Sixteenth Century,* Glasgow, 1904

Ranfurly, Countess of, *To War with Whitaker: The Wartime Diaries of the Countess of Ranfurly 1939–45,* William Heinemann Ltd., 1994

Rhodes James, Robert, ed., *Chips: The Diaries of Sir Henry Channon,* Weidenfeld & Nicolson, 1967

Rogers, Anthony, *Churchill's Folly: Leros and the Aegean,* Cassell, 2003

Rose, Kenneth, *Elusive Rothschild: The Life of Victor, Third Baron,* Weidenfeld & Nicolson, 2003

Roskill, Stephen, *Hankey, Man of Secrets, Volume I 1877–1918,* Collins, 1970

Soames, Mary, *Speaking for Themselves,* Black Swan, 1998

Steel, Nigel and Peter Hart, *Jutland 1916: Death in the Grey Wastes,* Cassell, 2003

Sutherland, David, *He Who Dares: Recollections of Service in the SAS, SBS and MI5,* Leo Cooper, 1998

Thompson, Julian, *War Behind Enemy Lines,* Sidgwick & Jackson, 1998

Windlesham, Lord, *Politics in Practice,* Jonathan Cape, 1974

Winton, John, *Jellicoe,* Michael Joseph Ltd., 1981

Wright, Peter, *Spycatcher,* Viking, 1987

Unpublished Sources

Diary of Lord Jellicoe from April to October 1939.

A 10,000 word, handwritten contemporaneous account by Lord Jellicoe covering the events from lunchtime on Tuesday 22 May 1973 to lunchtime on Thursday 24 May 1973 entitled 'The account of events last week'.

Letters, speeches and other documents among Lord Jellicoe's papers at Tidcombe Manor and referenced as such in the Notes on Sources.

The Naval and Military Record, 9 April 1919.

Papers of Lieutenant Colonel Count JA Dobrski, OBE, MC, (alias Lieutenant Colonel Julian Dolbey) King's College, London, Liddell Hart Centre for Military Archives.

Jack Sibard, *Récit Condensé: Mission Créte – Juin 1942,* copy in the author's collection.

Captain G W Read, *Raiding Forces and the Levant Schooner Flotilla: a Story of an Independent Command in the Aegean 1943–1945,* July 1945, given to members of raiding forces on disbandment, copy in author's possession.

The Parliamentary Debates (Hansard) Official Reports, referenced as such in the Notes on Sources.

The National Archives (formerly the Public Record Office [PRO]), referenced as such in the Notes on Sources.

Index

277